Volume XX

Medievalist Traditions in
Nineteenth-Century British Culture

MEDIEVALISM

ISSN 2043-8230

Series Editors
Karl Fugelso
Chris Jones

Medievalism aims to provide a forum for monographs and collections devoted to the burgeoning and highly dynamic multidisciplinary field of medievalism studies: that is, work investigating the influence and appearance of 'the medieval' in the society and culture of later ages. Titles within the series investigate the post-medieval construction and manifestations of the Middle Ages – attitudes towards, and uses and meanings of, 'the medieval' – in all fields of culture, from politics and international relations, literature, history, architecture, and ceremonial ritual to film and the visual arts. It welcomes a wide range of topics, from historiographical subjects to revivalism, with the emphasis always firmly on what the idea of 'the medieval' has variously meant and continues to mean; it is founded on the belief that scholars interested in the Middle Ages can and should communicate their research both beyond and within the academic community of medievalists, and on the continuing relevance and presence of 'the medieval' in the contemporary world.

New proposals are welcomed. They may be sent directly to the editors or the publishers at the addresses given below.

Professor Karl Fugelso
Art Department
Towson University
3103 Center for the Arts
8000 York Road
Towson, MD 21252-0001
USA
kfugelso@towson.edu

Professor Chris Jones
School of English
University of St Andrews
St Andrews
Fife KY16 9AL
UK
csj2@st-andrews.ac.uk

Boydell & Brewer Ltd
PO Box 9
Woodbridge
Suffolk IP12 3DF
UK

Previous volumes in this series are printed at the back of this book

Medievalist Traditions in Nineteenth-Century British Culture

Celebrating the Calendar Year

Clare A. Simmons

D. S. BREWER

First published 2021
Paperback edition 2023

D. S. Brewer, Cambridge

ISBN 978 1 84384 573 7 hardback
ISBN 978 1 84384 682 6 paperback

D. S. Brewer is an imprint of Boydell & Brewer Ltd
PO Box 9, Woodbridge, Suffolk IP12 3DF, UK
and of Boydell & Brewer Inc.
668 Mt Hope Avenue, Rochester, NY 14620–2731, USA
website: www.boydellandbrewer.com

A CIP catalogue record for this book is available
from the British Library

The publisher has no responsibility for the continued existence or
accuracy of URLs for external or third-party internet websites referred
to in this book, and does not guarantee that any content on such
websites is, or will remain, accurate or appropriate

To My Father,
Michael Simmons
and in Loving Memory of My Mother,
Pamela Simmons

Contents

Illustrations

The author and publisher are grateful to all the institutions and individuals listed for permission to reproduce the materials in which they hold copyright. Every effort has been made to trace the copyright holders; apologies are offered for any omission, and the publisher will be pleased to add any necessary acknowledgment in subsequent editions.

Preface

These facts, however, are not found in history.

(John Henry Newman, "The Life of St Bettelin")

Early collectors of British popular traditions[1] such as John Aubrey, Francis Grose, and Henry Bourne make frequent reference to activities tied to particular times of the year. In the nineteenth century, though, these references become more and more wistful. Britons acknowledge that if their country ever had a cohesive society, it is becoming increasingly divided between rich and poor, urban and rural, as lives are centered more around work than around community events.

This study examines how nineteenth-century Britons connected seasonal celebration with a conception of the medieval past that helped them think more sympathetically about what their ancestors' lives may have been like before the Reformation. At a time when Britain was the most industrially advanced nation in the world, many vaunted the superiority of the present to the past[2] – yet others, and not necessarily only those who imagined their forebears as feudal overlords, felt that if shadows of past ways of life haunted the present, they were friendly ghosts.

The focus here is on these ghosts: not on the discovery of to what extent nineteenth-century ideas about their inheritance from Middle Ages were accurate, but on how medievalist writings created a cultural idea of the Middle Ages and its traces in present practice. Some of the writings discussed, such as works by Tennyson and Dickens, have remained central to our own ideas about the nineteenth century. Many others, especially those in ephemeral publications, are not so well remembered – yet they both reflect and help create a new appreciation of the medieval period. Medieval-inspired works could be accessed not just by the most privileged members of society but by readers of a wide range of publications. While only the wealthy could afford to subscribe to the works of antiquarian clubs such as the Roxburghe and Percy Societies, magazines and almanacks aimed at middle-income households often lampooned the Middle Ages but nevertheless showed a grudging admiration for the medieval style; while works marketed to poorer readers, such as those printed by William Hone, were often socially critical in their comparisons between past and present. The tension between an imagined past and the sometimes

---

[1] I am avoiding the term "folklorists" since the term "folklore" only came into use after 1846, when it was coined by William Thoms. See *International Folkloristics*, ed. Alan Dundes (Lanham, MD: Rowan and Littlefield, 1999).
[2] For example, George Porter's *Progress of the Nation*, 2nd edition (London: John Murray, 1847) used statistics to demonstrate "the progress of the whole social system" (2).

grim realities of the present is especially acute in works that show a consciousness of time and season; and times of year, mapped against a sense of the past, shape the structure of this book.

The Introduction suggests that nineteenth-century Britons did not necessarily assume that the medieval period was a time of ignorance and oppression; some, indeed, were intrigued by the remnants of community celebrations and festivals that they believed had taken form in the Middle Ages. The first chapter surveys two competing models for the year: Christian attempts to retain the concept of the liturgical year by John Keble, John Henry Newman, and others; and a poetic venture by Robert Browning that presents medieval subject-matter but a more secular sense of the year. In Chapter 2, the focus is on what I am terming "calendar experiments," or ways of uniting the year with story. Succeeding chapters move through the calendar year from Christmas to Christmas. Chapter 3 focuses on some of the nineteenth-century attempts to return the national Christmas to what they believed it had been in early times, a season in its own right. Chapter 4 explores traditions of love through the Saint Agnes rituals of January and Valentine's Day in February. Chapter 5 moves to spring celebrations associated with Easter and May Day. Chapter 6 turns to more scholarly ideas about medievalism and the mystery plays and pageants of midsummer. Chapter 7 centers on competing autumnal medievalisms: harvest festivals, the lacuna of Hallowe'en, and another regional medievalism, the Lord Mayor's Show of the City of London. The study closes by circling back to Christmas and another form of return of the past in ghost stories. Yet much as the nineteenth-century idea of the medieval past might be dismissed as a phantasm, we should not reject the positive impulse behind it. We too are haunted by history and seek a community founded on equal justice, and finding ways to share in celebration might not be so bad a place to start.

Acknowledgments

This book explores the need for community, and a community of institutions, colleagues, and loved ones contributed to its completion.

I should first note the debt all scholarly study of medievalism owes to the late Leslie J. Workman and his wife Kathleen Verduin, who founded the journal *Studies in Medievalism* and first brought together scholars from all over the world to study the later reception of the Middle Ages. Versions of parts of two chapters of this book first appeared in *Studies in Medievalism*, now edited by Karl Fugelso. I am grateful to Kathleen, to Karl, and to Leslie's legacy.

I also owe a special debt of gratitude to the Armstrong Browning Library at Baylor University. During my Fellowship there in Autumn 2018, with access to the library's outstanding collection of nineteenth-century materials, my sense of this project became much clearer. I thank the Library Director Jennifer Borderud; Joshua King, the Margarett Root Brown Chair in Browning Studies; Melinda Creech; and many others at Baylor for making me so welcome and for helping the project move in some new directions.

My home institution, The Ohio State University, has also helped support my research in many ways. I have had the huge benefit of the learning and friendship of my colleagues in nineteenth-century British studies and medieval studies, Jill Galvan, Aman Garcha, Jamison Kantor, Ethan Knapp, David Riede, Jake Risinger, David Ruderman, Beth Sutton-Ramspeck, Robyn Warhol, and Karen Winstead. Thanks are also due to The Ohio State University Library and the help given me by the Billy Ireland Cartoon Library and the Special Collections Librarians Eric Johnson and Rebecca Hewitt.

Other institutions that have given me kind assistance include the Cleveland Public Library, the Alden Library of Ohio University, the Thomas Fisher Rare Books Library at the University of Toronto, and the Victoria and Albert Museum in London.

I had the opportunity to test out early drafts of many sections at conferences, especially the International Conference for the Study of Medievalism, Interdisciplinary Nineteenth-Century Studies, and the British Association for Romantic Studies, and I have learned from the generous feedback I received there. I have also benefited from the enthusiastic encouragement and valuable suggestions from Caroline Palmer and many of her associates at Boydell and Brewer.

Too many friends have contributed hints and wrinkles for me to name them all here, but I should mention David Brewer, Sara Crosby, Elizabeth Emery, Christopher

Highley, Joanna Kim, Lisa Kiser, Peter Manning, Joseph McQueen, Dorothy Noyes, Nils Holger Pedersen, Jessica Prinz, Kristin Flieger Samuelian, Mark Schoenfield, Frances Simmons, Michael Simmons, Richard Utz, Roxann Wheeler, and of course my husband and sons, Henry, Justin, and David Stern.

Abbreviations

Ancient Mysteries	Hone, William. *Ancient Mysteries Described.* London: William Hone, 1823.
Book of Days	*The Book of Days; A miscellany of popular antiquities in connection with the calendar, including anecdote, biography & history, curiosities of literature, and oddities of human life and character,* ed. Robert Chambers. London: W. and R. Chambers, n.d. (c. 1863).
Brady	Brady, John. *Clavis Calendaria, Or, A compendious analysis of the calendar.* 2 vols. London: Longman, 1812–13.
Bourne	Bourne, Henry. *Antiquitates Vulgares, Or, The Antiquities of the Common People.* Newcastle: Printed for author, 1725.
Brand	*Observations on Popular Antiquities, including the whole of Henry Bourne's Antiquitates Vulgares, With addenda to every chapter of that Work,* ed. John Brand. Newcastle: J. Johnson, 1777.
Brownings' Correspondence	Robert and Elizabeth Barrett Browning, *The Brownings' Correspondence,* ed. Philip Kelley and Ronald Hudson. 14 vols. Winfield, KS: Wedgestone Press, 1984–.
Comic Almanack	Cruikshank, George, et al. *The Comic Almanack, An Ephemeris in Jest and Earnest, Containing Merry Tales, Humorous Poetry, Quips, and Oddities, by Thackeray, Albert Smith, Gilbert à Becket, The Brothers Mayhew, With many hundred Illustrations by George Cruikshank and Other Artists.* London: Tilt, 1835–53. Rpt First Series, 1835–43. London: Chatto and Windus, n.d.
Ellis	Brand, John, ed. Henry Ellis. *Observations on Popular Antiquities; Chiefly illustrating the Origin of our Vulgar Customs, Ceremonies, and Superstitions. Arranged and Revised with Additions.* 2 vols. London: Rivington, 1813.
Every-Day Book	*The Every-day book and Table book: or, Everlasting calendar of popular amusements, sports, pastimes, ceremonies, manners, customs, and events, incident to each of the three hundred and sixty-five days, in past and present times; forming a complete history of the year, months, and seasons, and a perpetual key to the almanac,* ed. William Hone. London: William Hone, 1826–27.

Hampson	Hampson, R.T. *Medii aevi kalendarium; or,Dates, Charters, and Customs of the middle ages; with calendars from the tenth to the fifteenth century; and an alphabetical digest of obsolete names of days: forming a glossary of the dates of the middle ages; with tables and other aids for ascertaining dates.* 2 vols. London: H.K. Causton, 1841.
Hutton, Stations	Hutton, Ronald. *Stations of the Sun: A History of the Ritual Year in Britain.* Oxford: Oxford University Press, 1996.
Poems of Tennyson	Tennyson, Alfred, Lord. *The Poems of Tennyson*, ed. Christopher Ricks. London: Longmans, 1969.
Punch	*Punch*, ed. Mark Lemon et al. 301 vols. London: Punch Publications, 1841–1980.
Times	*The Times.* London: R. Nutkins, 1788.

Introduction: Medievalizing Time

In Sir Walter Scott's 1816 novel *The Antiquary*, published somewhat ominously at the beginning of what should have been summer in the notorious Year Without a Summer, Jonathan Oldbuck, the Antiquary of the title, asks for an "almanack."[1] From this he determines that his friends Sir Arthur Wardour and his daughter Isabel are in deadly danger from the oncoming high tide.

By the 1790s, when this story is set, "almanacks" had become a significant part of local infrastructure. *The Edinburgh Almanack and Scots Register* for 1794, for example, contains lists of important Scots officials, useful information such as postage rates and mail coach times, and what is proudly described as "a Correct Kalendar."[2] The Kalendar includes saints' and festival days; the phases of the moon; what times the sun and moon rise and set; and high and low tides at the nearby port of Leith. It thus combines ancient knowledge as preserved in the church ritual calendar with scientific observation and local use of time.

The Antiquary himself is acutely aware of time. Fascinated by anything ancient, he has invited his friends to enjoy an authentically antiquarian meal of "Solan Goose" (gannet) with his new friend Lovel. The invitation is for 4pm on "Tuesday the 17 current *stilo novo*" (36). The reference to the "new style" calendar (Britain had adopted the Gregorian calendar in 1752) seems remarkably precise. In point of fact, since the story started on Tuesday July 15 and several days seem to have elapsed, the precision is fictional rather than historical. If as David Hewitt has argued, the story takes place in 1794 (357), resources such as the *Edinburgh Almanack* reveal that that July 17 was not a Tuesday, and that the tide would not have been especially high any evening around that time. Nevertheless, within the fictional time of the novel, the Antiquary combines historical, local, and documented knowledge of time.

The Antiquary is, of course, a historical novel, even if the historical distancing is brief. Completed after the Battle of Waterloo, when the outcome of the wars with France was certain, the story turns back time a few years to a point when invasion seemed a possibility, and when an elderly man like Jonathan Oldbuck would have been able to recall the struggles between the houses of Stuart and Hanover: Jacobites and Jacobins are both real threats to him. Also in his own memory would be the

---

[1] Sir Walter Scott, *The Antiquary*, ed. David Hewitt and David Punter (1816; London: Penguin, 1998), 53. Subsequent references follow this edition.
[2] *The Edinburgh Almanack and Scots Register for 1794* (Edinburgh: David Ramsay, 1794), 1.

reform of a calendar that seemed to some who lived through it a theft of eleven days of their lives.[3] The story looks back to the recent past (the origins of Lovel), and the more historical past of Lovel's birth family, who still worship in the remnants of a ruined medieval abbey. Yet as the opening shows, when the coach is behind its appointed time and the ferry leaves on the tide without the coach's passengers, by the 1790s clock time was becoming increasingly important.

As the nineteenth century moved forward, an awareness of clock time became increasingly central to Britain's infrastructure. A village church bell ringing to summon people to services and festivals was of limited effectiveness in an industrial city (many of which lacked churches with bells). Coaches and trains required a posted schedule. As shipping moved from sail-power to steam, scheduling departures became more feasible. Factory workers, working indoors often under artificial light, were obligated to keep regular work hours. Elementary education became compulsory in 1870, but even before that, children had to know what times to go to school. Postal deliveries depended on reliable schedules and transportation. Almost every form of employment required regular hours, with very few days off. This would at first consideration seem to be a significant cultural shift away from the natural cycle of the year of earlier times, when long summer days and long winter nights dictated at least the working lives of the poor, and the outdoor activities of everyone. Not everyone saw this as positive progress: perhaps a sense of connection both with nature and with community was lost as everyone's lives became governed by the clock, rather than by the cycle of the year. Many were aware of this sense of loss. In his study of rural life, William Howitt remarked:

> Our ancestors were passionately fond of shows, pageants, processions, and maskings. They were fond of garlands and ribbons, dancing, and festive merriment. May-day, Easter, Whitsuntide, St John's Day, Yule, and many other times, were times of general sport and gaiety. Music and flowers abounded; mumming, morris-dancing, and many a quaint display of humour and frolic spread over the country. The times, and the spirit of the times, are changed: – we are become a sober people. England is no longer merry England, but busy England; England full of wealth and poverty – extravagance and care.[4]

This traditional cycle of the year had been marked by festivals both religious and secular, most of which were believed to have originated in or to have been adapted from earlier pre-Christian traditions during the Middle Ages.[5] The English word "holiday" takes its origin from "holy day," a day of religious festival that departed from the regular work week. Some of these festivals, especially those associated with saints' days, faded from popular memory after the Reformation: for example, by

---

[3]   On the cry of "Give us back our eleven days," see, for example, E.G. Richards, *Mapping Time: The Calendar and its History* (Oxford: Oxford University Press, 1999), 252–56.

[4]   William Howitt, *The Rural Life of England*, 2 vols (London: Longman, 1838), 2:142.

[5]   See R.T. Hampson, *Medii aevi kalendarium*. Hampson concedes that some traditional practices and superstitions derive from Celtic beliefs, but ascribes the majority to Roman pagan practices adapted to Christianity in the Middle Ages.

1800 Britons barely remembered Corpus Christi, or the origins of Lammas Day.[6] The most important seasons for Christianity, Christmas and Easter, continued to be an important part of social practices, but other days that had been, or that were believed to have been, important in rural communities, such as May Day and Midsummer, were fading from popular consciousness. For much of the nineteenth century, the only two universally recognized "holidays" from work in England were Christmas Day and Good Friday, marking Christ's birth and death.[7]

That by the mid-Victorian period writers frequently remark on Easter Monday outings or the unreliability of workers on what had become called Boxing Day suggests the power of cultural memory.[8] Presumably, both in rural and industrial communities, workers either negotiated additional holidays with their employers or simply did not show up for work on days that they felt should be traditional holidays, especially the day after Christmas and the day after Easter, which were also the start of new theatre seasons. In 1846, seven inmates of the East London Union Workhouse were ordered to appear in court for refusing to work on Easter Monday (*The Times*, April 14, 1846).

This book focuses on attempts, some conscious, some less so, to find a connection between the nineteenth-century world and a lost or fading medieval past preserved in cultural memory through an awareness of time and calendar. Stephanie Trigg has drawn attention to "the centrality of time – and our different ways of negotiating its mysteries – to the various ways we conceive the medieval past,"[9] and time provided one means of connecting with the lost world of the Middle Ages. The nineteenth-century preoccupation with medievalism is, as many commentators have remarked, a struggle with a sense of loss.[10] Most often the loss is depicted as of values embedded in the medieval way of life, although frequently the values are associated with aesthetics: A.W.N. Pugin, John Ruskin and many others claimed that the medieval period – which British writers generally defined as between the arrival of the Saxons and the English Reformation – had an artistic style that

---

[6]   Some believed Lammas Day was associated with lambs, and some with loaves; see, for example, Hampson, 2:234, or William Hone's *Every-Day Book* 1:1063.

[7]   The *Illustrated London Almanack* for 1855 shows varying "Holidays Kept at Public Offices"; the Exchequer recognized only Good Friday and Christmas Day, but the Bank of England and India House also kept May 1 (St Philip and St James) and November 1 (All Saints) as holidays; The Custom and Excise Office also took off May 24, Queen Victoria's birthday; and the Stamp Office took off the queen's birthday and then five days later the Restoration of Charles II.

[8]   On Boxing Day, see Chapter 3; *The Times* notes Easter Monday as an occasion for theatre, fairs, and political activism, at one point calling it a "mob-holyday" (April 23, 1840).

[9]   Stephanie Trigg, "Medievalism and Theories of Temporality." *The Cambridge Companion to Medievalism*, ed. Louise D'Arcens (Cambridge: Cambridge University Press, 2016), 207.

[10]   Alice Chandler's classic *A Dream of Order: The Medieval Ideal in Nineteenth-Century British Literature* (Lincoln, NE: University of Nebraska Press, 1970) discusses medievalism as loss; see also Kathleen Biddick, *The Shock of Medievalism* (Durham, NC: Duke University Press, 1998). Another helpful overview is David Matthews's *Medievalism, A Critical History* (Cambridge: D.S. Brewer, 2015).

embodied its beliefs.[11] My focus here, though, is on written texts showing how nine-teenth-century Britons detected, interpreted, created, and above all, enjoyed what they believed to be medieval survivals, especially in the form of celebration. I am choosing here to use the word "enjoyment" because, as I shall argue, frequently the religious connotations of the word "joy" are downplayed and a secular, or even a pagan, tradition is evoked. At a time of social change, the claims of tradition – we do this because we have always done it at this time of year – resonate particularly strongly. I am fully aware that the result is some circular arguments: we do this because we have always done this, which is why we continue to do this. But I also want to suggest that the hidden part of "we do this because we have always done this" is that "we do this because we've always enjoyed doing this; we look forward to this time of year because this is what we do." What especially interests me is that seldom do the writers and participants express themselves this bluntly: instead, they appeal to a vaguely medieval past, as though that in itself is a justification. My examples focus on the points where oral, antiquarian, and literary traditions blur together to create a vision of what life in medieval England must have been like.

Nineteenth-century medievalists implicitly or explicitly created comparisons between their own time and the Middle Ages. The main arguments tended to be:

1. The way of life of English people of the Middle Ages gave them a stronger sense of values than we have now.

Although commentators expressed the values in different ways (John Ruskin, for example, suggesting they were derived from a communal sense of religion and Thomas Carlyle stressing a society based on hierarchy) the picture created is of a more morally cohesive society.[12]

2. English people of the Middle Ages had a finer appreciation of artistic style than we have now.

The Victorian Medieval Revival in the fine and decorative arts fully shows this sense of artistic inferiority, and moreover connects style with values.

This study, however, will focus more on two further assumptions:

3. English people of the Middle Ages had a stronger sense of connection to tradition and to community both at the national and at the local level than we have now.

This leads to the aspect of the medieval world that given assumptions 1 and 2 might at first seem counterintuitive:

4. English people of the Middle Ages had more fun than we do now.

---

[11]   For example, A.W.N. Pugin's *Contrasts; A Parallel between the Noble Edifices of the XIVth and XVth Centuries and Similar Buildings of the Present Day, Shewing the Present Decay of Taste* (Alderbury: printed for author, 1836).

[12]   See John Ruskin, particularly *Seven Lamps of Architecture* (London: J. Wiley, 1849); Thomas Carlyle, *Past and Present* (London: Chapman and Hall, 1843).

Any study of "fun" in the Middle Ages must be indebted to Mikhail Bakhtin, who sees in François Rabelais's *Gargantua and Pantagruel* not just a scatological oddity in "isolation" from canonical medieval texts, but rather the embodiment of the popular spirit of the Middle Ages: "No dogma, no authoritarianism, no narrow-minded seriousness can co-exist with Rabelaisian images."[13] Yet some British authors of the nineteenth century anticipate his envisioning in *Rabelais and His World* of an irreverent, iconoclastic Middle Ages, sometimes a little coarse, sometimes disrupting hierarchy, but frequently more shaped by pleasure than the present. Moving through the year, the result is the creation of a festival calendar, or, as Brian Maidment has argued, of competing calendars,[14] referring back – sometimes playfully, sometimes regretfully – to the habits of past, especially as represented by an imagined medieval England.

Playing with Calendars

Earlier authors had, of course addressed times of year in their writings, especially in the pastoral tradition. Educated readers might have some familiarity with the bucolic worlds of Virgil's *Georgics*, not in strict calendar form but representing the farming practices of different times of year; and Edmund Spenser's *Shephearde's Calender* (1579).[15] Robert Herrick's poetry makes multiple references to festive occasions, including Christmas, May Day, and even Mothering Sunday; antiquarians of the later eighteenth and the nineteenth century often quote his work as a source. James Thomson's *The Seasons* (1730) was well known, and Robert Bloomfield's very popular *The Farmer's Boy: A Rural Poem* (1800) follow the same pattern of the changing seasons.

The earliest substantial historical study of the calendar itself that I have found is John Brady's *Clavis Calendaria*, first published in 1812–13. Brady's work provides a history of the calendar, explaining its historical development and the linguistic origin of months and days of the week; then moves day by day through the year, noting important festivals and anniversaries associated with each day. Brady, however, is unsure how his readers will react to his account of the Middle Ages. Assuming a cultural divide between his readers and medieval religious and cultural beliefs, he remarks that:

> In tracing the absurdities and inconsistencies of mankind through the dark ages of ignorance, a necessity has occurred of adverting to the advantages accruing to modern times, from the suppression of those superstitious usages, which for centuries deformed the Christian Religion; and to awake a proper sense of those blessings, the Author has described in strong colours the errors from which we are now happily emancipated.

[13] Mikhail M. Bakhtin, *Rabelais and his World* (1965), translated by Helene Iswolsky (Cambridge, MA: MIT Press, 1968), 3.

[14] Brian Maidment, "Re-Arranging the Year: The Almanac, the Day Book and the Year Book as Popular Literary Forms, 1789–1860." In *Rethinking Victorian Culture*, ed. Juliet John and Alice Jenkins (Basingstoke: Macmillan Press, 2000), 91–113.

[15] Spenser's poem, and Virgil's to a lesser extent, have a moral-allegorical component, but they could still both be read as describing the pastoral life at different times of year.

Apologizing in case this seems offensive to Roman Catholics of his own day, he adds, "The superstitious impieties of times long past, the Author is convinced, will find few advocates among those who are still professedly of the same Church."[16] Even though he is recreating a historical sense of time, Brady shows himself anxious to separate himself and his readers, even those who are Roman Catholic, from some of the beliefs of the medieval past.

Yet even before Brady's study of time, collectors of local traditions had noted that in areas of long-established residency, customs, and pastimes followed the year. Henry Bourne's *Antiquitates Vulgares, Or, The Antiquities of the Common People*, first published in Newcastle in 1725, lists general superstitions but then follows through the church year from Christmas to harvest. Bourne's expressed intent was a return to the "primitive Purity" of inoffensive popular customs and the abolition of those that were sinful: he explains,

> I would not be thought a Reviver of old Rites and Ceremonies to the Burdening of the People, nor an Abolisher of innocent Customs, which are their Pleasures and Recreation: I aim at nothing, but a Regulation of those which are in Being amongst them, which they themselves are far from thinking burdensome, and abolishing such only as are sinful and wicked. (Bourne, x)

Ironically, in recording the customs and practices derived from "Heathenism, or the Inventions of indolent Monks" (Bourne, xi) in order to regulate them, Bourne helped preserve them. In 1777 John Brand reprinted and expanded Bourne's study with the expressed intent of rescuing "many of these causes from oblivion." At the Reformation, he observes, "our sensible and spirited forefathers" were easily persuaded to change their religious beliefs – "Yet were *the People* by no means inclined to annihilate the seemingly innocent Ceremonies of their former superstitious Faith." Brand then notes the importance of person to person transmission: such practices, "consecrated to the Fancies of Men, by a usage from Time immemorial, though erased by public Authority from the *written Word*, were committed as a venerable Deposit to the keeping of *oral Tradition*" (Brand, vi). Brand may be making a class distinction between the "forefathers" of his readers and those "People" who wanted to preserve those parts of previous ceremonies inspired by the Roman Catholic calendar that were fun – but now he seeks to reinscribe those traditions passed down orally in writing for the good of the whole:

> The common People, confined by daily Labour, seem to require their proper Intervals of Relaxation; perhaps it is of the highest political Utility to encourage innocent Sports and Games among them. The Revival of many of these would, I think, be highly pertinent at this particular Season, when the general spread of Luxury and Dissipation threatens more than at any preceding Period to extinguish the Character of our boasted national Bravery. (vi)

---

[16]   John Brady, *Clavis Calendaria, Or, A compendious analysis of the calendar* (London: Longman, 1812–13), 1:vii–viii.

Although the connection between time of year and festive celebration is implicit in Brand's Preface, his information being partly derived from "one of those ancient Romish Calendars of singular Curiosity" (viii), his appendices added much information but disrupted Bourne's calendar format. When Henry Ellis revised the work again in the nineteenth century, he returned to a strict calendar format following through the year from January to December.[17]

This revision, however, was pre-empted by William Hone's *Every-Day Book*, which lists both events of historical significance and traditions for each day of the year. Kyle Grimes, who has created a digital edition, notes that Hone initially published this work in weekly installments starting in January 1825, but that production soon fell behind; the material was reprinted in a number of formats for many years.[18] Successive versions of the *Antiquitates Vulgares* had moved from an articulated sense of difference, where the reader is assumed to be distinct from the "common People" described, to a shared sense of heritage. The *Every-Day Book* emphasizes the pleasures and wonders of the Middle Ages: enlarging on the concept of what Benedict Anderson has called "imagined community" it connects British readers of the present with the national past, and especially with forms of celebration.[19] The words "our ancestors" occur dozens of times, as do the words "our Saxon ancestors," of whom Hone is particularly admiring. Eliding the "common people" and "the nation," Hone combines the traditional Anglican calendar with information from history and popular culture, especially seasonal recreations: for example, although the Calendar of Anglican feast-days merely describes October 31 as the vigil for All Saints' Day, the *Every-Day Book* lists folk activities associated with Hallowe'en.

In compiling this massive calendar, Hone uses some medieval sources; for example, he frequently references the *Aurea Legenda* or *Golden Legend* originated by the thirteenth-century Jacobus de Voragine, which was one of the first works to be printed in England, for more obscure saints. But he also quotes very new ones, such as Peter George Patmore's *Mirror of the Months* (1826), which describes the natural history and activities associated with each of the twelve months. Patmore in turn acknowledges a debt to Leigh Hunt's *The Months: Descriptive of the Successive Beauties of the Year* (1821). Hunt's *Months* is significant for representing not only cultural traditions but also literary ones: bringing together the earliest and most recent English poetry, he quotes Chaucer, Spenser, Shakespeare, Jonson, Herrick and others, but also Coleridge, Wordsworth, Shelley, and Keats as part of the national heritage.[20] Similarly, the Howitt family collaborated on *The Book of the Seasons; Or, The Calendar of Nature* (1831), where the claimed objective was to describe nature and rural activities throughout the year at a time when towns and cities were enlarging their

---

[17] Subsequent references distinguish these three editions as "Bourne," "Brand," and "Ellis"; see Abbreviations for bibliographic details.

[18] Kyle Grimes, ed., *The Every-Day Book*, honearchive.org/etexts/edb/home.html (accessed September 21, 2018). After Hone's bankruptcy, publication passed to Thomas Tegg.

[19] For the concept of "imagined community," see Benedict Anderson, *Imagined Communities* (1983, 2nd edition, London: Verso, 1991), especially pp. 5–7. See also E.J. Hobsbawm and T.O. Ranger, *The Invention of Tradition* (1983; rpt Cambridge University Press, 1996).

[20] Shelley's *Revolt of Islam* was published in 1817 and Keats's "To Autumn" only in 1820.

"boundaries, and the sweet face of Nature is hidden from the inhabitants."[21] William Howitt, the acknowledged author, seems to have supplied the descriptions of nature and presumably the information on birds and angling; his brother Godfrey helped create tables of insect-life and plant-life relevant to each month; and his wife Mary wrote "lays" – a medievalist choice of title – for each of the four seasons.

The most medievalist venture into calendars, though is R.T. Hampson's *Medii aevi kalendarium; or Dates, charters, and customs of the middle ages.* Hampson presents his researches as a service to, and to some extent a corrective of, other antiquarians, and he is one of the earliest English historians actually to use the word "mediaeval" (Hampson 1:1; 1:6).[22] Although his focus is on the tenth to fifteenth century, he does not seem to like the Middle Ages very much, and describes the "superstitions" associated with particular days of the year as surviving through the failure of "the authority of the church" to "remove the relics of paganism, which had thus been incorporated with the semi-christianity of the middle ages." He is nevertheless helping to preserve memory of traditions that will soon no longer exist:

> The absurdities, noticed in the following pages, exist in scarcely any other than rural districts; and the childish and boisterous sports which delighted our undisciplined ancestors, have nearly all disappeared before the intellectual amusements and occupations now generally within the attainment of the bulk of the people. (1:57)

Almanacks

The calendar was, of course, important to the church, as I will discuss in Chapter 1. A number of secular attempts to list calendar events, however, provide a fascinating bridge between oral and written tradition. Since 1697 Britons had been able to buy the *Vox Stellarum*, an almanack that included a detailed calendar of each month, including religious and secular festivals, significant anniversaries, phases of the moon, the times of sunrise and sunset, and other useful information. It also included astrological predictions of weather and events, at a time when long-range weather forecasts were more dependent on magic than meteorology. Founded by the astrologer Francis Moore, the book has become known as *Old Moore's Almanack*, its primary title from the 1850s.

In the 1830s the tax on publications was reduced, and following the development of a massive seasonal publishing industry focused on gift books and annuals for Christmas and the New Year,[23] publishers tried creating variations on the almanack,

---

[21] William Howitt [and Mary Howitt], *The Book of the Seasons, Or, The Calendar of Nature* (London: Henry Colburn and Richard Bentley, 1831), xvii.

[22] Hampson usually uses the phrase "of the middle ages" but the adjective "mediaeval" occurs a handful of times in early pages of the book, possibly suggesting that he wrote those pages last, just as the word "mediaeval" was becoming accepted; the spelling "medieval" also occurs twice in the Glossary volume, once capitalized.

[23] In *Forget Me Not: The Rise of the British Literary Annual, 1823–1835* (Athens, OH: Ohio University Press, 2015), Katherine D. Harris distinguishes between gift books, one-time publications, and annuals, published each year (62).

some of which contained no predictions whatsoever.[24] For example, the A. Schloss company, who claimed to be "Fancy Stationers" to Queen Victoria's mother the Duchess of Kent, published *Schloss's English Bijou Almanac*, a tiny booklet less than one inch tall that reproduced the calendar on bi-weekly pages. The 1843 edition, edited by Mary Russell Mitford, included a list of the birthdates and household members of the royal family; some images of famous people with short poetic addresses to each. The opening verses by Elizabeth Barrett, later Browning, begin: "Seven years are gone, since first we won/ A look from cordial faces. And now we strike our octave, like/ A minstrel used to praises."[25] The simile of a minstrel (later also used to honor the poet Samuel Rogers) creates a medieval picture in the reader's mind; while the phrase "strike our octave" marks this as the eighth annual issue, but also plays on the concept of a musical octave or poetic stanza.

The Tilt and Bogue engraving company, which produced expensive Christmas annuals, also published the *Comic Almanack*, with illustrations by George Cruikshank and humorous pieces by Thackeray, the Mayhew brothers, and others. With a medievalist flourish that suggests that somebody involved may have read older works such as Edmund Spenser's *Shepheardes Calender*, the cover announces that it is "Adorned with a Dozen of 'Righte Merrie' Cuts, Pertaining to the Months." At its commencement in the 1830s, the *Comic Almanack* was very much a parody of the work of Francis Moore and his successors, providing a month-by-month calendar in chart form and funny predictions. As I discuss in Chapter 2, the 1839 and 1840 issues experimented with a novel in calendar form. By this time, the "Almanack" aspect of the publication had become more subdued, some years providing calendars and some none, but the writers still included humorous predictions of the future from time to time.

Punch, published from 1841, also usually included a calendar of the year with humorous seasonal illustrations that remind readers of long-standing celebrations and anniversaries. The format varies from year to year, but the calendar for 1845 connects past, present, and future. Anglican religious feast days and Sundays are recorded in Gothic script, but most of the days are filled with odd facts or with humorous predictions, usually involving absurdities and bad puns. For example, January 20 states that "At Coventry, last week, a kitten was born with the head of a red herring." April 2 states that the little American actor "Tom Thumb exhibited in the evening at Buckingham Palace, as Napoleon, Her Majesty liking a *little nap* after dinner" (*Punch* 8:11–12). In creating jokes around specific dates, both *Punch* and the *Comic Almanack* are particularly fond of the humorous possibilities of Valentine's Day, a tradition that appears to be genuinely ancient. Yet they also pay attention to other festivals that have an embellished or imagined medieval aspect

---

[24] Peter Stockham, *Notes on Schloss's Bijou Almanacs* (London: Dillon, 1968). See also Brian Maidment, "Beyond Usefulness and Ephemerality: The Discursive Almanac, 1828–1860," *British Literature and Print Culture*, ed. Sandro Jung (Cambridge: D.S. Brewer, 2013), 158–94.

[25] Barrett's letters reveal that she drafted poems to match a number of other engravings, but in the end, MRM seems only to have used the introductory verses and those on the duchess of Orleans. *Brownings' Correspondence* 6:99.

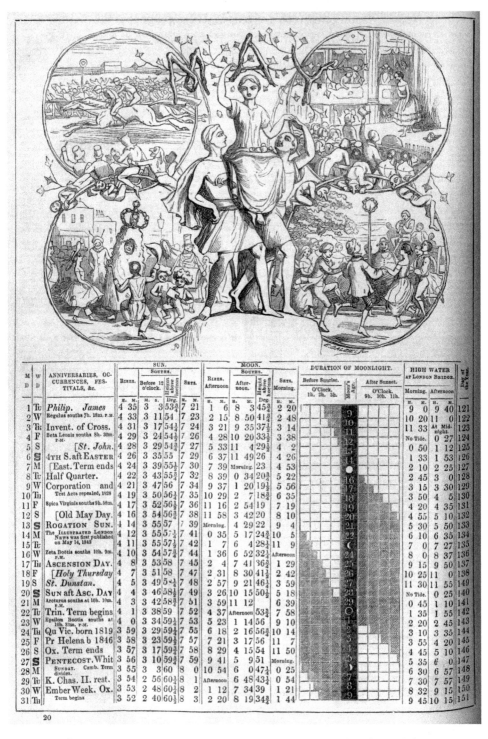

M D	W D	ANNIVERSARIES, OCCURRENCES, FESTIVALS, &c.	SUN. Rises. H.	M.	Souths. Before 12 o'clock. M.	S.	Height above horizon Deg.	Sets. H.	M.	MOON. Rises. Afternoon H.	M.	Souths. After-noon. H.	M.	Height above horizon Deg.	Sets. Morning. H.	M.	DURATION OF MOONLIGHT. Moon's Age.	HIGH WATER AT LONDON BRIDGE. Morning. H.	M.	Afternoon H.	M.	Day of the Year.
1	Tu	*Philip. James*	4	35	3	3	53¾	7	21	1	6	8	3	45¾	2	20	9	9	0	9	40	121
2	W	Regulus souths 7h. 18m. P.M.	4	33	3	11	54	7	23	2	15	8	50	41¾	2	48	10	10	20	11	0	122
3	Th	Invent. of Cross.	4	31	3	17	54¼	7	24	3	21	9	35	37½	3	14	11	11	33	At Mid-night		123
4	F	Beta Leonis souths 8h. 30m. P.M.	4	29	3	24	54½	7	26	4	28	10	20	33½	3	38	12	No Tide.		0	27	124
5	S	[*St. John.*	4	28	3	29	54¾	7	27	5	33	11	4	29½	4	2	13	0	50	1	12	125
6	S	4th S. aft Easter	4	26	3	35	55	7	29	6	37	11	49	26	4	26	14	1	33	1	53	126
7	M	[East. Term ends	4	24	3	39	55½	7	30	7	39	Morning.		23	4	53	●	2	10	2	25	127
8	Tu	Half Quarter.	4	22	3	43	55¾	7	32	8	39	0	34	20¾	5	22	16	2	45	3	0	128
9	W	Corporation and	4	21	3	47	56	7	34	9	37	1	20	19½	5	56	17	3	15	3	30	129
10	Th	Test Acts repealed, 1828	4	19	3	50	56¼	7	35	10	29	2	7	18¾	6	35	18	3	50	4	5	130
11	F	Spica Virginis souths 9h. 58m.	4	17	3	52	56½	7	36	11	16	2	54	19	7	19	19	4	20	4	35	131
12	S	[Old May Day.	4	16	3	54	56¾	7	38	11	58	3	42	20	8	10	20	4	55	5	10	132
13	S	Rogation Sun.	4	14	3	55	57	7	39	Morning.		4	29	22	9	4	21	5	30	5	50	133
14	M	The Illustrated London News was first published	4	12	3	55	57¼	7	41	0	35	5	17	24¾	10	5	22	6	10	6	35	134
15	Tu	on May 14, 1842	4	11	3	55	57½	7	42	1	7	6	4	28¼	11	9	☾	7	0	7	27	135
16	W	Zeta Boötis souths 10h. 9m. P.M.	4	10	3	54	57¾	7	44	1	36	6	52	32¼	Afternoon		24	8	0	8	37	136
17	Th	Ascension Day.	4	8	3	53	58	7	45	2	4	7	41	36¾	1	29	25	9	15	9	50	137
18	F	[*Holy Thursday*	4	7	3	51	58	7	47	2	31	8	30	41½	2	42	26	10	25	11	0	138
19	S	*St. Dunstan.*	4	5	3	49	58¼	7	48	2	57	9	21	46¼	3	59	27	11	30	11	55	149
20	S	Sun aft Asc. Day	4	4	3	46	58½	7	49	3	26	10	15	50½	5	18	28	No Tide.		0	25	140
21	M	Arcturus souths at 10h. 10m. P.M.	4	3	3	42	58¾	7	51	3	59	11	12		6	39	29	0	45	1	10	141
22	Tu	Trin. Term begins	4	1	3	38	59	7	52	4	37	Afternoon		53¾	7	58	○	1	35	1	55	142
23	W	Epsilon Boötis souths at 10h. 33m. P.M.	4	0	3	34	59¼	7	53	5	23	1	14	56	9	10	1	2	20	2	45	143
24	Th	Qu Vic. born 1819	3	59	3	29	59¼	7	55	6	18	2	16	56¾	10	14	2	3	10	3	35	144
25	F	Pr Helena b 1846	3	58	3	23	59½	7	57	7	21	3	17	56	11	7	3	3	55	4	20	145
26	S	Ox. Term ends	3	57	3	17	59¾	7	58	8	29	4	15	54	11	50	4	4	45	5	10	146
27	S	Pentecost. Whit	3	56	3	10	59¾	7	59	9	41	5	9	51	Morning.		5	5	35	6	0	147
28	M	Sunday. Camb. Term divides.	3	55	3	3	60	8	0	10	54	6	0	47¼	0	25	☽	6	30	6	57	148
29	Tu	K. Chas. II. rest.	3	54	2	56	60¼	8	1	Afternoon		6	48	43¼	0	54	7	7	30	7	57	149
30	W	Ember Week. Ox.	3	53	2	48	60¼	8	2	1	12	7	34	39	1	21	8	8	32	9	15	150
31	Th	Term begins	3	52	2	40	60½	8	3	2	20	8	19	34¾	1	44	9	9	45	10	15	151

Duration of Moonlight: Before Sunrise, O'Clock 1h. 2h. 3h.; After Sunset, O'Clock 9h. 10h. 11h.

20

Fig. 1. "May." Almanack page by Richard Doyle from the *Illustrated London Almanack* for 1849.

that I shall return to later in this study, including May Day, the Lord Mayor's Show, and of course the Christmas season.

A particularly medievalist example of an almanack is the *Illustrated London Almanack* for 1849, a sister publication of the *Illustrated London News*. The calendar for each month is headed by an illustration by Richard Doyle that combines past and present with the sign of the zodiac. For example, May (Fig. 1) shows a May Queen held up by two figures suggesting Gemini, flanked by vignettes of the present-day May races and theater and old May Day revels, an indication that memories of calendar reform were still current. In addition to astronomical (but not astrological) information, each month contains a description of traditional English rural festivals associated with the month. Here London readers could learn about customs passed down through generations but extinct in the city. An article on "Calendars, Almanacks, Wakes, and Fairs" gives a short history of how time was marked in the past, with a particular emphasis on "Village Wakes or Feasts, which in the progress of society are gradually growing obsolete."[26] The writer stresses the community of the past, even in his discussion of the social rather than superstitious religious origins of commemorative days: "Among the old Term days, it is believed that May Day is the only one which is not specifically distinguished by being a festival or office observed by the Church." Some examples of times of year containing the word "mass" follow, such as Lammas and Candlemas, concluding, "It may here be observed, that the word MASS, about the etymology of which there have been so many conjectures, is of Gothic origin; and that, in its primary meaning, it is nearly synonymous with the word *Mess*, as still used in the navy to signify a *community* of persons who take their meals together."

The author is probably Thomas Miller, whom the editors credit with the monthly listing of traditional festivals of year, each illustrated with an appropriately rural engraving. His first paragraph needs quoting in full:

Many of the old games, and masques, and mummings, which were in accordance with the simple habits of our homely forefathers, have long since passed away. Only a few remain, out of which it was their delight and amusement to witness; and even those are shorn of their ancient splendour; for, though still picturesque, they have a faded look, and seem no more in keeping with the manners and customs of the present day, than the murrey-coloured coats, and slashed doublets, and trunk hose would be, if dragged forth from the oak oaken recesses in which they have lain, disturbed only by the moth for many a long year, and worn again by the present generation. Such as have survived the stern mandates of Cromwell, lived through the Restoration of Charles, and withstood all the stormy revolutions which at last settled down, when the House of Hanover was securely seated upon the throne, we shall occasionally glance at in our descriptions of the months; for they are still within the ancient boundary-line which every year is rapidly cutting up, and into the opening of which the steam-boats and rail-roads are entering, and overturning nearly all that is

---

[26]   *Illustrated London Almanack for 1849* (London: Illustrated London News), 60.

picturesque and primitive, and that has for centuries given such life and beauty to the rural landscapes of England.[27]

Even medieval clothing, though it might be out of place in the Victorian world, seems more colorful and interesting than the present day's. This passage uses the word "picturesque" twice, and the following months attempt to present both a visual image and the cheerful spirit of the English rural past. In addition to drawing attention to nature as seen in the countryside throughout the year, Miller seemingly has no difficulty in finding at least one tradition for each month: for January, the focus is on "merry Plough Monday" (January 8 in 1849); February on Valentine's Day; and March on palm-bearing on Palm Sunday, with regret for "the abolition of these sacred emblems" that recall the Gospel and medieval pilgrims. Palm Sunday in 1849 actually fell on April 1, but Miller preserves this day to relate some pranks that he and his companions used to play on "April-Fool Day." May Day is one "of the oldest and most poetical of all our country amusements"; June discusses Whit Monday festivities (although Whitsun was in May in 1849); July represents sheep-shearing feasts; August harvest; and September sports at a country fair. October has least focus on organized activities, discussing nutting in the woods; then November is Guy Fawkes Day and December, of course, Christmas. Of these, only Christmas and Palm Sunday have any substantive religious content: readers need not fear that by celebrating they are returning to religious beliefs rejected by the English church, but instead, Miller hints, they should be regretting the loss of a community in touch with both spirituality and nature.

By the middle of the nineteenth century, then, Britons could obtain many works that recalled a historic sense of the festival year, and more were to follow. Robert Chambers published a substantial two-volume *Books of Days* in the early 1860s, and Bourne's researches of the early 1700s were again recast into William Carew Hazlitt's *Faiths and Folklore: A Dictionary* (1905). The heir of these works is the modern diary or calendar, but deserving of mention in this context is *The Oxford Companion to the Year*, edited by Bonnie Blackburn and Leofranc Holford-Strevens and first published in 1999.[28] For the structure of this study I am indebted to these works, and also to other discussions of the English year. Among these I should particularly note Ronald Hutton's important studies *Stations of the Sun: A History of the Ritual Year in Britain*; and *The Rise and Fall of Merry England 1400–1700*. Although my focus is on nineteenth-century discourse and festive representations in literature, rather than a quest for actual origins, his research is invaluable. Another very helpful study of festival is David Cressy's *Bonfires and Bells: National Memory and the Protestant Calendar in Elizabethan and Stuart England*; nineteenth-century antiquarians tended to be vague about what actually happened to traditions after the Reformation and Cressy's study helps fill in those forgotten spaces. Finally, I agree wholeheartedly with Eric Hobsbawm's assertion that "'Traditions' which appear or claim to be old are often quite recent in origin and sometimes invented." Hobsbawm

---

[27]   *Almanack for 1849*, 6. Thomas Miller (1807–74) had just published a series of books for boys on rural pursuits arranged by the seasons. Some of the text in the *Almanack* is copied from his *Pictures of Country Life* (1846).

[28]   See Bibliography for full details of these works.

further explains: "'Invented tradition' is taken to mean a set of practices, normally governed by overtly or tacitly accepted rules and of a ritual or symbolic nature, which seek to inculcate certain values and norms of behaviour by repetition, which automatically implies continuity with the past."[29] The examples in Hobsbawm and Terence Ranger's fascinating *Invention of Tradition* initially focus on royalty, but also demonstrate that others within a structure of power can develop their own traditions, sometimes at odds with the establishment. I am especially interested in those forms of celebration that assume "unofficial" forms and that emerge as memories of the Middle Ages.

My focus is primarily literary, tracing how this medieval tendency found its way into both historical and imaginative works, some of which have become canonical and many others of which were influential in their time in helping shape a conception of medieval Britain but are now largely neglected. I am aware that some of my readings, such as those of poems by Browning and Tennyson, may lay themselves open to the charge of being too literal. Yet in the case of works that can be read allegorically, the question remains: why choose the setting of the Middle Ages? The answer may vary somewhat from work to work, but writers consistently find something liberating in representing the Middle Ages and its survivals: thinking about the medieval not only provides a commentary on the political and social state of the present, but also opens up a world of wonder and activity that the present barely retains in the form of seasonal celebration. I hope that I can avoid the practice of the antiquarians of the late eighteenth and early nineteenth centuries who looked to literary texts for evidence of what the past was really like; and can focus instead on how texts and images both ephemeral and destined for posterity create a *story* of past and present festive customs and forms of celebration that made sense to nineteenth-century Britons.

The need to tell the story, and particularly the need to write it down, partly explains the constant refrain that a cultural practice is in decline or past and gone; after all, if everyone knew the story, it would not need to be told. Although this study pointedly avoids scholarly anthropology, focusing on the period before J.G. Frazer's *The Golden Bough* provided an overarching theory of comparative mythology suggesting everything derived from primitive religion,[30] the concept of *doxa* as expressed by Pierre Bourdieu might be helpful here. In a stable culture a ritual practice "*goes without saying because it comes without saying.*"[31] Hence the need to articulate the elements of a cultural practice – the expression of rules that create an orthodoxy – suggests the possibility that the practice may be facing a challenge. This is unquestionably true of many festivities in nineteenth-century Britain, where so

---

[29] "Introduction." Eric Hobsbawm and Terence Ranger, eds, *The Invention of Tradition*, 1.

[30] Ronald Hutton points out in *The Rise and Fall of Merry England 1400–1700* (Oxford: Oxford University Press, 1994) that "late medieval denunciations of popular festivities" never seemed inspired by supposed pagan origins (71); even in the mid-nineteenth century, discussions of popular celebrations are very different from those after Frazer's *Golden Bough*. Sir James G. Frazer, *The Golden Bough: A Study in Magic and Religion*, 3rd edition, 12 vols (London: Macmillan, 1911–15).

[31] Pierre Bourdieu, *Outline of a Theory of Practice*, trans. Richard Nice. (Cambridge: Cambridge University Press, 1977, rpt 1988), 167.

many recreations are re-creations of believed earlier practices whose origins have been lost. My conclusions are often the reverse of those of Johan Huizinga, who suggests that most play-elements have an origin in ritual; in nineteenth-century Britain, ritual origins may be the most imagined part of play as seasonal activities become inscribed as ritual.[32]

I should briefly state some limitations to this study. First, since historicizing festive occasions was so much part of the culture of nineteenth-century Britain, I have had to be selective in my choice of examples, focusing largely on instances where the story was centered in a sense of the medieval, in dispute, or evolved over time. Second, the majority of texts under discussion were published in London, and tend to reflect a London-centered point of view, sometimes from a position of superiority towards regional practices, but just as frequently with some level of recognition that those practices stemmed from or sustained a sense of community no longer possible in the metropolis. And finally, I will concede that the term "medieval" is open to discussion. Because this word only entered English vocabulary around 1830, and because many of the texts I discuss are very vague in their use of the past, it is sometimes difficult to know when "ancient times" or the days of "our ancestors" might be. I have tried, however, to differentiate between practices ascribed to Ancient Britons and Romans, and medieval practices believed to have survived the English Reformation. According to eighteenth- and nineteenth-century antiquarians, many medieval traditions were adaptations of Roman customs. My interest here, though, is in how such traditions influenced an emerging idea of Britain's Middle Ages. I leave it to readers to decide who had more fun: medieval Britons, or nineteenth-century Britons, who through imagining that they were re-enacting the celebrations of their ancestors, found a new justification for enjoying themselves.

---

[32]   See Johan Huizinga, *Homo Ludens; a Study of the Play-Element in Culture* (1949; London: Routledge and Kegan Paul, 1980).

1

The Christian and Not-So-Christian Year

THE ENGLISH CHURCH of the nineteenth century still maintained an elaborate calendar. The Elizabethan version of the Book of Common Prayer,[1] printed in 1559, expunged most of the saints' days recognized by Roman Catholics but retained those commemorating the Apostles. An explanatory statement, "Of Ceremonies, Why Some Be Abolished and Some Retained," claims that "some at first were of godly intent and purpose devised and yet at length turned to vanity and superstition, some entered into the Church by undiscreet devotion and such a zeal as was without knowledge." The goal is to retain the ceremonies "which pertain to edification," yet to recognize that "the burden of them was intolerable" even in early Christian times.[2] The calendar was still very important since the schedule of Bible readings was set out by date. In combination, Matins and Evensong, the two required services for every day, covered the entire Book of Psalms in a month. Moreover, while many holy days were fixed by date, those calculated in relation to Easter varied according to the "Golden Number," the nineteen-year table being included in the prefatory material and an "Almanac for Thirty Years" calculating the date of Easter between 1559 and 1588. The months are listed from January to December with the surviving saints' days and readings for morning and evening prayer, together with the signs of the Zodiac, perhaps implying a connection between the Christian year and the solar year. Complicating this further is the fact that before calendar reform in England, the new year was considered to start in March, and the Christian year in Advent.

By the Victorian period, the calendar-related materials in the Book of Common Prayer looked somewhat different, even though the book retained "Of Ceremonies." The signs of the Zodiac had been dropped from the calendar, but as early as the time of William Laud the number of saints' days had been expanded. *The Annotated Book of Common Prayer* (1867) lists in addition to the Apostles and other Gospel figures twenty "Martyrs in the Age of Persecution," twenty-one "Martyrs and other Saints especially connected with England," and a few more saints besides.[3] The comparative calendar that follows shows that the Victorian Church of England had far

[1] A Prayer Book was produced in the reign of Edward VI but this 1559 version stresses the beginning of English uniformity of worship.
[2] *The Book of Common Prayer 1559: The Elizabethan Prayer Book*, ed. John E. Booty (Charlottesville, VA: Folger Shakespeare Library, 1976), 18–19.
[3] *The Annotated Book of Common Prayer*, ed. John Henry Blunt (London: Rivington, 1867), 37.

less saints' days than before the Reformation, but still had several days of special religious significance every month.

The seasons of the year and related celebrations, then, were always a part of mainstream English Christianity, but the links between time, date and celebration became even stronger with the rise of the Oxford Movement. In 1827, John Keble published his *Christian Year*, poems inspired by Christian celebrations of Sunday and special holy days. By 1828, the book was already in its third edition, and it continued to sell well throughout the nineteenth century. In George Gissing's 1893 novel *The Odd Women*, the impoverished Virginia Madden spends money that she can ill afford to buy her younger sister Monica a copy of *The Christian Year*; as far as can be told, Monica never reads it, and I suspect that the fate of many real-life copies of the book was to be gifted to others and left unread. Nevertheless, *The Christian Year* reconciled the ancient ritual year with present-day Anglican belief. It was a major influence on the thinking of Charlotte Mary Yonge, who regarded Keble as a mentor. In *The Heir of Redclyffe*, itself an inspiration for Victorian medievalists such as Ruskin and Morris, Sir Guy Morville receives a copy from his guardian Mrs Edmonstone for his eighteenth birthday – Mrs Edmonstone has evidently read it, since she has previously quoted the line "the trivial round and common task" from the opening poem "Morning."[4]

The Christian Year is specific as to time of year, but at the same time depicts a rural England hardly changed from year to year since the Middle Ages. It is with "Morning" that the cycle begins, followed by "Evening," the times of Matins and Evensong. Christians are reminded to match their spirits with the time of day: "Oh, timely happy, timely wise,/ Hearts that with rising morn arise!"[5] The reader's duty is to live a Christian life in the world, and at first consideration the immediacy of the "new"-ness of every day is anti-medievalist: rejecting the monastic lives associated in England with the Middle Ages, Keble also elaborates: "We need not bid, for cloister'd cell" since self-denial can be found in the "trivial round, the common task" (1:3–4). Yet after "Morning" and "Evening," the poems that follow cycle through the weeks of the year, recalling the ancient Christian associations with those dates; in many instances, the epigraphs and footnotes refer to Bible readings associated with the day in the lectionary and the Prayer Book.

Although the reader is constantly reminded of Christians of the past, explicit references to the Middle Ages are rare in *The Christian Year*. The first seasonal poem, III, Advent Sunday, refers to the Crusades: after the time of Christ,

> Years roll away, again the tide of crime
> Has swept thy footsteps from the favour'd clime.
>> Where shall the holy Cross find rest?
>> On a crown'd monarch's mailed breast:
> Like some bright angel o'er the darkling scene,
> Through court and camp he holds his heavenward course serene. (1:12)

---

[4]   Charlotte Mary Yonge, *The Heir of Redclyffe* (1853), ed. Barbara Dennis (Oxford: World's Classics, 1997), 90, 54.
[5]   John Keble, "Morning." *The Christian Year* (Oxford: J. Parker, 1827), 1:2. Subsequent references given in text by volume and page number.

A footnote explains, "St Louis in the tenth century," which may show the vagueness of Keble's medieval history: the armor marked with the red cross suggests that Keble means the Crusader king Louis IX, who lived in the thirteenth century. Yet the poem's form is itself medievalist. Keble is fond of ending his stanzas with Alexandrines, and here the concluding Alexandrine provides an intertextual reference to another medievalist work, namely, to Edmund Spenser's *Faerie Queene* and the Red-Crosse Knight, upholder of the faith. Although no poem in *The Christian Year* is in true Spenserian stanzas, the stanza forms of about one-third conclude with Alexandrines.

Keble's poetics recall medievalism in other significant ways. First, his poetry is clearly influenced by William Wordsworth, and contains frequent echoes of the *Lyrical Ballads* in form and in the representation of nature. For example, Poem LIV, Fourth Sunday After Trinity, begins:

> It was not then a poet's dream,
>   An idle vaunt of song,
> Such as beneath the moon's soft gleam
>   On vacant fancies throng;
>
> Which bids us see in heaven and earth,
>   In all fair things around,
> Strong yearnings for a blest new birth
>   With sinless glories crown'd;
>
> Which bids us hear, at each sweet pause
>   From care and want and toil,
> When dewy eve her curtain draws
>   Over the day's turmoil,
>
> In the low chant of wakeful birds,
>   In the deep weltering flood,
> In whispering leaves, these solemn words—
>   "God made us all for good." (2:12–13)

Like Wordsworth's "Expostulation and Reply," Keble is using ballad form, claimed by Thomas Percy and other ballad scholars to have its origins in oral poetry of the Middle Ages, to lyrical effect. The poetic imagination focuses not on "vacant fancies" but on the exterior world of God's creation that provides confirmation of divine goodness and of the promise of heaven. Keble's nature is composed of physical, external objects that remind the observer of their Creator – and also of Wordsworth. Poem XVII, "Third Sunday after Epiphany," begins "I marked a rainbow in the north," then explains in sentiments and meter similar to Wordsworth's "I wandered lonely as a cloud,"

> It was a gleam of memory dear,
> And as I walk and muse apart,
> When all seems faithless round and drear,
> I would revive it in my heart ... (1:64)

Yet Keble finds in these external objects a stimulus not just to his own memory but to the soul, their value being not just in their beauty but in their message about creation: "Brighter than rainbow in the north, /More cheery than the matin lark,/ Is the soft gleam of Christian worth" (1:65).

Second, Keble refers his to devotional poetry on several occasions as "minstrelsy." Poem XII, "The Circumcision of Christ," for example, asks,

> Wouldst thou a Poet be?
> And would thy dull heart fain
> Borrow of Israel's minstrelsy
> One high enraptured strain? (1:46)

Yet although Keble follows the notion that the Psalmist David was a "minstrel," the term has stronger associations with the medievalism of the ballad revival than with the Bible. [6] XLIX, "Tuesday in Whitsun-Tide, which has the subtitle "(*Addressed to Candidates in Ordination*)," concludes:

> Listen, ye pure white-robed souls,
> Whom in her list she now enrolls,
> And gird ye for your high emprise
> By these her thrilling minstrelsies.
>
> And wheresoe'er, in earth's wide field,
> Ye lift for Him, the red-cross shield,
> Be this your song, your joy and pride –
> "Our Champion went before and died." (1:196–97)

Implicitly, the "her" is the church, and the newly-ordained pastors are her Crusaders, following the example of Christ.

And finally, his understanding of the relationship between past and present is strongly influenced by the Biblical typology of medieval theologians such as Augustine.[7] George P. Landow has characterized the Victorian use of Biblical typology as shaped by the Reformed reading of scripture, yet Keble seems fully aware of the structured typology of medieval theologians, where one story may represent a historical moment, a prediction of the life of Christ, a representation of the state of the human soul, and a prediction of the end times. Poem XII, "The Circumcision of Christ," connects the Gospel story of Jesus' circumcision with the tradition of Abraham and the prophets; Christ's death; the Eucharist; and the necessity of suffering in the Christian life. The shedding of Christ's blood brings together the old and new covenants, and Christians past and present: "O bond of union, dear/And strong as is thy grace! /Saints, parted by a thousand year, /May thus in heart embrace"

---

[6]   The word "minstrel" appears in only one verse in the King James version of the Bible; in II Kings 3:15, a minstrel is inspired to prophesy. II Chronicles 25:1–3 recounts that musicians were appointed to "prophesy" in David's temple. "Minstrels" is used once in the Gospels with pejorative overtones in the story of the raising of Jairus' daughter (Matthew 9:23).

[7]   See Joshua King, "John Keble's *The Christian Year*: Private Reading and Imagined National Religious Communities." *Victorian Literature and Culture* 40 (2012), 397–420.

(*Christian Year* 1:46). Incidentally, it shows the problem of the "year," since Christians connected the Circumcision with January 1, and Keble has started his year at Advent. Poem XXIII, Quinquagesima Sunday, contains the four typological levels. First, following the lectionary, the poem recalls the Genesis story of the rainbow as covenant between God and humans. Just as people cannot look at the sun but can contemplate the rainbow, so "The Son of God in radiance beam'd /Too bright for us to scan,/ But we may face the rays that stream'd/ From the mild Son of Man." Christians in the present "hail" these "tokens of a pardoning God" the same as the patriarchs. And the rainbow also suggests the future of heaven: "So home-bound sailors spring to shore,/To oceans safely past;/ So happy souls, when life is o'er/ Plunge in th'empyreal vast" (1:91–92).

Keble's poetry thus follows what he later termed "the universal adoption, by the early Christian writers, of the allegorical way of expounding the Old Testament."[8] Keble demonstrated his awareness of the medieval origins of Christian typology in his final contribution to the Oxford Movement's *Tracts for the Times*. In the 1830s John Henry Newman and his similarly-minded friends, most of them students at Oxford University or young clergymen, attempted "the practical revival of doctrines" and the "Apostolic" tradition within the Church of England (*Tracts* 1:iii). Observation of ritual in worship and of Christian holy days required an acute consciousness of time and date. "The Times" are stressed in the title, ostensibly referring to the present. Yet early in the development of the series the present is tied to tradition, most tracts end with a date marking a holy day in the Christian year. For example, Tract 18, "Thoughts on the Benefits of the System of Fasting, Enjoined by our Church," concludes, "OXFORD, *The Feast of St Thomas*" (that is, December 21, 1833). Tract 21, "Mortification of the Flesh, A Scripture Duty" appeared on the Feast of the Circumcision (January 1, 1834).

Keble's Tract 89 is titled "On the Mysticism Attributed to the Early Fathers of the Church." Openly showing his detailed study of early Christian thinkers who influenced the development of medieval theology such as Origen and Augustine, Keble sets himself the task of reevaluating the Protestant "notion, understood or expressed, that 'the Fathers [of the Church] were Mystics, and need not be regarded at all'" (89:3). Past and present are immediately contrasted: "Mysticism conveys the notion of something essentially and altogether remote from common sense and practical utility: but common sense and practical utility are the very idols of this age." This dislike of anything associated with mysticism causes "even respectable people" to think "meanly" of "the highest sort of poetry, – that which invests all things, great and small, with the noblest of all associations" (89:4). Keble does not entirely agree with those critics who question the Fathers' "discovering the tokens of our LORD'S Passion, and more especially the Sign of the Cross, in innumerable places of the Old Testament" without New Testament confirmation (89:4). He invites his readers to "go back to the days when Christians were used to carry about with them every where the Sign of the Cross" as "an outward and visible sign of their communion with Saints and Patriarchs of old, and of GOD's everlasting providence

---

[8]   *Tracts for the Times by Members of the University of Oxford*. New edition. London: Rivington, 1839, 89.12. Subsequent page references given in the text.

over both" (89:21). This almost poetic use of symbol unites the Christians of the early Middle Ages (a term Keble seems deliberately to avoid) with Biblical times.

Keble returns to the question of poetry later in the tract, when he advocates:

> the way of regarding external things, either as fraught with imaginative associations, or as parabolical lessons of conduct, or as a symbolical language in which GOD speaks to us of a world out of sight: which three might, perhaps, be not quite inaptly entitled, the Poetical, the Moral, and the Mystical, phases or aspects of this visible world.

Following, and justifying, the Fathers, Keble asks whether Christ "condescends ... to have a Poetry of His own, a set of holy and divine associations and meanings, wherewith it is His will to invest all material things?" (89:143–44). Just, then, as Keble's admired Wordsworth wrote the Preface to *Lyrical Ballads*, alluded to here when Keble calls poetry "the expression of an overflowing mind," after the initial publication of the poems, so Keble's discussion of mysticism justifies his own approach to poetry in *The Christian Year* while stressing the connection with medieval Christian thinking.

Lives of the English Saints: A Failed Christian Year

Whereas Keble's *Christian Year* was widely popular, John Henry Newman's series *Lives of the English Saints* was a less successful attempt to remind English Christians of the age-old connection between the calendar and devotion. The best-remembered sentence from *The Lives of the English Saints* does not actually appear where claimed. When Newman gave him the task of writing the history of St Neot, the very legendary contemporary of King Alfred, James Anthony Froude is reported to have concluded his account with the words, "This is all, and perhaps more than all that is known of the life of the blessed St Neot."[9] This sentence is itself a legend, yet it demonstrates the tension between historiography and hagiography confronting Victorians who wanted to believe that their medieval heritage was inscribed in the calendar.

John Henry Newman's Tract XC is the most notorious example of Tractarian medievalist historiography: by describing the beliefs of the English church as consistent with its medieval origins, Newman brought about his own exit from the Church of England. Recalling this moment in his *Apologia Pro Vita Sua*, Newman acknowledged the rewriting of English history. The Anglican tradition characterized the English Reformation as a "continuation ... of that one Church of which in old times Athanasius and Augustine were members. But" (and here Newman is thinking) "if so, the doctrine must be the same; the doctrine of the Old Church must live and speak in Anglican formularies, in the 39 Articles."[10] Whereas orthodox Anglican theologians characterized the Reformation as a return to the purity of the primitive Church, Newman attempted to erase the Reformation and to argue for the continuity of the present-day Church with its medieval form.

---

[9]   Quoted by Ciaran Brady, *James Anthony Froude, An Intellectual Biography of a Victorian Prophet* (Oxford: Oxford University Press, 2013), 87.

[10] John Henry Newman, *Apologia Pro Vita Sua* (Oxford: Clarendon Press, 1967), 122.

Less well remembered than Tract XC is Newman's editorship of the *Lives of the English Saints*, a series that he conceived between his departure from his position at Oxford University and his acceptance into the Roman Catholic Church. Devon Fisher, one of the few critics to have analyzed the project, describes it as "originally intended to focus the attention of the second generation of the Oxford Movement, men who generally had a greater sympathy for medieval Roman Catholicism than did the Movement's founders, on antiquity."[11] Newman mentions the series in a letter to Thomas Mozley in October 1842 and by March 1843 he was soliciting contributions from his enthusiastic followers.[12] Newman created a catalogue for the project based on the calendar of saints' feast days; ominously for a project conceived around the calendar, the agreement to publish came from Rivington's on April Fools' Day, 1843 (9:298). Newman must himself have known that such an undertaking was likely to be controversial, recalling medieval works such as the *Golden Legend* and individual hagiographies that the Church of England had largely disavowed. He nevertheless told J.W. Bowden, who does not seem to have contributed, that the plan was "to be historical and devotional, but not controversial. Doctrinal questions need not enter. As to miracles, I think they may be treated as matters of fact, credible according to their evidence" (9:299). What may have seemed simple in the proposal, however, was to prove immensely difficult in execution, as the hagiographers found their own medievalist credulity strained to the limits.

Ciaran Brady justly describes the *Lives of the English Saints* as "at once clever, ambitious, and insufficiently thought through" (Brady, 93). When Newman commissioned young Oxford scholars to research and write a history of the early English church, the goal was clearly to remind their fellow countrymen of the authentic Catholic tradition represented by early Christians of the British Isles: as Arthur Wollaston Hutton notes, "its original object was to illustrate, or to attempt to illustrate, the continuity of the existing Church of England with the mediaeval Catholic Church."[13] The plan was to include three hundred English saints that in effect would map the Christian year.[14]

Newman's writers, however, soon discovered that the lives of the English saints as recorded in their sources, mainly chronicles and hagiographies, were so filled with miraculous actions and events that scientific-minded Victorians could hardly be expected to accept the constant breaking of the laws of nature as historical. By the 1840s, British historians were becoming familiar with the concept of "scientific" history as practiced by Leopold von Ranke and others. If the impartial historian evaluated all of his – the historian was assumed to be male – sources, he would be able to assess their credibility and come to a reasoned conclusion as to what actually

---

[11] Devon Fisher, *Roman Catholic Saints and Early Victorian Literature* (London: Ashgate, 2013), 53.

[12] *The Letters and Diaries of John Henry Newman*, ed. Francis J. McGrath et al., 32 vols (Oxford: Oxford University Press, 2004–08), 9:128; 9:289. Subsequent references quoted in text by volume and page number.

[13] *Newman's Lives of the English Saints*, ed. Arthur Wollaston Hutton, 6 vols (London: S.T. Fremantle, 1900–01), 1:viii.

[14] See Newman, appendices to the *Apologia*.

occurred. "History," Ranke proclaims, "reminds us of the conditions of existence."[15] Since these saints were inscribed in the English calendar and the process of becoming a saint involves breaking normal "conditions of existence" through posthumous miracles, it seemed reasonable that they might be credited with some supernatural power. More problematic were the miracles recorded of their lives: for example, John Walker, writing the life of St German, feels obliged to warn his readers: "The following pages will record a series of miracles, which finished only with his death, and among which were some were of the most astonishing nature."[16] The stories that follow involve many encounters with demons. While their project's goal was to fill in the calendar of the saints and thereby create a "truer" history of the English Church than that believed by orthodox Anglicans, the apprentice historians constantly had to confront the problem of truths that defied even the most medievalist credulity.

Only a few years earlier, another writer had used legendary material on saints in a very different way. R.H. Barham's *Ingoldsby Legends*, published piecemeal in *Bentley's Miscellany* under the pen-name of Thomas Ingoldsby, tells many stories of the marvelous in the form of "legends"; some claim descent from the thirteenth-century *Golden Legend* as translated into English by William Caxton. Two of these, "A Lay of St Dunstan" (January 1, 1839) and "The Lay of St Cuthbert, or, The Devil's Dinner-Party, A Legend of the North Countree" (January 1, 1842) depict figures from the English saints' calendar, although ones that Newman's group did not survive long enough to discuss. In both of these verse stories, the author's tongue is firmly in his cheek. Saint Cuthbert only appears in the "Lay" bearing his name as a *deus ex machina* to extricate the lord of Bolton Hall from an ill-advised oath, "the DEVIL MAY EAT UP THE DINNER FOR ME."[17] "St Dunstan" assumes that readers will know about the Saxon-era patron of goldsmiths and his encounter with the devil: "Every one knows How the story goes:/ He took up the tongs and caught hold of his nose" (157). The tale that follows is a version of the "Sorcerer's Apprentice" in which Dunstan is an alchemist-cabalist and his "Lay-brother" Peter uses his master's demonic broomstick to bring large quantities of beer, resulting in his own drowning. Even the narrator recognizes inconsistencies here, noting of Dunstan's use of "Abracadabra," "it must be confess'd, for a Saint to repeat/ Such language aloud is scarcely discreet" (158). The flippant tone, however, deflects possible critiques: should anyone claim the Ingoldsby account as irreverent, the semi-fictional author could claim that it was all a joke. Even though the view of the Middle Ages in generally affectionate, the verses frequently step outside the historical frame to include topical references, reminding readers that the medieval world is different from the present.

---

[15]   See, for example, "On the Character of Historical Science." *The Theory and Practice of History*, trans. and ed. Georg G. Iggers, Wilma A. Iggers and Konrad von Moltke (Indianapolis, IN: Bobbs-Merrill, 1973), 33–44. Many of Ranke's works were available to Victorian readers in English translations.

[16]   *Lives of the English Saints*, various authors (London: James Toovey, 1844–45) 3 [St German]:70). Cited in text by series number, saint's name – pagination of most saints was separate – and page number.

[17]   R.H. Barham, *The Ingoldsby Legends* (1839–42; London: T. Nelson, n.d.), 382. Subsequent references given in text.

The Lives of the English Saints is thus significant in affecting a new earnestness towards medieval materials. The entries that were actually completed were the work of around a dozen of Newman's disciples, plus Newman himself. Newman was self-admittedly the inspirer of the *Lives of the English Saints* – indeed, the new edition published around 1900 by Arthur Wollaston Hutton calls its six volumes *Newman's Lives of the English Saints* – but relatively soon into the project he found himself under attack. In his voluminous "Life of St Stephen Harding," J.B. Dalgairns seemed from the outset to proclaim the superiority of Roman Catholicism; his opening page says of the present day, "We have much that is amiable and domestic amongst us, but Saints, the genuine creation of the cross, with their supernatural virtues, are now to us a matter of history" (*English Saints* 5 [Stephen Harding]:1). Later, of private contemplation he observes that it "can only exist without danger in the Catholic Church, whose creed is fixed, and her faith unchangeable, while she herself is an external body, the image of her Lord" (5 [Stephen Harding]:84).

Francis Rivington, who reviewed the work after having agreed to publish it, wrote to Newman in protest, stating his opinion that "tendency" of "St. Stephen Harding" is "essentially Roman Catholic" and arguing that its opening page appears "to deplore the condition of our Church as separated from Rome and to desire its union with the latter in her present corrupt state" (*Letters and Diaries* 10:22). Newman found a different publisher, James Toovey, but a year later attempted to distance himself from the project, and published a note in the *English Churchman* stating "Mr Newman is not Editor of the Series of Lives of the English Saints now in course of publication. His responsibility as Editor ceased with the first two numbers, as he expressly stated in the Advertisement prefixed to them" (10:396). Yet although he seems to have planned to give up the editorial role by December 1843, in late July 1844 he mentions to Pusey that "the Lives of the Saints are coming out *monthly*," and seems to be working on them with Dalgairns (10:307). Most likely, nobody really edited the essays, which are highly inconsistent in editorial titles, style, and even chapter divisions. Hardly surprisingly, then, although almost all of the writers display what Devon Fisher calls "an acute anxiety over the question of how the genre could be used to convey truth" (Fisher, 74), different solutions are presented to the question of whether miracles are history.

The simplest solution was, of course, rationalizing away. For example, Frederick William Faber smooths over the story of St Wilfrid (saint's day, October 12) bringing the Gospel and fish to the South Saxons. Although versions exist where Wilfrid miraculously brings rain and fish to the pagans residing near his Selsey retreat, Faber follows, and even tones down, the version in Bede's *Ecclesiastical History*, where timing of long-awaited rain on the day of the South Saxons' baptism is coincidental enough to be miraculous but Wilfrid teaches the people to fish: Wilfrid's catch of three hundred fish prompts "the joyous surprise of the poor natives, who perhaps thought the draught had somewhat of a miraculous nature about it" (*English Saints* 3 [Wilfrid]:135. Wilfrid, however, is a historical figure whose existence can be verified from a variety of sources; Bede, who writes about him, actually knew him (although he seems not to have liked him). Ironically, Wilfrid was in a calendar struggle of his own, in a dispute with others of the English clergy over the date of Easter.

Even problematic is the cluster of early "hermit saints," about whom very little is known, and towards which Newman himself contributed. The first strategy is simply to exercise medievalist credulity and present the stories as received. If God has the power to work miracles, as the Biblical and apostolical accounts suggest, then surely England is of sufficient importance to the divine plan to have found the true faith through the mediation of miracle workers. For example, when some robbers stole St Neot's oxen, four stags miraculously arrived, "gracefully bending their heads over the yoke" (3 [Neot]:108–09). The stags brought in the harvest until the robbers were so terrified that they returned the oxen.

The second is to note the "legendary" nature of these stories. Even though James Anthony Froude includes the story of the stags, he begins his contribution "A Legend of St Neot" with the observation that "It is not pretended that every fact in the following Legend can be supported on sound historical evidence." He then adds, "It is enough that we find them in the writings of men who were far better able to know the certainty of what they said than we can be." He claims to be unsure whether the "extreme minuteness" of some of the accounts is "the highest evidence in their favour" or evidence of the writers' "free use of their imagination to give poetic fullness to their compositions" (3 [Neot]:73–74). The Lives may not be "so much biographies as myths, edifying stories compiled from tradition." Yet still Froude wavers, pointing out that "Even ordinary history, except mere annals, is more or less fictitious." It becomes clear that Froude is really not committed to Newman's project when he says, "here are certain facts put before us, the truth or falsehood of which we have no means of judging" (3 [Neot]:81). If the plan was to base a belief system on the origins of the English church as represented by the lives of the saints, Froude's assertion that the material upon which faith should be based may be false throws the entire venture into question.

Even though the other authors of "Hermit Saints" may have been more commit-ted to the project than Froude (who seems to have been involved because of New-man's friendship with his late brother Richard Hurrell Froude), they have a similar struggle with the problem of historical fact. In some instances, they adopt the same kind of rationalization seen in the story of St Wilfrid. Dalgairns is apparently unable to swallow the story how after pirates had cut off his head, St Helier picked it up and carried it to shore in his arms. When after his martyrdom Helier's master finds him, "the head was resting so tranquilly on the breast between the two hands, and its features still smiling so sweetly, that he thought that God, to preserve the body of the Saint from infidel hands, had endued the limbs with life to bear the head across to the shore" (3 [Helier]:31–32). In recording how angels transported the body to its resting place, Dalgairns shifts the point of view to the local people, who see a ship that "they took for a phantom, a vessel driving on without sail or helmsmen, its whole crew a sleeping man [Helier's disciple] and a headless body." Dalgairns cannot help remarking, "But however this be," before noting Helier's contributions to the spread of the true faith.

"A Legend of St Helier" shows Dalgairns struggling with his material; a little more theory as to how to approach miracles occurs in the two "Legends" where Newman is believed to have played the largest part, namely, "A Legend of St Bettelin" and "A Legend of St Gundleus." Newman's introductory note calls "St Bettelin" "the work of more than one author," and he is believed to have been one of them.[18] The introduction contains a long quotation of a passage on miracles from "Bollandus" that concludes, "Suppose the very things were not done; yet greater things might have been done, and have been done at other times. Beware, then, of denying them on the ground that they could not or ought not to have been done" (2 [Bettelin]:60). The reference is to the Jesuit Jean Bolland (Johannes Bollandus) who in the sixteenth century had produced a similar Lives of the Saints (*Acta Sanctorum*) in an attempt to preserve the values of the Christianity of the Middle Ages. Quoting a Jesuit and thus reminding his readers that previous saints' lives were Roman Catholic endeavors hardly helped prove to English readers that this was an Anglican project.

A major problem with writing a true history of St Bettelin is that the stories about him contradict each other; he apparently committed a great sin in youth, but it remains unclear whether it was having a baby with his girlfriend, both mother and child being subsequently eaten by wolves; or contemplating the murder of St Guthlac while shaving him. In an odd echo of the *Ingoldsby Legends*, the story lapses into doggerel verse for the legend of how when the local prince challenged St Bettelin to find a champion to take on his fiendish giant in single combat, St Michael arrived on a white palfrey and sent the giant back to Hell: "The black knight had fallen beneath the glance/ Of that angelic countenance" (2 [Bettelin]:70). Returning to prose, the narrator proclaims that whatever happened, "some facts are needed to account for the honour with which St Bettelin was held at Stafford." The claim to have recorded "more than is known" that legend ascribes to Froude is probably a misremembering of the conclusion of the life of St Bettelin: "And this is all that is known, and more than all, – yet nothing to what the angels know, – of the life of a servant of God, who sinned and repented, and did penance and washed out his sins, and became a Saint, and reigns with Christ in heaven" (2 [Bettelin]:71–72).

In his acknowledged contribution to the Hermit Saints, "A Legend of St Gundleus," Newman looks for a theory of miracles. He explains that the "divinely illuminated mind" will meditate on truth, "whether in matters of sacred doctrine or of sacred history." The sincere historian, aware of the shortage of detail, must be a like a painter, who allows "his imagination to assist his facts." Hence

> holy men have before now put dialogues into the mouths of sacred persons, not wishing to intrude into things unknown, not thinking to deceive others into a belief of their own mental creations, but to impress upon themselves and upon their brethren, as by a seal or mark, the substantiveness and reality of what Scripture has adumbrated by one or two bold and severe lines. (2 [Gundleus]:1–3)

The conclusion drawn from this example, "Hence it is, that so much has been said and believed of a number of Saints with so little historical foundation," seems very questionable logic. That the modern-day biographers might include speculative details about the early saints is not unreasonable: Dalgairns, for example, repeatedly uses the phrase "must have" as he fills in the historical background for his saints, and while the effect is wordy, it brings the history into the realm of humanity. It is

---

[18] Arthur Wollaston Hutton's edition provides a table of attributions (6:399).

one thing to guess what a saint must have had for breakfast, however, and another to depict him raising the dead. Nevertheless, Newman concludes, an early saint's life "develops its small portion of true knowledge into something which is like the very truth though it be not it, and which stands for the truth when it is but like it. Its evidence is a legend; its facts are a symbol; its history is a representation; its drift is a moral." This seemingly does not even convince Newman himself, as he goes on to insist: "It is but collateral and parallel to the truth"; or even, "It is the picture of a saint who did other miracles, if not these" (4–5); and finally, "At the best it is a true record of a divine life; but at the worst it is not less than the pious thoughts of religious minds" (2 [Gundleus]:3–6). Here Newman is in deep trouble. If history is a "representation," then the entire claim of the *Lives of the English Saints* to show the true origins of English church practice and belief does not work.

Neither does the account of St Gundleus that follows help the case, since it mentions a miraculous spring of water during the saint's life, and dire consequences for pirates and robbers who tried to plunder his tomb. The short piece concludes,

> Whether St Gundleus led this very life, and wrought these very miracles, I do not know; but I do know that they are Saints whom the Church so accounts, and I believe that, though this account of him cannot be proved, it is a symbol of what he did and what he was, a picture of his saintliness, and a specimen of his power. (2 [Gundleus]:8)

Such a statement privileges institutional, and to some extent folk, tradition over individual interpretation, and it is tempting to connect Newman's theory of miracles in "St Gundleus" with the directly contemporary development of folklore as an area of scholarly study.

Yet even if the reader is able to find in medieval faith an allegorical truth that transcends the limits of both the Victorian sciences of history and of nature, the conclusion of the "Legend of St Gundleus" seems to surrender Newman's original historical purpose of demonstrating to English readers the continuity of the English Church through an enhanced calendar. Rather than showing the early medieval English church and its representatives as connected to the present day, the stories largely serve show the difference between medieval thinking and that of the Victorian present. Newman's theory of historical continuity did not just fail to convince not the readers of the *Lives of the English Saints*, but also failed to convince its authors. Within a few years, most had moved away from the High Church of England, many, including Newman and Dalgairns, to the Roman Catholic Church; others gave up ritualistic beliefs to focus more on the academic life of Oxford; and one at least, James Anthony Froude, abandoned conventional Christian belief entirely.[19] Far from uniting the English church through a historical calendar of the saints, *The Lives of the English Saints*, itself fragmentary, was an exercise in medievalism that contributed to the English church's further fragmentation and a more secular sense of the calendar.

---

[19]   For the processes of Froude's disillusionment, which Brady only partly attributes to the *Lives of the Saints*, see Ciaran Brady, 86–111.

More Lives of the Saints: Christina Rossetti and Sabine Baring-Gould

Despite the unhappy end of Newman's *Lives of the English Saints*, a market for saints' lives apparently existed since in the 1870s Sabine Baring-Gould, an Anglican clergyman with a keen interest in legends, published a *Lives of the Saints*. Rather than following the church calendar starting at Advent, Baring-Gould arranged the saints according to the Roman calendar, so that Volume One covered saints commemorated in January, Volume Two those for February, and so on – except that for some months the entries were so extensive that they were divided into two volumes. Baring-Gould's objective was to include all credible accounts of saints of all nations and all ages: he explained that he included "only those miracles which are most remarkable, either for being well authenticated, or for their intrinsic beauty and quaintness, or because they are often represented in art, and are therefore of interest to the archaeologist." Noting that his retellings should not give offense to either Anglicans or Roman Catholics, Baring-Gould defends the evidence for miracles as "overwhelming." Of his own time, he remarks that "in its vehement naturalism," it "places itself, as it were, outside of the circle of spiritual phenomena, and is as likely to deny the supernatural agency in a marvel, as a mediæval was liable to attribute a natural phenomenon to spiritual causes."[20] As a result, Baring-Gould makes bolder editorial decisions than Newman's team: some stories of raising the dead are presented without comment, but St Helier's head is simply lopped off by pirates without even mentioning the possibility that he had walked around without it (July 404). Baring-Gould's attitude towards the English medieval period is apparent in some of his accounts of their lives: he remains vehemently pro-English. The account of St Wilfrid uses a similar description of Wilfrid and the fishes to that of Faber in Newman's *Lives*: "By his prayers he obtained rain, and by teaching the rude men of Sussex how to use their eel-nets in the sea, he obtained draughts of fishes which were regarded as miraculous" (October 1:308). He cannot resist adding that Wilfrid was encouraged to return from Rome to England at the end of his life so that he might continue "combating the liberties of the national church" (October 1:310).

Neither can the hagiographer can see much good in King Edward the Confessor, whose devotion to God he concedes but whose ability to rule he questions; he is far more favorably inclined towards Earl Godwin and his family. Denying the story that Godwin was struck down for lying under oath, Baring-Gould claims that "the English wept for Earl Godwin as for their friend and father" (October 1:340). Although Baring-Gould is insistent on the reality of miracles, the account ends on a sarcastic note. Edward was the first to claim to cure the King's Evil (scrofula) by touch, and he gave those who were cured a gold medal, to which Baring-Gould adds, "It was marvelous how many succeeded in persuading the king that they were healed, and thus securing the piece of gold" (October 1:346). The stories of Edward the Confessor, St Wilfrid, and Wilfrid's associate St Etheldreda show Baring-Gould, a father of fifteen children, deeply suspicious of religious celibacy: he goes as far as he dares to hint that Wilfrid's support for Etheldreda's desire not to have marital relationships with her husbands might have been personally motivated. When the series was complete,

---

[20] S. Baring-Gould, *Lives of the Saints: January*, 3rd edition (London: John Hodges, 1882): January ix–x. Subsequent references in text by month volume and page number.

a further volume provided not only an index but also a calendar containing just the saints of Britain and Ireland.

Baring-Gould's *Lives of the Saints* was a major source for Christina Rossetti's *Time Flies, A Reading Diary*. Published by the Society for the Promotion of Christian Knowledge, the book provides an interesting example of a year-long Christian "Reading Diary" with a meditation for every day. Unlike Keble, whose *Christian Year* starts at Advent, she starts the year on January 1. Yet whereas Baring-Gould set himself the task of representing the saints as accurately as he could, Rossetti's few references to the medieval saints in the Anglican calendar show her to be more interested in the spiritual applications for the contemporary reader than in historical authenticity. In particular, she seems more attracted to the asceticism of the medieval period than Baring-Gould, for whom it is a significant mark of difference in thinking between the medieval mind and the present day. Rossetti's account of Bede for May 27, for example, quotes Bede's words exactly as Baring-Gould phrases them, but she sees him as embodying "the tranquil happiness of a devout ascetic student."[21] Etheldreda (October 17) is not a fanatic but "triumphed" over those who sought to restrict her "freedom" through marriage. Rossetti's short meditation on Edward the Confessor, though, shows her thinking about the nature of tradition. She follows Baring-Gould in listing Edward the Confessor's weaknesses and remarks, "I accept him on trust as Saint and Confessor: for, by studying the brief summary I write from, I discern him not as such by the aid of my own faculties" (198).[22] If church tradition has declared Edward a saint, then tradition trumps Rossetti's own powers of observation. As she writes on October 16, "Whatso it be, howso it be, Amen."

In most instances, then, Rossetti shows that she can reconcile legend and Christianity in a way that Newman's writers never quite managed. Of England's patron Saint George she relates the bare facts, then adds the English folk traditions: "Who does not think of St George as a quasi-impossible personage slaying a dragon and rescuing a princess?" She adds that this is acceptable provided that readers turn "the wild legend into a parable of truth" of Christ defeating evil to save the church. She reminds her readers that "Fabrications, blunders, even lies, frequently contain some grain of truth" (78).

The conflict between rational thought and the tradition of faith is also clear on May 19, the Feast of St Dunstan. The history of Dunstan is "full of turmoil and conflict": Rossetti sees him as waging "battles for the right," but in the reader's imagination, "he rises before as a legendary personage in the act of routing a besetting devil by dint of a pair of tongs!" (5). Whereas Baring-Gould records that "In Art S. Dunstan is chiefly honoured by a foolish representation of the devil caught by the nose by a pair of blacksmith's pincers" (May, 288), Rossetti sees behind the legend "the grave lesson of self-conquest and sin-conquest." Stories such as these cannot simply be dismissed as medieval superstition, since they create pictures the struggle of the Christian soul to resist temptation and follow the good. Medieval saints' lives

---

[21]   Christina G. Rossetti, *Time Flies: A Reading Diary* (London: SPCK, 1885), 101. Subsequent references in text by page number.
[22]   Baring-Gould's views of the Saxon and Norman periods are influenced from E.A. Freeman's *History of the Norman Conquest*, published in 1870–79.

provide the opportunity both to see the workings of faith in the past; to reflect upon the state of one's soul in the present; and to anticipate a blissful eternity in the future. Thus in a way that continued to elude Newman and his disciples, Rossetti seems to have made peace with the English Church's medieval heritage. Fittingly enough for three thinkers who cared so much about dates, Keble, Newman, and Rossetti are all commemorated in the latest Anglican calendar in the *Book of Common Worship*.[23]

The Not-So-Christian Year: The Case of *Sordello*

Unlike *The Christian Year*, Robert Browning's *Sordello* is explicitly set in medieval times, the age of troubadour poets and "minstrelsy." Although some of the more pedantic scholars of the time made a distinction between troubadours and minstrels, Browning, like Keble, more frequently uses the term "minstrel."[24] The problem is that even if he was famous in his lifetime, little is known historically about Sordello, best-remembered as a character in Dante's Purgatorio who associates for a while with Dante and Virgil. The *Divine Comedy* was at this time prompting new interest among British readers through widely available translations, the most popular being the one by Henry Francis Cary. Cary self-published his translation in 1814, but after approving reviews by Coleridge and others, it was widely reprinted in the United States and Britain, including an 1831 three-volume edition by John Taylor of London: Elizabeth Barrett, for example, mentions that she has "reverenced" him as "the translator of Dante & Pindar" (*Brownings' Correspondence* 4:2). It is most likely this edition that attracted the attention of poets such as Tennyson (whose "Ulysses" draws on Dante) and Browning. Dante and Virgil encounter Sordello after they have been meeting with souls of those who died a violent death, which has led some critics to surmise that Dante thought Sordello was murdered.[25] Cary writes, "The history of Sordello's life is wrapped in the obscurity of romance. That he distinguished himself by his skill in Provençal poetry is certain; and many feats of military prowess have been ascribed to him."[26]

Browning probably supplemented this scant account from other sources based on commentaries on Dante, but the lack of information about Sordello, beyond his skill both in poetry and war and his devotion to a married woman, may have appealed to him. The story is set in the first half of the thirteenth century. Yet Browning even changes Dante's version: the *Purgatorio*, at least in Cary's translation, makes a clear distinction between Sordello, who, at the sound of his own dialect is "prompt to greet a fellow citizen/ With such glad cheer" (Cary 2:52); and most of the

---

[23] Rossetti is commemorated on April 27; Newman on August 11 (he is listed as "Tractarian"); and Keble on July 14. Baring-Gould is not on the list.

[24] See Joseph Ritson, "A Dissertation upon Romance and Minstrelsy." *Ancient Engleish Metrical Romanceës* volume 1 (London: Bulmer, 1832). George Shuffelton discusses the terminology in "Is there a Minstrel in the House: Domestic Entertainment in Late Medieval England." *Philological Quarterly* 87 (2008), 51–76.

[25] Edward Berdoe provides exhaustive accounts of what is known of Sordello and of the struggle between Guelfs and Ghibellines in *The Browning Cyclopaedia* (London: George Allen, 1912), 477–515.

[26] H.F. Cary, *The Vision; or Hell, Purgatory, and Paradise of Dante Alighieri*, 2nd edition (London: Taylor and Hessey, 1819), 2:51.

other warring Italians of both life and afterlife. Sordello seems a cheerful individual, although perhaps not quite as helpful in guiding Dante and Virgil through Purgatory as they might have hoped. In contrast, Browning's Sordello is both enmired in factional struggles and gloomily introspective.

Browning's *Sordello* begins, "Who will, may hear Sordello's story told," echoed in the final line of the poem: Tennyson notoriously claimed that they were the only lines that he understood, and they were both lies.[27] (Evidently, Tennyson did not read the poem through, because the line recurs with minor variations multiple times.) Unlike the poet-preacher of *The Christian Year*, who can share with his readers the eternal present of the annual cycle, the poet-narrator of *Sordello* cannot share his readers' experience and "hear the story": historic time dictates that he knows what is to happen in his tale of Italy "six hundred years and more" in the past.[28]

A clear appeal of the medieval period from a poet's point of view is that during the Middle Ages, at least as represented in literature, poets had a recognized profession as minstrels and troubadours that could bring them eternal fame. It is easy to see the attraction for Robert Browning, who in the 1830s was still living with his parents and publishing his work at his own expense. Yet if "minstrelsy" made Sordello famous, Browning's poetic envisioning of Sordello's life became infamous. The poem's setting makes the reader conscious of differences in time and place, and a sense of time, place, and season is apparent in Browning's correspondence about the poem. Browning was apparently working on *Sordello* as early as 1834, since in early December he mentions having completed *Paracelsus* and exclaiming "3000 verses in 3 months!" (*Brownings' Correspondence* 3:107). Simultaneous progress with *Sordello* was not to be so rapid. In the same letter he mentions more work to do on *Paracelsus*, but adds that he is changing his conception of *Sordello*. Later in the letter he observes that "any production of my mind, is invariably followed by an after-birth – a very abortion – who delivery I accelerate & in whose perishing (of which I take good care) I rejoice..." He imagines that "some little monster's intervention" might delay *Sordello* from being his next publication.

But the reference to working on *Sordello* in the summer may be significant. Apart from this December letter (where Browning is thinking of working on *Sordello* but not actually doing so), the references to work on *Sordello* in surviving letters are mainly written in spring and summer. For example, in May 1836 Browning describes himself in a letter to William Charles Macready as "now engaged in a work which is nearly done: I allow myself a month to complete it; from the first of July I shall be free ..." (3:173). Yet here he seems to have abandoned *Sordello* and to have worked

---

[27] Isobel Armstrong states "'Will' is Browning's word for the imagination, and this willed and willful poem includes its own self-conscious virtuosity as its subject." See her discussion of Sordello book 3 in *Language as Living Form in Nineteenth-Century Poetry* (Brighton: Harvester Press, 1982), 141. The conception of "imagination" here, however, does not, as Keats seems to hope it does, include a transcendent escape from the self. On initial reactions to *Sordello*, see, for example, Sarah Wood's "*Sordello* and the Reviewers." *Robert Browning, A Literary Life* (Basingstoke: Palgrave, 2001), 40–51.

[28] Robert Browning, *Sordello* (1840), Book 1 line 77. Quotations follow *The Poetical Works of Robert Browning*, ed. Ian Jack and Margaret Smith (Oxford: Clarendon Press, 1984), 2:198.

on the "little monster's invention" of his verse-drama *Strafford* for Macready. *Strafford* was published and performed in May 1837: another indicator of Browning's consciousness of season is that he addresses a note to Fox along with his review copy of *Strafford* "May-day" (3:238). In July 1837, he claims he is about to "begin the finishing Sordello" (3:256),[29] while on August 9 he writes, "In a few months I hope to produce 'Sordello'" (3:265). Later that month he claims to be "working well enough at *Sordello*" (3:280).

The next surviving reference is in another note to John Robertson dated Good Friday, presumably in 1838. Here Browning states that "I sail this morning for Venice – intending to finish my poem among the scenes it describes" (4:24). Yet on his return he states in a letter to his friend Euphrasia Fanny Haworth that he "did not write six lines" of *Sordello* during his Italian travels. Still, he optimistically claims, "You will see Sordello in a trice, if the fagging-fit holds" (4:67).[30] The phrase "fagging-fit" suggests that in the English summer, he is indeed writing – but *Sordello* was only completed in 1839, finally being published on March 7, 1840.[31] In a note to his friend Alfred Domett, sending him a copy with the apparent hope that he would give his opinion of it, Browning concludes, "Saty. Night. /St Perpetua's Day! (see Almanack)" (4:253). March 7 was the Anglican date for the celebration of the martyrdom of St Perpetua. The Carthaginian noblewoman Perpetua and the slave Felicity (in some calendars but not the Anglican Book of Common Prayer, they share the date), were young mothers among a group of Christians martyred in gladiatorial games in 203 CE; a document survives purporting to be Perpetua's personal diary of her imprisonment and martyrdom.[32] Browning's language describing his poetry in his December 1834 letter (conception, abortion, sending into the world) might have caused him to think of this date as auspicious since it commemorates a rare example of a saint who had given birth.

A more unfortunate parallel with St Perpetua was that she was savaged by wild beasts (oddly, by a mad cow) before being dispatched by the sword of a nervous gladiator. In the next few days, Browning sent out multiple copies of *Sordello*,[33] which was published at his own expense, to friends and potential reviewers. If he was expecting praise from individuals or publications, he was disappointed. A

---

[29] Ian Jack and Margaret Smith ascribe some of the hesitation to the publication of Mary Margaret Busk's *Plays and Poems*, including a six-canto "Sordello," around July 1837 (*Poetical Works* 2:159). Given the quantity of poetry then under publication, however, this seems an inadequate explanation of why Browning took so long to complete his poem. Incidentally, Busk's poem also contains the idea of Sordello's beloved dressing as a minstrel – except that Busk's Cuniza thinks better of it and remains chaste.

[30] July 24, 1838; date calculated by editors.

[31] According to *The Brownings' Correspondence*, *Sordello* was advertised for publication on February 29 (Leap-day), but Browning's notes make it clear that it was not available until March 7 (4:xiv; 253).

[32] *The Catholic Encyclopedia* vol. 6 (New York: Robert Appleton, 1907). The date of the martyrdom is disputed.

[33] The Armstrong Browning Library has identified some twenty copies that appear to be presentation copies, rather than copies signed at the owner's request. Ian Jack and Margaret Smith note that Browning's account with Moxon revealed that "of an edition of 500 copies, only 157 had been sold, while 86 had been given away to reviewers and friends ..." *Poetical Works of Robert Browning* 2:163.

number of recipients expressed their thanks but added that they had not read the poem yet. For example, Walter Savage Landor, who claimed on March 18 to have received the book three days earlier, noted that he had been entertaining visitors (*Brownings' Correspondence* 4:257). Harriet Martineau claimed to be writing "at once" when the book finally reached her on April 8, given Browning's expression of concern for her health (4:268). Of course, given the difficulty of establishing the whereabouts of busy people at this time, it is possible that these recipients really did experience delays before *Sordello* reached them – but the delays also provided an excuse as to why they had not read *Sordello* and an easy loophole for not having to praise it. Euphrasia Haworth apparently said "roses and lilies and lilac-bunches and lemon-flowers" about the poem, but she asked for elucidation of the part of Book 3 that Browning had mentioned as referring to her, since "Eyebright" is an English name for the flower Euphrasia (4:269). Browning in reply said not what she was presumably hoping to hear, namely, that she was his inspiration, but that she should be "glad" that he found inspiration "one sunny June day." Sordello Book 3 states:

> I muse this on a ruined palace-step
> At Venice: why should I break off, nor sit
> Longer upon my step, exhaust the fit
> England gave birth to? Who's adorable
> Enough reclaim a – no Sordello's Will
> Alack! – be queen to me?[34]

The narrator scans the local women for someone who could be his "queen" of inspiration, just as Palma was to Sordello. He identifies the date as "this end of June," which, if linked to the time Browning was actually in Venice in 1838, would be around the same time as the coronation of Queen Victoria. This suggests that either Browning wrote more in Venice than he mentioned in his earlier letter to the same recipient, or (as seems to me most likely), when he returned to the poem in the summer of 1839, he was imaginatively placing himself both in Venice and in the month of June, the season of the lily and "green wheat-spike" being as much inspiration as the place.

Fanny Haworth at least said something positive, even if we only have evidence that she read the part of *Sordello* that might be about herself. Reviewers found in the poem not the continuity with the Middle Ages that the Tractarians had argued, but multiple disconnections: between ages, language, and the idea of poetry. The earliest reviews focused on unreadability: *The Spectator*, for example, writes: "It is not necessary to wade all through a mud-puddle to become aware that it is a mud-puddle. What this poem may be in its extent, we are unable to say, for we *cannot* read it."[35] David E. Latané has made the argument that at a time when the Annuals were publishing simplistic stories and poems, "booksellers looked to find easy poems that would sell, and poets and critics looked for difficult poems that would exercise their

---

[34] *Poetical Works: Sordello* 3:676–81. Subsequent references to the poem are given in text by book and line numbers.
[35] *The Spectator*, March 14, 1840. Quoted in *Brownings' Correspondence* 4:416.

readers."[36] If that was the case, Browning overestimated the patience of his readers and reviewers. The *Metropolitan Magazine* wrote, "If it were possible to understand the meaning of the writer of this poem, we should be delighted to impart it to our readers."[37] The *Athenaeum* gave a number textual examples to support the case that "it might be worth Mr. Browning's while to use the language of ordinary men, and to condescend to be intelligible, which need not prevent his being profound."[38]

But Browning is not, as the *Athenaeum* seems to be suggesting he might try to be, another Wordsworth, depicting scenes of everyday life in "the language of ordinary men." The obscure historical setting (the contest between the Guelfs and Ghibellines in Crusader-era Italy) seems at first consideration to suggest alterity, yet Sordello himself is both in time, enmeshed in the political struggles of the age; and, in the way that he thinks as a poet, out of time. Browning uses a different approach from Keble to be medievalist in poetic form; like Chaucer's *Canterbury Tales*, *Sordello* is in rhyming couplets, although Browning goes farther than Chaucer – or, indeed, most English poets – in systematically contorting English word order to preserve meter and rhyme.

Browning's knowledge of medieval English literature was probably limited, since relatively few medieval works in English had been printed at this time. From sources such as Thomas Warton's *History of English Poetry*, however, he would have known enough to use the calendar as an identifiable aspect of medieval literature, where the seasons mark moods: the Prologue to the *Canterbury Tales*, for example, starts with a very precise description of April. In the same year as the publication of *Sordello*, a number of poets, including Browning's future wife Elizabeth Barrett, participated in an attempt to popularize Chaucer. The stated goal of the volume was to increase awareness of Chaucer's poetry since even "in his own country, only a very small class of his countrymen ever read his poems."[39] In his introduction to *The Poems of Geoffrey Chaucer, Modernized*, Richard Hengist Horne, who three years later noted *Sordello*'s "impracticable style,"[40] defended Chaucer's meter as regular, and criticized the rigid heroic couplets (and attempts to rewrite Chaucer) of eighteenth century. He attributes the "restoration of a more free, manly, varied, and harmonious versification" to "Wordsworth, Coleridge, Shelley, and Leigh Hunt" (Wordsworth and Leigh Hunt both contributed to the volume). To some extent, he implies, these new poets' methods are more compatible with Chaucer than those of the Augustans. Chaucer is, Horne maintains, "a poet, and a founder of the language of his country."[41]

Horne's insistence that Chaucer's methods of versification, far from being crude and uncouth as other commentators had characterized them, were regular and familiar seems incompatible with Browning's choice to make the medieval period

---

[36] David E. Latané, *Browning's* Sordello *and the Aesthetics of Difficulty* (Victoria, British Columbia: University of Victoria English Literary Studies Monograph Series, 1987), 16–17.

[37] *Metropolitan Magazine*, April 1840. Quoted in *Brownings' Correspondence* 4:417.

[38] *Athenaeum*, May 30, 1840, 431–32.

[39] R.H. Horne, ed., *The Poems of Geoffrey Chaucer, Modernized* (London: Whittaker, 1841), v.

[40] R.H. Horne, *The New Spirit of the Age*, 2 vols (London: Smith, Elder, 1844), 174. Overall, Horne still finds much to admire in *Sordello*.

[41] Horne, *Chaucer*, viii.

seem unfamiliar. At the beginning of the poem the narrator claims a presence in the poem that will keep Sordello distant; he could have made him "speak, myself kept out of view, /The very man as he was wont to do"; but he will not observe Sordello telling his own story, but narrate. Given that this poem reminds the reader of Dante the Pilgrim and his encounter with Sordello, it seems appropriate to call the narrator Browning the Narrator, especially given the self-identifications in Books 2 and 3.

At first introduction Sordello associates the cycle of the calendar not with the divine plan or Christian festivals but with nature: he also identifies himself with what he loves, so that the natural cycle of the year is associated with points in Sordello's process of maturation. The narrative opens in a troubled autumn but then goes back thirty years to a castle in Mantua, where

> Still in loneliness,
> A slender boy in a loose page's dress,
> Sordello: do but look on him awhile
> Watching ('tis autumn) with an earnest smile
> The noisy flock of thievish birds at work
> Among the yellowing vineyards; she him lurk
> ('Tis winter with its sullenest of storms) ... (1:447–53)

As Sordello grows up not unhappy but isolated from human society in Mantua, absorbing the natural world around him (for example, "as if the poppy felt with him" (1:705)), various markers of the seasons show how "springs, /Summers, and winters came and went" (1:697). Yet as time goes by, he discovers "Apollo," an experience associated with summer. He sees what appears to be a dark forest, but on closer inspection, as the clouds pass, he realizes that it is an illusion:

> Yet could not he denounce the stratagem
> He saw through: 'till, hours thence, aloft would hang
> White summer-lightnings, as it sank and sprang
> To measure, that whole palpitating breast
> Of heaven, 't was Apollo, nature prest
> At eve to worship. (1:921–26)

Summer is the time of Apollo, but in medieval literature spring is the season of love, and Book Two opens as "Pink leaflets bud[] on the beech" and Sordello imagines that he is "born to be adored" by the crowd, and by Palma, the woman for whom his "soul /Shook" when he first saw her (1:752–23). Sordello's performance displaces the troubadour Eglamor, who ponders "was he brought/ So low, who stood so lofty this Spring morn?"; and thus wins the poetry contest of the "Court of Love" as Palma chooses him "for her minstrel" (2:122).

After this April defeat of Eglamor, in "a sunrise of blossoming and May," which Browning the Narrator identifies as "my own month" (Browning was born on May 7), Sordello, reclining beneath a "flowering laurel thicket" (laurel, of course, being the poet-victor's crown) senses a "wretched whisper" that the mythology that he is already creating about himself cannot be sustained: "All was quite false and sure to fade one day" (2:295–313). Not simply the child of Apollo, Sordello is the child of political warring between parties: "In short, Apollo vanished; a mean youth, just named/His lady's minstrel, was to be proclaimed – How shall I phrase it? – Monarch of the World!" (3:352–55). Sordello uses "Language" to satisfy his audience and in effect becomes a kept minstrel; it is not under he returns to the mountain landscape of the Goito of his childhood in winter (with "leafless and groveling vines") that he has a return of the dream that he should be "Apollo" and not "a pettish minstrel" (2:954–61). Yet the voice saying "Come home Sordello!" is not an external source of inspiration but his own, and he returns to see the castle where he had been a boy "dwindled of late years, but more mysterious; gone to ruin – trails of vine/ Through every loop-hole" (2:978–80).

Yet in the year he spends in Goito, he is less sure both of his place in the cycle of nature and of his own nature, which makes him ponder whether being "Apollo" is possible:

> To need to become all natures, yet retain
> The law of my own nature, to remain
> Myself, yet yearn … as if that chestnut, think,
> Should yearn for this first larch-bloom crisp and pink,
> Or those pale fragrant tears where zephyrs stanch
> March wounds along the fretted pine-tree branch! …
> Will and the means to show will, great and small,
> Material, spiritual, – abjure them all,
> Save any so distinct, they may be left
> To amuse, not tempt become! And, thus bereft,
> Just as I first was fashioned would I be!
> Nor, moon, is it Apollo now, but me
> Thou visitest to comfort and befriend! … (3:39–51)

The narrator slides "Over a sweet and solitary year/ Wasted," until a "declining Autumn day," when "their moods according, his and nature's. Every spark/ Of Mantua life was trodden out; so dark/ The embers, that the Troubadour, who sung/ Hundreds of songs, forgot, its trick his tongue …" (3:68–76). The natural cycle only makes him more aware that he "Must perish once and perish utterly" (3:102). He thinks back to the Court of Love and April:

> Who heard you first
> Woo her, the snow-month through, but ere she durst
> Answer 'twas April. Linden-flower-time-long
> Her eyes were on the ground; 't is July, strong
> Now; and because white dust-clouds overwhelm
> The woodside, here or by the village elm
> That holds the moon, she meets you, somewhat pale,
> But letting you lift up her coarse flax veil
> And whisper (the damp little hand in yours)
> Of love, heart's love, your heart's love that endures
> Till death… (3:107–17)

Although the beloved is here referred to as the idealized poetic subject "Elys," Palma had given Sordello the prize in April; whether "linden-flower-time-long" (May and June) she had remained modest, only to meet him in a tryst in July, or whether this is Sordello's imagining of what might have happened, is not entirely clear. Yet it is this scene that inspires him to pursue "Happiness" (3:171). Although he has sought refuge in nature, his conclusion is, "Mantua's yoke,/ My minstrel's-trade, was to behold mankind" (3:198–99). He obeys the summons to return to the court of the now-betrothed Palma, who hopes that he will embrace the cause of the Holy Roman Emperor and the Ghibellines, and proposes that she should dress "in some gay weed/ Like yours" (that is, as a minstrel) and that the two of them should act as leaders of their faction (3:545–47).

At this point the narrative has caught up with autumn in which poem began, with the figures now identified as Sordello and Palma asleep. Browning the Narrator says "They sleep, and I awake/ O'er the lagune, being at Venice" (3:614). Although his childhood has been marked by regular cycles, "with sleep and stir in healthy interchange" (1:630), Sordello is never seen to sleep in the rest of the narrative, which frequently depicts him as awake in the night. There follows the section giving the Narrator's thoughts on the poetic process, and particularly on the intersection between poetry and the poet's own person that had so puzzled his friend Euphrasia Haworth. The Narrator is, or thinking as though he is, at Venice in the summer of 1838, a time marked by Venice as just after the religious festival of Corpus Christi (June 10, 1838) but by the English as the time of the coronation of Queen Victoria, which took place on June 28 (1838). Yet a few lines later the Venice of the present is merged with the Venice of six hundred years previously as Browning the Narrator, his apparent only audience a young beggar girl who has asked him for money, is able to listen in on conversations about the poetic imagination, and especially the ability to transport oneself imaginatively. If the poet "Plara," confined to the Doge's prison, can write of the idyllic vale of Tempe, then, as I have suggested, Browning need not be in Venice to write of being in Venice – but significantly, he seems to have needed the season to be summer to write of summer. The Book ends with an anecdote of a saint – not a minor saint but John the beloved of Christ – who responds in a very human way to his own portrait. A picture may be misread, even by its subject, and St John, who according to scripture has seen visions of the fate of the entire universe, does not know what he looks like in a mirror.

If Book Three folds back 1839 on 1838, and 1838 on six hundred years previous, Book Four continues the moment of the beginning of the book, in autumn. It opens with a scene of the devastated city of Ferrara, as the factions of Guelfs, led by Palma's betrothed Richard St Boniface,[42] and Ghibellines, led by Taurello Salinguerra, ravage the city and its inhabitants. Up to this point, although the people have drawn inspiration from Sordello and have continued to flock to him, he has felt little connection with them. Now, with Boniface the hostage of Taurello, Sordello comes to the understanding that his power over the people could give him the opportunity to

---

[42]   In Browning's sources Cunizza, the inspiration for Palma, marries Richard St Boniface, but although Palma summons Sordello to be her minstrel at her wedding, seemingly no wedding takes place.

"impress/ With his own will, effect a happiness/ By theirs" (4:201–03); he now ponders whether the result might be "incidental good" to the people "as well,/ And that mankind's delight would help to swell/ His own" (4:279–81). Reaching the conclusion that he must "confront Taurello," Sordello emerges from his meditation "older by years/ Than at his entry" (4:332–33). Taurello, while noting that Sordello looks "lean, outworn, and really old" dismisses the minstrel's career as "doing nought" (4:420). Taurello has become practiced at reading others' "hearts" in order to "catch/ Their capabilities and purposes"; he thus sees himself in contrast with Sordello, who "only cared to know/ About men as a means whereby he'd show/ Himself" (4:617–22). When the scene returns to Sordello and Palma, one of their followers suggests the deeds of ancient Rome as the "subject for a ballad" (4:954).[43] As a poet Sordello could have the power to "build up Rome" again (4:1025). Ironically, then, Sordello has the idea that he will not be a Dante revealing the truth of medieval Christianity, but a Virgil proclaiming the glory of the pre-Christian Roman republic.

Yet the vision of ancient Rome fades, and Sordello turns instead to thinking about the form in which Rome has prevailed, namely the church. The figure who stands out in Sordello's thinking in Hildebrand, who as Pope Gregory VII argued for the supremacy of the church over secular power, but this would involve shifting his own followers and those of Taurello to the Guelf cause. The narrator ponders, "Who'd suppose, before/ This proof, that he, Goito's god of yore,/ At duty's instance could demean himself/ So memorably, dwindle to a Guelf?" (5:337–40); it seems to the narrator "unseasonably off" (5:349). Even though this book has acknowledged the influence of the Christian tradition on Italian affairs, Sordello still thinks in pagan terms, of Saturn's displacement by Jupiter (5:539–56). Asking "What shall I unlock/ By song?" (5:581–82) he proceeds to question the Dantean approach of allotting "Hell, Purgatory, Heaven" (5:589), except as an example of what the poet can do. And maybe poetry can offer to

> … unveil the last of mysteries –
> Man's inmost life shall have yet freer play:
> Once more I cast external things away,
> And natures composite, so decompose
> That…

Here the Narrator interrupts, "Why, he writes *Sordello*!" (5:617–20). But ultimately he must "cast aside such fancies, bow/ Taurello to the Guelf cause" (5:657–58). Taurello seems swayed, gives Sordello a badge of authority as "Romano's Head" (5:734) and recommends that he wed Palma. At this point, Palma reveals that Sordello is not actually sprung from the poet-sungod Apollo but is the son of Taurello and his first wife (5:750). What seems to Taurello and Sordello divine destiny is in fact the human contrivance of Palma, who at seeing the father and son's reactions recites one of Sordello's Goito verses that compares a lady to nature in summer (5:905–10).

---

[43] The German historian Bertold Georg Niebuhr had suggested that the early history of Rome would have been preserved in the form of ballads; after this book became available in English translation in the 1830s, T.B. Macaulay took the hint and published *The Lays of Ancient Rome* in 1842: it sold far more copies than *Sordello*.

For Sordello, however, summer is not to come again. In Book 6, Sordello ponders the "symbols of immensity" (Eglamor's phrase) of the cosmos and the possibility of "a soul, in Palma's phrase, above his soul" controlling the ebb and tide of human destiny as the moon does the sea (6:41–43). Sordello has always looked to the moon for inspiration, and in this musing the moon may represent Palma – after all, if destiny has been manipulated, it was done by her. Even then, the possibility that the marker of the months and tides might be emblematic for the divine control of the cosmos recedes as he ponders whether if no "external power" is there, he himself might "stand forth (a prouder fate)/ Himself a law to his own sphere?" (6:111–13). Thinking back to the Mantua of his youth and poetic images of spring, he wonders why "Evil's beautified/ In every shape" (6:238). Nature is not always beautiful – there is of course "the season's strife/ With tree and flower" (6:241) – and even helping others does not necessarily drive evil away. The heightened consciousness of time that has always been part of Sordello's thoughts is even more acute as he ponders the symbolism of the badge given him by his father, yet he is still inclined to cling to the now: "Oh, t'were too absurd to slight/ For the hereafter the to-day's delight!" (6:383–84). He concludes, "I, for one,/Will praise the world, you style mere ante-room/To palace – be it so!" (6:397–98): an image both of his renunciation of earthly rule and heavenly hope; he comes to an understanding that he is "alone/ Quite out of time and this world" (6:485–86). The narrator reminds Sordello of the "Power above" him, but just as this sense of time and immensity falls upon him (6:612) he dies with his foot on his father's badge of earthly power and with a seemingly triumphant rejection of a confession of faith.

Keble's *Christian Year* creates a continuity between medieval devotional practice and the present, whereas *Sordello* connects medieval Italy both with the Roman past and the increasingly skeptical thought of Browning's present, but each uses the cycle of the year to make a vision of the Middle Ages. Even if life is a "sorry farce," though, the last image is of Sordello's song of summer, as a child in Asolo chants its lyrics: "the few fine locks/ Stained like pale honey oozed from topmost rocks/ Sun-blanched the live-long summer" (6:868–70). Sordello's poetry and the medieval world that it represents survive through oral tradition, although remembered just as fragments. A fragmentary sense of the medieval, however, might in itself be a source of inspiration, as in the calendar experiments discussed in the next chapter.

2

Medievalist Calendar Experiments

DURING THE FASHIONABLE years of the Christmas gift almanack, William Makepeace Thackeray experimented with writing novels in parts to create calendars, raising the question of how calendar time and narrative time might work together. *Stubbs's Calendar; Or The Fatal Boots* appeared in twelve chapters in *The Comic Almanack* for 1839. Each month has a title (almost invariably involving a pun) and illustration appropriate both to the characterization of the season and to a moment in the narrator Bob Stubbs's life: as he explains, "Twelve of my adventures, suitable for meditation and perusal during the twelve months of the year, have been arranged by me for this work."[1] In his narrative Stubbs repeatedly complains of his "ill-luck" – which he terms "the slugs and harrows of outrageous fortune" (163). Yet although he seems completely unaware that he has caused his own problems through deception and greed, he is acutely conscious of the relationship between his story and the calendar. In "January – the Birth of the Year" he includes a letter from his mother complaining of the expense that his birth has caused. "February – Cutting Weather" begins with Stubbs's own reflections on his chosen title and the calendar:

> I have often thought that January (which is mostly twelfth-cake and holiday time) is like the first four or five years of a little boy's life; then comes dismal February, and the working-days with it, when chaps begin to look out for themselves, after the Christmas and New Year's heyday and merrymaking are over, which our infancy may well be said to be. (166)

He starts at "Doctor Swishtail's academy" on a "bitter first of February"; this episode tells of the young Stubbs's schooldays, and how his skills in making the other boys indebted to him led to a flogging. Showery March leads him to contract for, but not pay for, the fatal boots. In April, "when spring begins to bloom" and Stubbs is a teenager, he makes a fool of himself by throwing over his pretty sweetheart for a wealthier woman seventeen years his senior. This lady he also abandons before his planned marriage of May 10, 1792 when he learns that she is a relative of the German bootmaker. As the months and also years pass, he quarrels with everyone, including his own mother, and by December, "The Winter of our Discontent," he is in debtors' prison for never having paid for the boots.

---

[1] *Stubbs's Calendar*, in *The Comic Almanack* for 1839, rpt (London: Chatto and Windus, n.d.), 163. Subsequent references in text from this edition.

Although *Stubbs's Calendar* was originally published anonymously in a multi-authored publication, it appeared in early collected editions of Thackeray's works and there is little reason to question that it was entirely or mainly by Thackeray. The story is a contemporary one, yet later editions adopted a medievalist presentation. When Smith and Elder reissued the story in a large-format sixpenny edition around 1880 that proclaimed Thackeray's authorship, each month included not only the *Comic Almanack* illustration, but also an illuminated letter in the style that Thackeray had used in *Vanity Fair* that served triple duty. The illumination functioned as a medieval-style first initial to the chapter; as the sign of Zodiac; and as a marker of Stubbs's age. For example, in February (Fig. 2), when Stubbs is a schoolboy, the initial letter "I" includes two plump boys in a fishpond (Pisces); and in June (Fig. 3), when Stubbs is a militiaman, a huge crab (Cancer) is closing in on two soldiers, who hold their arms aloft for the letter W.

In this as in many later editions, "Stubbs's Calendar" is dropped from the title. Yet the reader is still reminded of the calendar form, since the sixpenny volume also contains Thackeray's month-by-month novel from the 1840 *Comic Almanack*, there titled *Barber Cox and the Cutting of his Comb*, and here retitled *Cox's Diary*. The Diary starts on January 1, 1838 and like Stubbs's tale presents a moment in the London barber's life for each of the twelve months; rather than spanning his life, though, the story covers one exceptional year in the life of the Tuggeridge-Cox family. Barber Sam Cox describes himself as "master of a lovely shop in the neighbourhood of Oxford Market," living comfortably on the income from his shop and the sale of his uncle's patented hair tonic "Cox's Bohemian Balsam of Tokay."[2] At this time, although he works in central London, his home is presumably further east, since his daughter goes to school in Hackney and his father-in-law's business was on the Whitechapel Road.

The family unexpectedly inherits a large property in January through his wife, and the succeeding episodes show their attempts to enter a different class of society at Portland Place (fairly close to the old shop) and Tuggeridgeville, their estate in the new neighborhood of Croydon, south of London. The name "Tuggeridgeville" is based on Cox's wife's family name, rather than his, and he is even compelled to start spelling his own name "Coxe." Cox is a more self-aware narrator than Stubbs, and realizes that he is out of place in the world of the wealthy. Whereas the self-centered Stubbs is very much at the center of his own narrative and never learns from his mistakes, once Cox has tried something and made a fool of himself, such as hunting or high-stakes gambling, he is disinclined to try again. As the year passes, Cox is pushed into the role of sideline observer in many of the episodes as his family and hangers-on try to work out how rich people spend their time. Readers would both be able to experience vicariously the pleasures of the wealthy, and to laugh at them.

Significantly, aristocracy begets medievalism. In August, neighbors inspire Cox's wife to organize a tournament: she ensures that the *Morning Post* announces, "THE PASSAGE OF ARMS AT TUGGERIDGEVILLE! The days of chivalry are *not* past. The fair Castellane of T-gg-r-dgeville, whose splendid entertainments have so often

---

[2]   *Barber Cox and the Cutting of His Comb*, in *The Comic Almanack* (London: Charles Tilt, 1840), 4. Subsequent quotations cited from this edition, by page number.

FEBRUARY — Cutting Weather

FEBRUARY—CUTTING WEATHER.

HAVE called this chapter 'cutting weather,' partly in compliment to the month of February, and partly in respect of my own misfortunes, which you are going to read about. For I have often thought that January (which is mostly twelfth-cake and holiday time) is like the first four or five years of a little boy's life; then comes dismal February, and the working-days with it, when chaps begin to look out for themselves, after the Christmas and the New Year's heyday and merry-making are over, which our infancy may well be said to be. Well can I recollect that bitter first of February, when I first launched out into the world and appeared at Doctor Swishtail's academy.

I began at school that life of prudence and economy which I have carried on ever since. My mother gave me eighteenpence on setting out (poor soul! I thought her heart would break as she kissed me, and bade God bless me); and, besides, I had a small capital of my own, which I had amassed for a year previous. I'll tell you what I used to do. Wherever I saw six halfpence I took one. If it was asked for, I said I had taken it, and gave it back;—if it was not missed, I said nothing about it, as why should I?—those who don't miss their money, don't lose their money. So I had a little private fortune of three shillings, besides mother's eighteenpence. At school they called me the copper-merchant, I had such lots of it.

Now, even at a preparatory school, a well-regulated boy may better himself; and I can tell you I did. I never was in any quarrels: I never was very high in the class or very low; but there was no chap so much respected:—and why? *I'd always money.* The other boys spent all theirs in the first day or two, and they gave me plenty of cakes and barley-sugar then, I can tell you. I'd no need to spend my own money, for they would insist upon treating me. Well, in a week, when theirs was gone, and they had but their threepence a week to look to for the rest of the half-year, what did I do? Why, I am proud to say that three-halfpence out of the threepence a week of almost all the young gentlemen at Doctor Swishtail's, came into my pocket. Suppose, for instance, Tom Hicks wanted a slice of gingerbread, who had the money? Little Bob Stubbs, to be sure. ‘Hicks,’ I used to say, ‘ *I'll* buy you three halfp'orth of gingerbread, if you'll give me threepence next Saturday.’ And he agreed; and next Saturday came, and he very often could not pay me more than three-halfpence. Then there was the threepence I was to have *the next* Saturday. I'll tell you what I did for a whole half-year:—I lent a chap, by the name of Dick Bunting, three-halfpence the first Saturday for threepence the next: he could not pay me more than half when Saturday came, and I'm blest if I did not make him pay me three-halfpence *for three-and-twenty*

Fig. 2. "February." By George Cruikshank. *Stubbs's Calendar, or The Fatal Boots.*

JUNE — Marrowbones and Cleavers.

JUNE—MARROWBONES AND CLEAVERS.

AS there ever such con-
founded ill-luck? My
whole life has been a
tissue of ill-luck: al-
though I have laboured
perhaps harder than any
man to make a fortune,
something always tum-
bled it down. In love
and in war I was not
like others. In my
marriages, I had an eye
to the main chance; and
you see how some un-
lucky blow would come
and throw them over.
In the army I was just
as prudent, and just as
unfortunate. What with judicious betting, and horse-
swapping, good luck at billiards, and economy, I do
believe I put up my pay every year,—and that is
what few can say who have but an allowance of a
hundred a year.

I'll tell you how it was. I used to be very kind
to the young men; I chose their horses for them,
and their wine: and showed them how to play
billiards, or écarté, of long mornings, when there was
nothing better to do. I didn't cheat: I'd rather die
than cheat;—but if fellows *will* play, I wasn't the
man to say no—why should I? There was one
young chap in our regiment of whom I really think I
cleared 300*l.* a year.

His name was Dobble. He was a tailor's son,
and wanted to be a gentleman. A poor weak young

creature; easy to be made tipsy; easy to be cheated;
and easy to be frightened. It was a blessing for him
that I found him; for if anybody else had, they would
have plucked him of every shilling.

Ensign Dobble and I were sworn friends. I rode
his horses for him, and chose his champagne, and did
everything, in fact, that a superior mind does for an
inferior,—when the inferior has got the money. We
were inseparables,—hunting everywhere in couples.
We even managed to fall in love with two sisters, as
young soldiers will do, you know; for the dogs fall
in love, with every change of quarters.

Well, once, in the year 1793 (it was just when the
French had chopped poor Louis's head off), Dobble
and I, gay young chaps as ever wore sword by side,
had cast our eyes upon two young ladies by the name
of Brisket, daughters of a butcher in the town where
we were quartered. The dear girls fell in love with
us, of course. And many a pleasant walk in the
country, many a treat to a tea-garden, many a smart
riband and brooch used Dobble and I (for his father
allowed him 600*l.*, and our purses were in common)
to present to these young ladies. One day, fancy
our pleasure at receiving a note couched thus :—

'DEER CAPTING STUBBS AND DOBBLE—Miss Briskets
presents their compliments, and as it is probble that
our papa will be till twelve at the corprayshun dinner,
we request the pleasure of their company to tea.'

Didn't we go! Punctually at six we were in the
little back-parlour; we quaffed more Bohea, and
made more love, than half-a-dozen ordinary men
could. At nine, a little punch-bowl succeeded to the
little teapot; and, bless the girls! a nice fresh steak

Fig. 3. "June." By George Cruikshank. *Stubbs's Calendar, or The Fatal Boots.*

AUGUST—A Tournament.

Fig. 4. "August – A Tournament." By George Cruikshank. From *Barber Cox, The Comic Almanack*, 1840.

been alluded to in this paper, has determined to give one, which shall exceed in splendor even the magnificence of the Middle Ages" (32). Mrs Cox and her advisors here slightly misquote Edmund Burke's lament that "the age of chivalry is gone"[3] as they attempt to improve upon the Middle Ages, which they associate with "magnificence." In planning a tournament in for August 1838, Mrs Cox is ahead of her time: readers of the *Almanack* at Christmas 1839 or New Year 1840 would be aware that in August 1839 the famous Eglinton Tournament brought the nobility and gentry together for a grand but damp tournament reenactment.[4] Cruikshank's illustration (Fig. 4) alludes to the Eglinton Tournament by depicting those not under the canopy as holding umbrellas; a poem about it precedes the illustration, which serves double duty as the *Barber Cox* picture for August and a topical reference. The Eglinton Tournament was closely modeled on the accounts of a tournament in Scott's *Ivanhoe*;[5] the Cox family, in contrast, seem dependent on scraping together their fragments of awareness of the Middle Ages. Drawing on their limited knowledge of

---

[3]   Edmund Burke, *Reflections on the Revolution in France*, 5th edition (London: Dodsley, 1790), 113.

[4]   On the Eglinton Tournament, see Mark Girouard, *The Return to Camelot: Chivalry and the English Gentleman* (New Haven, CT: Yale University Press, 1981).

[5]   Scott's account of the tournament of Ashby-de-la-Zouch spans multiple chapters and is modeled on his antiquarian reading. See Sir Walter Scott, *Ivanhoe* (1819), ed. Ian Duncan (Oxford: Oxford University Press, 1996), 88–149.

horseback riding, the family "had hopes to have had Miss Woolford [a well-known horseback entertainer] in the character of Joan of Arc, but that lady did not appear" (32);[6] others, though, dress as Queen Elizabeth and Henry V's queen with little regard for chronology. Cox is able even to borrow the "famous suit" of brass armor from the City of London's Lord Mayor's parade for his son.[7]

By the end of the year, the family has lost the estate to the true heir of the Tuggeridge fortune, Mrs Cox's uncle's Indian son, although perhaps the biggest fairy-tale of the whole of this Cinderella story is that the legal case determining ownership would have been wrapped up in a month. Cox ends up in the Fleet prison, and reminding his family of their follies, remarks, "it's a most extraordinary thing, but I'm blest if seeing them so miserable didn't make me quite happy. – I don't think, for the twelve months of our good fortune, I had ever felt so gay as in that dismal room in the Fleet, where I was locked up" (45). Thackeray, whose half-sister had an Indian mother, often makes use of racial stereotypes, but here the heir whom his wife wishes to dismiss as "black Tuggeridge" shows true Christmas feeling. In December, the season of good will, Mr Tuggeridge helps them pay their debts and resume their barbershop business, and all ends happily with punch-bowls and a bad pun: "I say," says Cox (now without the final e), "I am like the Swish people, for I can't flourish out of my native *hair*" (48). The reader is left to conclude that the Cox family's medievalism in future will consist of visits to the Circus and the Lord Mayor's Show.

About the same time, another calendar story was changing the history of the novel. Although published in monthly installments, the publishers' original conception of what was to become *The Pickwick Papers* was similar to the Christmas gift-books since the writer, in this case the twenty-four-year-old Charles Dickens, was to be supplied with illustrations by Robert Seymour and use them as an inspiration for episodes of *The Posthumous Papers of the Pickwick Club*. Years later, Seymour's widow asserted that her late husband had been the originator of the concept; Dickens claimed in the Preface to later editions that Seymour "never originated or suggested an incident, a phrase, or a word to be found in the book."[8] A close examination of the calendar form suggests that Seymour did have a plan for the work.[9] Seymour had previously created multiple pictures of comical sportsmen,[10] and illustrations of a "sagacious dog" and recalcitrant horse, plus Mr Pickwick chasing his hat on a windy day, suggest that the original conception may have been a kind of sporting calendar, with the members of the Club attempting different seasonal sporting

[6]   Miss Woolford was an equestrian performer at Astley's Circus; she is also mentioned in Dickens's *Sketches by Boz*. Astley's performances sometimes included medieval spectacle, such as a version of *Ivanhoe*; see www.vam.ac.uk/content/articles/t/the-first-circus/

[7]   The City, though did not own the armor but borrowed it for the occasion; see Chapter 7.

[8]   Dickens, Preface to 1867 edition of *The Pickwick Papers*. First published 1836–37. *The Pickwick Papers*, ed. James Kinsley (Oxford: Oxford University Press, 1986, rpt 1992), 723. Subsequent quotations follow this edition.

[9]   For a detailed if subjective discussion of what Seymour might have contributed, see Stephen Jarvis's novel *Death and Mr. Pickwick* (New York: Farrar, Straus and Giroux, 2015).

[10]   Collected in *Seymour's Humorous Sketches, comprising Eighty-Six Caricature Etchings*, ed. Alfred Crowquill (London: Bohn, 1866).

activities over the course of the year. Mr Pickwick is not a hereditary landowner born to the sporting life but a retired businessman. The conception would thus be similar to Robert Smith Surtees's "Jorrocks" stories of sporting misadventures. John Jorrocks was originally a character in Surtees's monthly journal *The New Sporting Magazine*. This monthly magazine provided seasonal information on hunting and racing, along with a few other articles on sports such as fishing and cricket; most engravings featured horses, dogs, deer and dead ducks. Publication began in May 1831, but took on a more specifically calendar form from January to December 1832, where "Sylvanus Swanquill"[11] wrote an account of the traditional countryside and sporting and recreational pursuits for each month.[12] By 1832, John Jorrocks was already a featured character in stories by Surtees; initially, these stories are narrated by a "Yorkshireman" but from time to time, Jorrocks speaks in his own voice. He is a London Cockney wholesale grocer, successful enough not just to have a warehouse near Eastcheap but also a house in Bloomsbury, who participates in the sporting life of racing and hunting with mixed success. His hunts take place in the Croydon area, the same emergent suburb as the Tuggeridge-Cox's family's new home. Although in some of Jorrocks's adventures the sporting aspects are merely tangential,[13] a number of hints connect these early Jorrocks stories with the months in which they appear. For example, some of Jorrocks's letters are dated, and in October, home brewing season, he intrudes into Swanquill's monthly calendar with a drinking song.[14]

Seymour thus had a "calendar" model for his proposed monthly publication on the sporting life, and the cover illustration shows shooting, fishing, and equipment for archery. Dickens, who was no sportsman, had to work hard to connect early chapters with Seymour's pictures: for example, the "sagacious dog" apparently reading a notice proclaiming "The Gamekeeper has orders to shoot dogs found in this inclosure" serves to illustrate one of Mr Jingle's far-fetched stories rather than the main narrative. Seymour committed suicide in April 1836, and later illustrations by Hablot Browne (Phiz) were planned around Dickens's description of the text, rather than the other way around as was common in the Christmas annuals.

Nevertheless, the monthly episodes show Dickens's own awareness of the calendar. The first couple of episodes, published in March and late April 1836,[15] take place in May 1827, but from the May episode onwards the story advances roughly

---

[11]   The *Oxford Dictionary of National Biography* identifies "Sylvanus Swanquill" as the pen-name – a double pun since a female swan is a pen and a quill is a pen – of John Hewitt (1807–78). Hewitt later curated the Tower of London's arms and armor and wrote antiquarian works under his own name, so he is likely also the author of entries on the history of hunting in the *New Sporting Magazine*.

[12]   February is missing, perhaps because Hewitt was busy writing the lengthy "Antiquity and Advantages of Field Sports," part of which appeared in the February 1832 issue.

[13]   Troy Gregory notes the frequent lack of sporting emphasis in the "Jorrocks" stories in "Mr. Jorrocks's Lost Sporting Magazine," *Victorian Periodicals Review* 36:4 (2003), 331–50. The article provides a valuable overview of Surtees' multiple pen-names and identities.

[14]   *New Sporting Magazine* (October 1832), 438. Later revisions, published as *Jorrocks's Jaunts and Jollities* after the *Pickwick Papers* had proved successful, dilute the "calendar" form.

[15]   Issue II contains a prefatory note dated April 27, 1836 acknowledging Seymour's death and confirming that "arrangements are in progress" to continue the series "on an improved plan." *The Posthumous Papers of the Pickwick Club* (London: Chapman and Hall, 1836–37).

a month each episode, frequently making reference to the month of the year in which each episode was published, and giving readers, many of whom would have been city-dwellers, a taste of long-surviving rural traditions. Episode III (May 1836) depicts rook-shooting and the summer sport of cricket; the June 1836 episode makes reference to "a pleasant afternoon in June"; in the September 1836 episode the Club goes pheasant-shooting on September 1, a day noted on many almanacks as the start of the season; the Christmas scenes (to which I shall return later) line up with Christmas; and Pickwick's Valentine's Day trial for breach of promise appeared in February 1837. Although there was a gap in May 1837 occasioned by the death of Dickens's young sister-in-law Mary, Pickwick and Sam's three months in the Fleet prison allow time to be compressed so that by the end of July 1837, the numbers and calendar months line up again. The original title *The Posthumous Papers of the Pickwick Club* suggested from the outset that the "Pickwick Club" would be extinct by the end of the narrative; the calendar format lives on, though, in the reader's mind since the most medievalist episode of all, the "large family merry-making" of Christmas at Dingley Dell becomes an annual event, connecting years old and new.

Medievalist Calendar Epics

Whereas the calendar novels make repeated but often comical gestures towards medievalism, two of the longest medieval epics of the Victorian period draw their structure from the calendar while making the medieval central to their poetic conception. Both Alfred Tennyson and William Morris represent the medieval world as a time of wonder, but also elusive. In *The Earthly Paradise* and *Idylls of the King*, omniscient narration is fragmented by memory, dreams, and oral tradition. In the half-remembered world of the Middle Ages, times of the year therefore often serve as points of reference for the narrative and for readers. In *Stubbs's Calendar, Cox's Diary*, and *The Pickwick Papers* medievalism is represented by choices of printed style or by specific parts of the story, but *The Earthly Paradise* and *Idylls of the King* take the reader into a medieval world. Medievalism raises the question of whether there has been, or can be, a golden age of virtue, justice, and peace, possibly Anglo-Saxon England, England just before the Reformation, or, perhaps most familiarly, a "Return to Camelot," with the fabled Arthurian realm symbolizing a lived ideal.[16] Both *The Earthly Paradise* and *Idylls of the King* have been much discussed as epics and as political allegory;[17] I shall here discuss them as calendar experiments that attempt to match narrative time with times of the year, emphasizing the significance of season to the imagined medieval world.

William Morris's huge cycle of stories *The Earthly Paradise: A Poem* (1868–70) suggests that if nineteenth-century Britons were seeking a golden age, earlier generations may have had similar desires. Even though such an Earthly Paradise might have stasis, with no aging or seasons, Morris's epic is declaredly structured

---

[16]   See, for example, Mark Girouard; also Alice Chandler's foundational study *A Dream of Order* (Lincoln, NE: University of Nebraska Press, 1970).

[17]   For example, Herbert F. Tucker, *Epic: Britain's Heroic Muse 1790–1910* (Oxford: Oxford University Press, 2008), especially 430–36 and 449–55.

around the months of the year. Twelve "Wanderers," who are seafaring Norsemen escaping the Black Death, roam the seas in search of the Earthly Paradise, one of the many stories in their collective folk memory. They finally encounter twelve "Elders" descended from the Ancient Greeks who preserve a sometimes fragmentary knowledge of classical mythology. Each month for a year, they gather for a feast towards the beginning of the month, when one of the Elders tells a story derived from classical tradition, although sometimes as shaped by medieval retellings. Towards the end of each month, a Wanderer tells a story, usually derived from sagas, folk-tales, and fairy-tales of northern Europe. A theme recurring in many of the stories is things forgotten or only partly remembered, and the calendar format serves as a locus for memory.

In structuring his poem as storytelling of the fourteenth century, Morris is drawing on poems of that time, notably Boccaccio's *Decameron*, where the storytellers are also a group seeking to escape the plague; and of course, Chaucer's *Canterbury Tales*: in the concluding Envoi, he pays tribute to Chaucer as his "Master."[18] Although he composed this poem in the later 1860s, Morris was later to use his own Kelmscott Press to produce versions of both *The Canterbury Tales* and *The Earthly Paradise* according to his own medievally inspired ideas of what books should look like (Fig. 5).

The Earthly Paradise complicates the relationship between written and oral tradition. The "Elders" explain that some at least of their stories have been written down: before the first tale for March, "Atalanta's Race," the Elder who tells the tale apologizes that "perchance it is/ That many things in it are writ amiss,/ This part forgotten, that part grown too great" (1:158). The teller of the classical story for April, "The Doom of King Acrisius," claims to have his story in a "book, writ wholly by mine hand" (1:263), although he too fears his story may have acquired "base metal" along with the gold over the centuries. The Elder for the May "Story of Cupid and Psyche" makes use of a book written since their departure from Greece. Morris's own sources for the "classical" tales include common reference works such as *Lemprière's Classical Dictionary*; Latin poetry such as Ovid's *Heroides* and *Metamorphoses*; and the Greek *Bibliotheca* or Library ascribed to Apollodorus, a book well read in the Middle Ages.[19]

Whereas all the classical stories are presented as distant memories passed down through generations, the medieval stories vary in the degrees of removal between teller and tale. The Wanderers explain that they have a tradition of winter storytelling; the first story will be "such a tale/ As folk with us will tell in every vale/ About the yule-tide fire" (1:189). The tellers of the "medieval" tales generally explain how they learned the stories orally, in most cases recalling who told it to them.

---

[18]   William Morris, *The Earthly Paradise* (1867–70); ed. Florence Boos (New York: Routledge, 2002) 2:773. Subsequent references are given in text following this excellent edition.

[19]   According to James G. Frazer, who translated the Loeb edition published in 1921, Apollodorus's *Bibliotheca* is not mentioned by other authors until the ninth century. Apollodorus, *The Library*, trans. Sir James G. Frazer, 2 vols (Cambridge, MA: Harvard University Press, 1921), 1:xiii. For extensive information on Morris's sources, see Florence Boos's notes in her edition of *The Earthly Paradise*.

Fig. 5. Introductory page from the Kelmscott *Earthly Paradise* (1896). By William Morris.

Interesting exceptions are the May story of "The Writing on the Image," which "Laurence, the Swabian priest" seems to have read in the *Gesta Romanorum* (1:461); and "January: The Ring Given to Venus." In the latter case, "the old Swabian," having caught the eye of a "maiden," produces a "yellow book" from his pouch that contains the story, which, he claims, was told "by a crone/ At some grand feast forgotten long agone" (2:567). Both the teller and the protagonist are named Laurence, but Father Laurence says nothing about a personal connection to the tale, whereas in the medieval story the follows, "February: The Hill of Venus," he claims to have been at the spot where the story took place; Morris could have found this story in Sabine Baring-Gould's *Curious Myths of the Middle Ages* (1866). Beside the *Gesta Romanorum*, another source for tales of a seasonal nature is Benjamin Thorpe's *Yule-Tide Stories: A Collection of Scandinavian and North German Popular Tales and Traditions*.[20] For other stories, Morris adapted other fairy-tales and Icelandic sagas, and in once instance, the source is a tale from *The Arabian Nights* that Rolf, a Wanderer leader, claims to have heard from his father, a Varangian guard at Byzantium.

Each story is framed first by a poem in rhyme royal (the verse form that Chaucer introduced into English) on the month, in which the poet appears to be speaking in his own voice, sometimes addressing the month and sometimes his wife; and by an internal frame in pentameter couplets marking the time in the month when the story is told with related seasonal details. The year starts in March, following English "Old Style," and ends in February. Within the stories themselves, however, the references to time of year do not necessarily coincide with the time of year at which the story is told. For example, of the March stories, "Atalanta's Race" opens in April and the race takes place around midsummer. The corresponding "medieval" tale for March, "The Man born to be King," is heavily associated with the September festival of Michaelmas, when both the boy known as "Michael" and the king's daughter that he will eventually marry are born on the same day. (Plot-wise, it connects with the January and February stories of Bellerophon in featuring a letter designed to bring about the bearer's death.) The medieval story for July, "The Watching of the Falcon," involves magic that only occurs at Eastertide. Other stories cover multiple seasons and years – even centuries. Thematically, though, even though the stories do not match up to the months as neatly as the calendar novels, Morris makes some interesting use of time, paradoxically both in an acute consciousness of season and in the recurrent desire for an Earthly Paradise that will escape seasonal constraints.

As passed down by word of mouth or from half-remembered books, the Earthly Paradise would be unaffected by times of the year: as the Northmen say during their first wanderings, "Let us seek news of that desired gate/To immortality and blessed rest … Certes no Greenland winter waits us there" (1:83). Hints of the Earthly Paradise are given to a certain characters in the stories; Psyche, for example, finds herself in a land outside the seasons at Cupid's palace, where she sees "The pomegranate, the apple, and the pear/ That fruit and flowers at once made shift to bear,/ Nor yet

---

[20] This work appeared in multiple editions; Morris probably had access to the 1851 text published by Henry Bohn. Interestingly, Thorpe claims that a Cinderella story in the collection, "The Little Gold Shoe," is related to one of Morris's "classical" offerings, "The Story of Rhodope."

decayed therefore" (1:401). Ogier the Dane has a similar experience in the eternal May of "Avallon." Avallon, as Boos notes, is the Isle of Apples, and apples function as a recurrent symbol in the epic, one that crosses from classical to medieval. Apples mark both fall of the year, or autumn; and other kinds of fall: the fall of Adam and Eve from their own Earthly Paradise, symbolized here by the story of Atalanta's race; and the fall of Troy, here represented by the "Death of Paris."

To demonstrate Morris's acute consciousness of season, my analysis here will focus on three stories in sequence, the late August story of "Ogier the Dane" and the September stories, "The Death of Paris" and "The Land East of the Sun and West of the Moon." Rolf, the teller of "Ogier the Dane," first explains that he heard it from another Wanderer, Nicholas, when they were dreaming of the Earthly Paradise. Ogier's story, which Thomas Keightley had included in his 1831 *Fairy Mythology*,[21] bears some similarities to the "Sleeping Beauty": as the June night of his birth grows oddly chill, six fairies grant him gifts, which may be summarized as virtue, honor, success, courtesy, women's love, and the love of the fairy herself. "Ogier's noble life" of good deeds, glory, and human love is covered in some thirty lines, until the hundred-year-old Ogier is shipwrecked and dying on a "loadstone rock" (1:231). He recalls how as a youth he was sent "a helpless hostage" to Charlemagne (1:650), which locates his story in the ninth century. When he hears mysterious sounds, including "his own name" he responds, "Lord, I am ready, whither shall I go?" (1:651), in language that echoes Tennyson's "Morte d'Arthur."[22] To this point, Ogier has seemed at peace with the prospect of his death, but when a boat appears, he responds like Tennyson's Ulysses, musing, "this must be what I have got to do,/ I yet perchance may light on something new/ Before I die" (1:654). The boat takes him to a garden with the hawthorn blossoms of May. When a female figure addresses him, he assumes it is his dead wife and that he has reached "the very Paradise" (1:658). But it is the sixth fairy, Morgan le Fay, and she gives him a ring as her consort in the earthly Paradise of Avallon.

Yet after a hundred years, Ogier's mortal life seems like a dream, and Morgan has to remind him that just as his fame is fading on earth, so is his memory of it: "thy name is waxing dim/ Upon the world that thou rememberest not" (1:667). Unlike King Arthur, whose promised return from Avalon is still to come, Ogier returns to France to fight the enemies of Christendom. He has the odd experience of realizing that he has become a legend that he himself barely remembers, as he reads a book chronicling "his own deeds ... grown strange and dim" (1:669); at the same time, he has "little remembrance" of the "bliss" of Avallon. When invited by the Queen to her garden – queens are generally to be avoided in this epic – Ogier dimly recalls having been there in the time of Charlemagne. Although the Queen discovers that Ogier's seeming youth is tied to his magic ring, she still seeks his love, and in May she throws him the symbol of love that has hitherto been associated with Avallon, a "wreath of flowering white-thorn" (1:679). By the following May, when he has

---

[21] Thomas Keightley, *Fairy Mythology*, 2 vols (London: J. Whitaker, 1833), 1:75–82.

[22] Sir Bedivere exclaims "Ah! My Lord Arthur, whither shall I go?" in Tennyson's "Morte D'Arthur," as three queens bear away the King in a funereal boat: Morris surely intended that his readers should see parallels with the King Arthur stories.

again won glory fighting for France, "Must he be crowned King of the twice-saved land" (1:681). But he hears a voice reminding him of his past lives, and the present is "grown a dream" (1:685). Leaving that "sweet morn of May," a temporary state in the "land of Death and Fear," he returns to the eternal May of Avallon. As Rolf finishes the tale, his hearers are reminded of coming of autumn and the fading of their memories of their past ways of life and the hopes associated with them.

Of the September stories, "The Death of Paris" is truly autumnal, and its subtle similarities to the wide-ranging "Land East of the Sun and West of the Moon" help to connect the latter tale with the season. Both the invocation to September, which mentions "thy gold-hung, grey-leaved apple tree" (2:4) and the prefatory narrative of the feast under "young September's fruit-trees" as apple-gathering takes place, mention apples, yet this autumn story of Paris, whose award of the Golden Apple is mentioned in March and December stories, avoids naming them. Philoctetes wounds Paris with a poisoned arrow (which, like the Golden Apple, is associated with the Labors of Hercules) when, as he says, "Late grows the year, and stormy is the sea" (2:11). Recalling their meeting in the beech woods, the wounded Paris calls on his wife Oenone, who seems to him to be the "image of his youth and faith gone by" (1:23), believing that the nymph has power to cure him. This Oenone refuses to do unless Paris will say he loves her. She refers to apples as symbols of fulfilled promise but as representing the loss of youthful hope when she says,

> Alas! It may not be; it may not be;
> Though the dead blossom of late spring-tide
> Shall hang a golden globe upon the tree
> When through the vale the mists of autumn glide. (1:26)

Paris, though, cannot even lie that he still loves her, and dies with Helen's name on his lips shortly before Troy becomes a tomb, remembered in story but whose location is forgotten. (Troy was to be rediscovered by Heinrich Schliemann in the following decade.)

The title for the medieval story for September, "The Land East of the Sun and West of the Moon," relates to a place whose whereabouts, like that of Troy, is unknown by humans. The complicated narrative framing brings together multiple seasons of the year: it is an autumn story of a summer story of a Christmas story of a story starting in summer but passing through many seasons before finding a final escape from them. In summer, "Gregory the Star-Gazer" (a figure who resembles astrologers in other stories such as "The Writing on the Image" and "The Ring Given to Venus"), falls asleep and dreams he is at King Magnus's Christmas feast. A "gold-clad" man comes in from the snow and announces "News from over sea/ Of Mary and the Trinity,/ And goodman Joseph, do I bring;/ Nowell, Nowell, Nowell, O King!" Having reminded the assembly of Christmas, he begins "Great marvels of far lands to tell" (2:38); but to help them remember the night, the visitor, who now seems to Gregory "as his other self to be," tells a story of their own land.

This story starts at midsummer, the time of hay harvest, when a farmer discovers that his hay is being mysteriously trampled in the night. Set to watch the hay, his elder two sons fail to stay awake, but his youngest son John sleeps in the day so that he can stay awake in the "hawthorn-brake" at night. Soon he is in love with a swan-maiden, and like Paris and Oenone, they experience love in a beech wood (2:55). Following a break in the dream, Gregory now dreams he is fully the "stranger-guest" telling the story at the Christmas feast, and continuing the story of John. After three years dwelling with the swan-maiden in "that wondrous land" with her ring to mark their marriage, she tells him he must return to the human realm. He appears at a family feast in rich clothing in an echo of how the stranger had come to King Magnus, and claims to be a traveler who has lost his horse. At this point in the story it is autumn, and Christmas preparations are beginning. John's memory is stirred by a cloak and hood with "sun and stars and moons" – a stargazer's garment – that he had worn for "Yule sport four years agone," and this causes him to "break out/ Into a song remembered well,/ That of the Christmas joy did tell" (2:72–73).

The Christmas song replays multiple memories: of "Yule sport" associated with pre-Christian times; of the Nativity story, described as though by an eyewitness; of the bringing of the Gospel "news" to Norway some decades earlier; and of Christmases in John's own past in the human realm. It also stirs memories in his mother: she recognizes him and he is received back into the family, but he still yearns for the swan-maiden. At Yule, by the "thorn,/ Where first that bitter love was born," he cries aloud for her, but is overheard by his sister-in-law Thorgerd, who has been eyeing him amorously since his arrival. Like Lanval in the Lai of Marie de France,[23] but also recalling Paris' refusal of Oenone, John proclaims his devotion to his faerie lover, who appears at the family's Yule feast, then departs again. Gregory is now seeing the story as though he is John himself. The rest of the long tale relates John's wanderings in attempt to find the way back to "The Land East of the Sun and West of the Moon," telling as he goes "the story of his hapless love" (1:100). Finally, he comes to place where, reversing Oenone's lament, the trees' blossom does not have to decay to bring forth fruit: "marveling he stood still,/ Because to one bough blossoms clung/ As it were May, but ripe fruit hung/ Upon the other" (1:110). He passes ghost-like through a town and comes at last his beloved, where their "joy fulfilled" enlivens the static world around them. Gregory awakes but is able to recapture much of the experience in memory, and this version of the story is a shadow of his "verses smooth." The teller ends his story of how "twain grew one and came to bliss" by acknowledging how distant the medieval world has become: "Woe's me! An idle dream it is!" (2:125).

Idylls of the King and Arthurian Cycles

In *Idylls of the King*, Tennyson also makes use of the cycle of the year – or again, two different conceptions of the cycle of the year. In *The Earthly Paradise*, the cycle begins in March, so that the poem presents Spring, Summer, Autumn, and Winter, the many allusions both to the month of May and to its namesake the may-tree or hawthorn suggesting that May is best (Morris named his daughter May). Nevertheless, the "January" Narrative prefacing the story of "Bellerophon at Argos" begins, "The year has changed its name since that last tale" (2:436), acknowledging the

---

[23] Florence Boos notes that Morris's daughter May first noticed the echo of "Lanval" (*The Earthly Paradise* 2:32).

Roman and modern calendar. And although the Wanderers have been looking for the Earthly Paradise beyond the reach of winter, the island that they now share with the Elders has four distinct seasons, and the January stories are told from indoors as "Deep buried under snow the country lies."

As far as can be told, the Elders and Wanderers are all men, but women play a significant role in most of the stories in *The Earthly Paradise*. Some are faeries and goddesses who foster desire that is generally followed by temporary or permanent misery; some are scheming queens eager to satisfy their desire at others' expense; and some are young girls becoming aware of their own womanhood. The first four of Tennyson's *Idylls*, published in 1859, focus on women in the Arthurian stories, and the connection with times of year is not so apparent. In the original 1859 version, the only introduction is an epigraph, "Flos Regum Arthurus" (The Flower of Kings, Arthur). Over time, Tennyson extended the cycle, concluding it with the piece he had published earlier as "Morte d'Arthur."

"Morte d'Arthur" suggests that Tennyson had some consciousness of a connection between the Arthurian cycle and the calendar cycle relatively early in his poetic career. Tennyson claimed to have loved Malory's version of the Arthurian cycle since boyhood. The "Bibliomania" of the time of Tennyson's youth, reviving an interest in early printed books, may have been a contributory factor in the reissues of Malory. William Caxton's text of the *Morte d'Arthur* was last printed in 1634, and probably would have been outside Tennyson's price-range at this time. Yet the work appeared in two modest editions in 1816, one from R. Wilkes of Chancery Lane titled *La [sic] Mort D'Arthur: The Most Ancient and Famous History of the Renowned Prince Arthur and the Knights of the Round Table*; and one from J. Walker and Company of Paternoster Row, titled *The History of the Renowned Prince Arthur and His Knights of the Round Table*. The titles of each, designating the hero "Prince" Arthur, suggest that they were based on the 1634 printing (or that one simply borrowed from the other). The following year Robert Southey produced an edition, called, like Caxton's, *The Byrth, Lyf, and Actes of Kyng Arthur*, published by Longman. Southey was friendly with the bibliophile Richard Heber, who gave him access to a number of Arthurian romances; and with Lord Spencer, who owned a copy of Caxton's 1485 edition that formed the basis of Southey's text.[24] Hallam Tennyson states in his biography of his father that Tennyson acquired the Walker edition; the poet's early travels included visits to locations associated with King Arthur, such as Tintagel and Glastonbury.[25] "Morte d'Arthur" indicates that he had read the text closely, even though other early poems influenced by Arthurian legend, such as "The Lady of Shalott" and, I shall suggest in a subsequent chapter, his "St Agnes" poem, show that he was willing to create his own variations on Arthurian themes. I agree that these poems can be read

---

[24]   *The Byrth, Lyf, and Actes of Kyng Arthur; of his noble Knyghtes of the Rounde Table, their merveyllous enquestes and adventures, theachyevyng of the Sanc Greal; and in the end Le Morte Darthur, with the dolourous death and departing out of thys worlde of them al*, ed. Robert Southey, 2 vols (London: Longman, 1817), 1:xxii, xxviii.

[25]   It is unclear from correspondence between Leigh Hunt and Tennyson as to whether Tennyson already owned the Walker *Prince Arthur* in 1835, or whether Hunt was obtaining him a copy; Hallam Tennyson, writing in 1898, notes that this "much used" copy was still extant. *Alfred, Lord Tennyson, A Memoir*, 2 vols (London: Macmillan, 1898), 1:156; 1:274.

allegorically as a commentary on Tennyson's own society,[26] but my interest here is the ways in which for Tennyson, as it is for Browning and Morris, reading and recreating stories of the Middle Ages is a way of rethinking the medieval inheritance of a sense of calendar.

As critics have pointed out, the original composition of "Morte d'Arthur" was most likely part of Tennyson's poetic response to the loss of his friend Arthur Henry Hallam in 1833.[27] It first saw publication, however, as part of "The Epic" in the 1842 poems, when it is framed as a Christmas eve recitation by "the poet Everard Hall." Christmas at the home of "Francis Allen" is a syncretistic festival; the parson is present, so any church celebration is presumably over, and the girls have been kissed beneath the "sacred bush" of Druidic mistletoe ("The Epic" 3).[28]

The syncretistic elements of Christmas at Francis Allen's house require a little further consideration. In Malory's version of the final battle, the time of year is some time after Trinity (usually June), when Arthur has an ominous dream; a treaty and attempted negotiations with Mordred last at least a month.[29] Fighting begins as the result of a fateful mistake: a knight draws his sword to kill an adder, another indication that is summer, rather than Christmas, when adders would be hibernating. The question remains as to whether Tennyson needed other sources to associate Arthur with Christmas. In the 1940s W.D. Paden proposed that Tennyson might have had some access to theories about the common origins of religion in works such as G.S. Faber's *Origin of Pagan Idolatry* (1816).[30] Faber noticed similarities in "the various systems of Pagan Idolatry," and since he believed that all humanity was descended from the survivors of the flood in Noah's Ark, he concluded that religious beliefs descended "from a common source."[31] Faber pointed out the use of water imagery and boats in the Arthurian stories as part of this memory of the flood filtered through Druidic practice (Faber 2:367). Faber's account of the Arthurian stories, however, does not connect them with the cycle of the year. While it is possible that given his interest in King Arthur, Tennyson may have read other works that encouraged a typological approach to Arthur, references to time of year are found in Malory's version, when Arthur first pulls the sword from the stone and anvil at Christmas, and thus Tennyson might have had in mind that Arthur's departure

---

[26]   On Tennyson's adaptations of Malory for political purposes, see Stephanie L. Barczewski, *Myth and National Identity in Nineteenth-Century Britain* (Oxford: Oxford University Press, 2000), 174–86.

[27]   Discussed in Christopher Ricks's headnote in *The Poems of Tennyson*, ed. Ricks (London: Longman, 1969), 585; also John D. Rosenberg, *The Fall of Camelot: A Study of Tennyson's "Idylls of the King"* (Cambridge, MA: Belknap Press, 1973, 14). Unless otherwise stated, subsequent references to Tennyson's poems are quoted from Ricks's edition by title and line number.

[28]   Hone's *Every-Day Book*, Tennyson's likely source for poems such as "St Simeon Stylites" and "St Agnes," lists mistletoe as a pagan/Druidic survival (1:6; 1:1614–15; 1:1634).

[29]   Sir Thomas Malory, C.XX.3. Quoted from *Le Morte Darthur*, ed. P.J.C. Field (Cambridge: D.S. Brewer, 2017). Subsequent quotations follow this edition.

[30]   W.D. Paden, *Tennyson in Egypt: A Study of the Imagery in his Earlier Work* (Lawrence, KS: University of Kansas Humanistic Studies No. 27), 78–88.

[31]   George Stanley Faber, *The Origin of Pagan Idolatry Ascertained from Historical Testimony and Circumstantial Evidence*, 3 vols (London: Rivington, 1816), 1:vii–viii.

should parallel his arrival. By the time that he made his "Morte d'Arthur" fragment into Everard Hall's "Epic" for his 1842 poems, he may also have been associating his own lost Arthur, Hallam, with Christmas, as in *In Memoriam*.

To return to the scene in "The Epic," the group holds "a talk,/ How all the honour had from Christmas gone,/ Or gone, or dwindled down to some odd games/ In some odd nooks like this" ("The Epic" 6–9). The conversation then turns to contemporary issues such as "Geology and schism" and finally, "the decay of faith." Francis Allen jokingly sees his life's anchor in Everard, and Everard in "the wassail-bowl," the festive drink still bearing a medieval name.[32] The narrator asks what happened about Everard's gift of poetry, and learns that all but a fragment of an epic on King Arthur has been burned since Everard came to question why anyone should remodel "models" (38).

The fragment that remains, however, captures the Arthurian cycle in miniature, and also the linking of times of year to the rise and fall of Camelot. The opening lines set the battle scene "Among the mountains by the winter sea" ("Morte d'Arthur" 2). Arthur's death is associated with winter, but his prime with summer, since in "those old days, one summer noon" an arm emerging from the lake had given him Excalibur (29–36). Bedivere now finds that not just the landscape, but even Excalibur seems a thing of winter: "the winter moon,/ Brightening the skirts of a long cloud, ran forth/ And sparkled keen with frost against the hilt:/ For all the haft twinkled with diamond sparks ..." (52–56). Twice Bedivere lies to Arthur that he has returned the sword to the lake, but Arthur knows his narrative is incomplete; only when Bedivere is able to tell him that the sword was reclaimed by "an arm,/ Clothed in white samite, mystic, wonderful" as previously described by both Arthur and the narrator do they move to the lakeside.[33] A "dusky barge" with three Queens has come for Arthur, the King tells Bedivere that he is going

> ... To the island-valley of Avilion;
> Where falls not hail, or, rain; or any snow,
> Nor ever wind blows loudly; but it lies
> Deep-meadowed, happy, fair with orchard-lawns
> And bowery hollows crowned with summer sea,
> Where I will heal me of my grievous wound. (259–64)

Although Everard's recitation ends with the "wailing" of the Queen's dying away, the epilogue ties King Arthur's death and promised return to the cycle of the year. Like Ogier the Dane, Arthur will live again in the timeless, seasonless Avalon until his return in a time of need. The conclusion is in darkness, and focuses on sound. After the eerie crowing of a cock at midnight, the folk-belief of Christmas rationalized

---

[32] According to the *Oxford English Dictionary*, "Wassail" probably derives from a Norse toast, but Victorian antiquarians generally accepted Geoffrey of Monmouth's claim that it originated in a toast between the Saxon Rowena and the Briton Vortigern. Francis Palgrave states, "the memory of the event was preserved in merry old England by the *wassail-cup*." *History of the Anglo-Saxons* (London: John Murray, 1831), 35.

[33] The reference to the arm in "white samite" is indicative that Tennyson had also read the early part of the cycle, "King Uther and King Arthur," where this description of the arm appears.

away by the narrator by the remark that "at that time of year/ The lusty bird takes every hour for dawn" (284–85),[34] the narrator imagines a "bark" returning and the people crying, "Arthur is come again; he cannot die." Next voices echo, "Come/ With all good things, and war shall be no more." Then he is awakened by a real, rather than imagined sound: "The clear church-bells ring in the Christmas morn."

"The Epic/Morte d'Arthur," itself a fragment, thus brings together fragments. The ancient pre-Christian world is present in the disembodied arm of the Lake faerie that reclaims the sword that has defended Christianity. Fragments of ancient belief about the winter solstice, the dawn of the New Year, bring together the loss of the medieval in the person of Arthur and the promise of new birth represented by the coming of Christ and the foretelling of Arthur's return. Finally, the whole is told in a present where science is attacking traditional belief, yet fragments of customary practice (mistletoe, wassail) still remain. For many readers in the 1830s, when Tennyson drafted the "Morte d'Arthur," King Arthur was still a very shadowy figure, the reissues of Malory being virtually the only narratives available in English. King Arthur had a continued presence in ballads, but even some of these were fragmentary in form; Thomas Percy, for example, had published in the third volume of the *Reliques of Ancient English Poetry* "King Arthur's Death: A Fragment." In the preface to his edition of Malory, Robert Southey had remarked that in his boyhood his experience of Malory was limited to a similar fragmentary state in the form of a "wretchedly imperfect copy," adding that "there was no book, except the Faery Queen, which I perused so often, or with such deep contentment."[35]

Even after the printings of 1816 and Southey's edition, awareness of the Arthurian stories as related by Malory seems to have been limited. In Charlotte Mary Yonge's 1853 *Heir of Redclyffe*, for example, young Sir Guy Morville declares his admiration for the "two fat volumes" of Malory, but his less privileged and more practical-minded cousin Philip proclaims it unreadable.[36] In 1858, however, the tireless antiquarian editor Thomas Wright published a new two-volume edition of Malory, which was part of, or perhaps prompted, a new wave of interest in Arthurian stories: a Google ngram search of "King Arthur" shows a sharp spike around 1860. Many of the works produced make little connection between the Arthurian cycle and the cycle of the year, but Thomas Westwood's poems fall in the category of such calendar experiments.

Westwood originally privately printed *The Sword of Kingship: A Legend of the "Mort d'Arthure"* as a Christmas gift for his wife in 1866. Among his Arthurian poems it was, as he acknowledged, closest to Malory as he had read it in Wright's edition, yet he gives additional emphasis to times in the Christian year. Arthur is born at "Christmas-tide, while wassail mirth ran high."[37] The child is taken away by Merlin, as a "luminous star" rises in heaven, so that a young witness thinks, "Surely our blessed Lord is born again!" In case the point is missed, a footnote adds, "The

[34] Ricks's note refers both to *Hamlet* and Thomas Keightley's 1828 *Fairy Mythology* (597).
[35] Southey, *Arthur*, 1:xxviii.
[36] Charlotte Mary Yonge, *The Heir of Redclyffe*, 150. The description of "two fat volumes" suggests that Guy may own Southey's edition.
[37] T. Westwood, *The Sword of Kingship: A Legend of the "Mort d'Arthure"* (London: privately printed, 1866), 7. Subsequent references quoted in text by page number.

old chivalric romance writers established a sort of parallel between King Arthur and Christ" (8). Years after King Uther's death, Merlin requests that "Archbishop Engelbert" summon "all true knights" to London, "at the time of Yule." On Christmas morning, the knights attempt in vain to remove a sword from an anvil; at the New Year's Day joust, however, young Arthur, is able both to remove the sword from the anvil and to return it into place. Dissension following among the knights, the Primate delays a decision on Arthur's kingship until significant seasons for Christianity: first, Candlemas – the time of Christ's presentation in the Temple – and then Easter – Christ's death and resurrection – and then Pentecost – the coming of the Holy Spirit. Each time Arthur alone can draw the sword, and when he draws it on Pentecost, "a luminous star" again arises, marking him as "God's Elect" (22).

There can be little doubt that Westwood was aware of Tennyson's "Epic/Morte d'Arthur," so his linkage of Arthur's birth with Christmas, just as Tennyson had linked Arthur's death with Christmas, equates Arthur's life with the solar year and with Christ. When Westwood returned to Arthurian stories in *The Quest of the Sancgreall* (1868), he also made times of year significant. Galahad is first inspired on the ominous day of "all-hallows eve," and, as in Malory's account, sits in the Siege Perilous in June.[38] Malory specifically connects the Siege Perilous and the Grail vision with Pentecost: Galahad arrives and sits in the seat on the eve, and on the feast day the vision of the covered Grail causes the knights to be like the Apostles at the first Pentecost and "alyghted of the grace of the Holy Goste" (Malory XIII.6). Westwood's *Quest* repeatedly equates Galahad with virtue and summer and the more fallible characters with winter. The effect is sometimes comic, as in the description of Galahad riding along with a nightingale overhead and a wren on his shoulder as rabbits and squirrels frisk around him, while Sir Galheron only hears the "croak and caw" of a raven (*Sancgreall* 31). The initial vision of the Sancgreall brings joyful associations of summer such as "fragrance on the air/ Of mead-flowers, honey-sweet; birds on each bough," contrasted with the "black and bitter night" of the knights' own world. The vow made to find the Sancgreall is thus a way "to cheer the darkness of these evil days" (*Sangreall* 7). The quest does not, however, bring summer. Some knights return at harvest-time, and the Queen is shown praying in repentance as she hears the bells "Ring out the old year, welcome in the New." And Galahad, the knight of summer, receives the eucharist from the Grail at Christmas and is borne up by angels, leaving his companions to return to Camelot by the following Pentecost, four years after their departure.

Meanwhile, Tennyson had been working on epic cycles of his own. The seasons are less clear in the four Idylls published in 1859, yet they are still quietly present.[39] Some minor reordering creates a sense of seasonal progress through the year. The story of Enid begins at Whitsuntide, when after the Queen is insulted during a hunt, Geraint goes on a quest to avenge her honor and meets Enid; the main action takes

---

[38] T. Westwood, *The Quest for the Sancgreall, The Sword of Kingship, and Other Poems* (London: John Russell Smith, 1868), 7.

[39] Tennyson had originally considered publishing "Enid" and "Nimue" (the name for "Vivien" in Malory) in 1857 as representing "The True and the False." According to Richard Jones, only one copy of the printing by Moxon still exists. See Richard Jones, *The Growth of the Idylls of the King* (Philadelphia, PA: Lippincott, 1894), 45–46.

place a year later, in summer. "Elaine," in which the weather is again mild, is placed next, even though the story takes place after Lancelot and Guinevere have been lovers for many years. Lancelot has won the diamond in the tournament for the past eight years, and when Guinevere upbraids him for choosing to stay at her side rather than competing, he has to remind her of "that summer, when you loved me first," a time when she cared little for what others thought.[40] Guinevere compares Arthur to "the Sun in heaven," but notes that now "There gleam'd a vague suspicion in his eyes" of her relationship with Lancelot (153–54). The narrative uncertainties of *The Earthly Paradise* are here represented by reported accounts, rumors, and gossip. At Camelot the story soon becomes "The maid of Astolat loves Sir Lancelot,/ Sir Lancelot loves the maid of Astolat" (185). "Vivien" is set against a backdrop of stormy weather. Even though Arthur is "Vext at a rumour rife about the Queen" (101),[41] which implies that this is after he has suspected a relationship between Lancelot and Guinevere, he ignores Vivien's advances, and so she turns her attention to Merlin. First, she uses Lancelot's language in an attempt to prove her sincerity, and later repeats gossip about the Knights of the Round Table. Merlin finally calls her to "shelter in the hollow oak, 'Come in from the storm'" (140), and here, when the storm abates, she traps him with his own charm.

"Guinevere" takes place shortly before Arthur's final winter battle, after Modred has made the Queen's infidelity public and she has sought refuge in a convent. The young novice, who like the other nuns does not know the Queen's identity, sings, "Late, late, so late! And dark the night and chill!" (233). Her song connects replays the parable of the wise and foolish virgins, who need to replenish their lamps and are shut out from the wedding feast, but for Guinevere they suggest that it may be too late for repentance. The novice's father has told her of the Earthly Paradise of the founding of Arthur's realm "before the coming of the sinful Queen" (239). Guinevere recalls "the golden days" of "maytime" when she first saw Lancelot, who came to bring her to Arthur, and they rode "under groves that look'd a paradise/ Of blossom, over sheets of hyacinth/ That seem'd the heavens upbreaking thro' the earth" (245). Just as her first meeting with Arthur spoiled Guinevere's dreams of an earthly paradise, so Arthur upbraids her with having caused the fall of his kingdom founded on the ideals of medieval chivalry, "To serve as model for the mighty world." The qualities agreed on by the Round Table are very like Ogier's gifts from the fairies:

> Not only to keep down the base in man,
> But teach high thought, and amiable words
> And courtliness, and the desire of fame,
> And love of truth, and all that makes a man.

To this he adds, "And all this throve until I wedded thee!" (250). As he leaves in the dark and mist, whereas in the previous Idylls individuals have been challenged to

[40]   Tennyson, *Idylls of the King* (London: Moxon, 1859), 152. Because Tennyson later made significant revisions, I am quoting the first four Idylls from the 1859 edition, by page number, in text.

[41]   After 1870, when Tennyson was working on the calendar order, he changed this line to read "Vext at a rumour issued from herself" ("Merlin and Vivien," line 151).

prove their love to the real or feigned object of their affections, Guinevere recognizes her love for Arthur and, the earthly paradise gone, can only hope for reunity in heaven.

If "Morte D'Arthur" is an epic in miniature, and the first four Idylls a calendar cycle in miniature, the *Idylls* as fully constructed into epic reinforce the idea of Spring, Summer, Autumn, and Winter. A note in the 1870 volume *The Holy Grail and Other Poems* recommends that the poems are read in the following order: The Coming of Arthur; Geraint and Enid; Merlin and Vivien; Lancelot and Elaine; The Holy Grail; Pelleas and Ettarre; Guinevere; and The Passing of Arthur, footnoted as "the earliest written of the poems."[42] By 1872, Tennyson had a conception of the whole epic as marking the rise and fall of Camelot, and also that the stories should be tied to seasons echoing the rise and fall. An introductory note in the volume containing "Gareth and Lynette" and "The Last Tournament" explains that "Of these two Idylls, GARETH follows THE COMING OF ARTHUR, and THE LAST TOURNAMENT immediately precedes GUINEVERE. The concluding volumes of the Library Edition will contain the whole series in its proper shape and order." After the final story, "Balin and Balan," was added in the 1880s, the whole work, like *The Earthly Paradise*, comprised twelve books, and, like the calendar novels of the early years of Victoria's reign, the books in order loosely echo the months of the year.

The Idylls published in 1870 and 1872 show Tennyson formulating the structure of his calendar epic, while incorporating a respect for the problems of story transmission similar to Morris's *Earthly Paradise*. In "Gareth and Lynette," for example, Gareth's journey to Camelot begins early in the year, "past the time of Easterday" ("Gareth and Lynette," line 183). Having promised the same to his mother Arthur's sister (here named Bellicent), Gareth is preparing to serve a year and a day as a kitchen scullion, but even before he reaches Camelot he sees a vision of the city that raises questions about truth and is told, "there is nothing in it as it seems/ Saving the King; tho' some there be that hold/ The King a shadow, and the city real" (260–62). The disguised Gareth discovers that Arthur's justice depends on accepting the petitioners' words as truth. His mother soon permits him to reveal his identity to Arthur, who sends him on a quest to rescue Lyonors, the sister of Lynette. To a Baron whose life he saves, Gareth self-identifies as a Cinderella, whose fortune will be "all as fair as hers, who lay/ Among the ashes and wedded the King's son" (881–82). Despite Lynette's insults, Gareth defeats knights who call themselves after times of day and stages of life, Morning-Star, Noonday Sun, Evening-Star, and Night and Death. Even in this "Spring" episode the concluding lines recall the narrative uncertainty of Morris's *Earthly Paradise*: "And he that told the tale in older times/ Says that Sir Gareth wedded Lyonors,/ But he, that told it later, says Lynette" (1392–95).

Westwood had suggested that when the Knights of the Round Table had their initial vision of the Grail, their world was already wintry. Tennyson's approach is different (and perhaps, since Westwood had beaten him to a Grail poem, he felt that it needed to be). After an optimistic Spring, "The Holy Grail" stands as a marker of the symbolic "midsummer" of Camelot before its decline, but as John D. Rosenberg has

---

[42]   Alfred Tennyson, *The Holy Grail and Other Poems* (London: Strahan, 1870), prefatory note.

pointed out, it has its own internal annual cycle at story level.[43] Whereas Westwood imagined the quest for the Grail as taking multiple years, in Tennyson's version there is a "year of miracle" ("Holy Grail," 166). The story as narrated in retrospect by Sir Percivale begins with his own sister, a nun who hears about the Grail from her confessor, and who, with a heart that her confessor describes as "pure as snow," prays and fasts until she sees a vision that convinces her that "now the Holy Thing is here again" (124). In Tennyson's reworking of Malory's account Percivale's sister's interaction with Sir Galahad, including the presentation of a sword-belt made of her hair, comes before Sir Galahad sits in the Siege Perilous. Percivale recalls how:

> And all at once, as there we sat, we heard
> A cracking and a riving of the roofs,
> And rending, and a blast, and overhead
> Thunder, and in the thunder was a cry.
> And in the blast there smote along the hall
> A beam of light seven times more clear than day:
> And down the long beam stole the Holy Grail
> All over covered with a luminous cloud,
> And none might see who bare it, and it past.
> But every knight beheld his fellow's face
> As in a glory ... (182–90)

Tennyson is less precise than Malory about the feast day and about the vision, but this episode explicitly takes place on a "summer night." Percivale's own account tries to make certainty out of uncertainty: he states that he did not see the Grail, and that therefore he would ride "A twelvemonth and a day in quest of it,/ Until I found and saw it, as the nun/ My sister saw it"; the other knights join with his vow. Arthur is absent during this episode; when he returns and questions the knights, only Galahad claims to have actually seen the Grail, raising the possibility that perhaps the most famous quest in European literature was inspired by delusion (195–99).[44] Arthur wishes that the vow had not been made, and when the year is over many knights have not returned, including Galahad. "The Holy Grail" thus functions as a cycle in itself, and as the summer point of Camelot, after which the ideals of the Round Table begin to fade, and with them the idea that medievalism might provide a foundation for Tennyson's present.

"The Last Tournament" is therefore an autumn poem as Camelot stands "high above the yellowing woods" ("Last Tournament," 3). The time is after the death of Elaine, when the jealous Guinevere had thrown the diamonds from nine years' tournaments out of the window, and they fell in the "stream" near Elaine's barge. Arthur and Guinevere decide to hold "the Tournament of the Dead Innocence," using as a trophy the jewels found with an unknown child now deceased, whose full story remains an unknown. Yet even as trumpets announce this chance for glory "from Camelot in among the faded fields/ To furthest towers," a mutilated "churl"

---

[43] Rosenberg, 56–59.
[44] Herbert F. Tucker suggests that "Tennyson treats the Grail quest as an unmitigated disaster for the Arthurian program of national reform" (454).

tells of a Red Knight who is establishing a rival Round Table mocking the hypocrisy of Arthur's court (56–88). The tournament takes place on a windy Autumn day, and the mood is not improved when Sir Tristram says "This day my Queen of Beauty is not here," referring to Isolt whom, contrary to the ideals of the Round Table, he has taken from King Mark. While some ladies murmur that "The glory of our Round Table is no more," one with dark brows and complexion tries to see the positive:

> Praise the patient saints,
> Our one white day of Innocence hath past,
> Tho' somewhat draggled at the skirt. So be it.
> The snowdrop only, flowering thro' the year,
> Would make the world as blank as winter-tide. (209–21)

If an all-white, seasonless world would be boringly blank, perhaps a world of spotless virtue would be the same, providing a cynical new context for Guinevere's first response to Arthur, that in comparison with Lancelot he was "cold,/ High, self-contained and passionless," a cynicism echoed in the story that follows. As in the "yellowing Autumn-tide" Dagonet the Fool dances "like a wither'd leaf," Tristram's song rejects the idea of an Earthly Paradise:

> Free love – free field – we love but while we may:
> The woods are hush'd, their music is no more:
> The leaf is dead, the yearning passed away:
> New leaf, new life – the days of frost are o'er:
> New life, new love, to suit the newer day:
> New loves are sweet as those that went before:
> Free love – free field – we love but while we may. (275–81)

"We love but while we may" suggests the transience of life and love, but Tennyson was to end what had become his epic where he had begun fifty years earlier: with the Morte d'Arthur. Everard Hall may have burned his "twelve books," but Tennyson finally succeeded in making an epic calendar that despite the imperfections of the chivalric world that it portrays would help kindle enthusiasm for an imagined Middle Ages. The ending may seem less explicitly Christian than the version published in 1842, since the sign of hope at Arthur's departure is not the sound of the bells of Christmas but the sight of the sun of the New Year. Yet the centrality of Christmas to Tennyson's Arthurian vision is one example of how nineteenth-century Britons used medievalism in the recreation of Christmas as a season, the subject of the following chapter.

3

Christmas Becomes a Season

I N THE 1860s the composer Charlotte Alington Barnard (1830–69) wrote to Ann Margaretta Higford Burr (1817–92) thanking her for her invitation and regretting that she would be unable to visit due to prior engagements. She adds, "We have spent a very cheerful Christmas this year as the Yarboroughs entertained for three weeks and it was delightfully like the old fashioned Christmas wh: so few keep up now."[1] Barnard says nothing more on the subject, but the assumption is that Mrs Burr will agree that the celebration of Christmas is in decline.

The notion that Christmas celebration was on the wane in the 1860s is significant since over the course of the nineteenth century, multiple attempts had been made to revive the "old Fashioned Christmas." In Washington Irving's *Sketch-Book* and "Bracebridge Hall" stories written around 1820 but reprinted in many forms, Christmas traditions are depicted as fading away. The sketches that open the second volume depict the dying traditions of the English Christmas season, which enhance the American visitor Geoffrey Crayon's feeling that in "those honest days of yore … the world was more homebred, social, and joyous than at present."[2] Those residing in the English countryside were, says Crayon, "in former days, particularly observant of the religious and social rites of Christmas" that seemed:

> to throw open every door, and unlock every heart. It brought the peasant and the peer together, and blended all ranks in one warm generous flow of joy and kindness. The old halls of castles and manor houses resounded with the harp and the Christmas carol, and their ample boards groaned under the weight of hospitality. (2:8)

Although Crayon is vague as to when these times might have been, references to Gothic and baronial halls and harps suggest that he is memorializing not just the past of a century ago, but the Middle Ages. "Christmas" further notes that "traditionary customs of golden-hearted antiquity, its feudal hospitality and lordly wassailings" have passed away.

Later editions of Irving's collected sketches are dedicated to Sir Walter Scott, probably in recognition of Scott's role in uncovering traditions, but perhaps partly because of the lament of the decline of Christmas in *Marmion*, a passage quoted

---

[1]   Armstrong Browning Victorian Letters (Higford-Burr correspondence). Reproduced by permission of the Armstrong Browning Library, Baylor University, Waco, Texas.
[2]   Washington Irving, *The Sketch Book of Geoffrey Crayon, Gent*, 2 vols (London: Thomas Davison, 1821), 2:3–4. Subsequent references in text by volume and page number.

by almost every antiquarian of the period.[3] The six cantos of Scott's 1808 poem *Marmion, A Tale of Flodden Field* are each prefaced by a poetic epistle to one of Scott's literary and antiquarian friends, headed like letters with the name of the addressee and the location from which Scott is (supposedly) writing. Most make reference to the time of year. The sixth and final epistle is addressed to the bibliophile Richard Heber, and dated and addressed "Mertoun-House, Christmas," with the poet supposedly writing from the fireside: "Heap on more wood! – the wind is chill;/ But let it whistle as it will,/ Well keep our Christmas merry still."[4] Adding that "Each age has deem'd the new-born year/ The fittest time for festal cheer," he first describes the feast associated with the "Iol" solstice fires of the pagan Danes. He then turns to the medieval Christian Christmas:

> And well our Christian sires of old
> Loved when the year its course had roll'd,
> And brought blithe Christmas back again,
> With all his hospitable train.
> Domestic and religious rite
> Gave honour to the holy night;
> On Christmas Eve the bells were rung;
> On Christmas Eve the mass was sung:
> That only night in all the year,
> Saw the stoled priest the chalice rear.
> The damsel donn'd her kirtle sheen;
> The hall was dress'd with holly green;
> Forth to the wood did merry-men go,
> To gather in the mistletoe.
> Then open'd wide the Baron's hall
> To vassal, tenant, serf and all;
> Power laid his rod of rule aside
> And Ceremony doff'd his pride.

Christmas is also associated with food, such as the "grim boar's head," Christmas pie,[5] and Scotland's "savory goose." After the banquet,

> Then came the merry makers in,
> And carols roar'd with blithesome din;

---

[3]   For example, William Sandys, *Christmas Carols, Ancient and Modern* (London: R. Beckley, 1833), cxliii–cxliv; Thomas Kibble Hervey and Robert Seymour, *The Book of Christmas* (London: William Spooner, 1836), 32.

[4]   Sir Walter Scott, *Marmion* (1808), Introduction to Canto Sixth. *Poetical Works* (London: Henry Frowde, 1904), 152.

[5]   I am not here discussing Christmas foods that became "traditional," since the antiquarians generally agreed that although feasting was ancient, Christmas treats such as plum pudding and mince pies became part of English Christmas after the Reformation, or even after the Restoration. See, for example, Hervey and Seymour, *The Book of Christmas*, where plum pudding is described as "a truly national dish." Thomas Kibble Hervey and Robert Seymour, *The Book of Christmas* (London: William Spooner, 1836), 277. Subsequent references given in text.

If unmelodious was the song,
It was a hearty note, and strong.
Who lists may in their mumming see
Traces of ancient mystery;
White shirts supplied the masquerade,
And smutted cheeks the visors made;
But, O! what maskers, richly dight,
Can boast of bosoms half so light!
England was merry England, when
Old Christmas brought his sports again.
'Twas Christmas broach'd the mightiest ale;
'Twas Christmas told the merriest tale;
A Christmas gambol oft could cheer
The poor man's heart through half the year.

Scott touches on many of the many of the details pointed out by antiquarians: the merging of the Christian Christmas with the Northern Iol or Yule; games and pastimes; mumming and carols; and specific food. Above all, Christmas is associated with benevolence: not merely generosity from the rich to the poor, but the actual mingling of social classes, with general good cheer. In Scott's time, the Scottish Kirk still disapproved of Christmas merriment, but the epistle to Heber suggests that Christmas may have been celebrated in the English style at Mertoun House, in the Scottish Borders. This was the ancestral home of the Scott family who frequently showed hospitality to the poet, their distant relative. Just as *Marmion*'s historical setting is the border country, on the border of the medieval times represented in the ballads that Scott had collected as *The Minstrelsy of the Scottish Border*, so this account of Christmas displays a murky sense of history. The first lines recall Viking times; then feudal days; and the references to food – the "Boar's Head Carol" is known to date from the 1500s – and to "masquerade" suggest the sixteenth and seventeenth centuries.

Besides Scott, Irving seems to have made use of the work of Joseph Strutt as a conduit to the medieval past. Joseph Strutt published *The Sports and Pasttimes of the People of England* in 1801. He quotes Polydore Virgil as mentioning the distinctive English customs of celebrating Christmas with "plays, masques, and magnificent spectacles," and of a "Christmas prince, or lord of misrule ... a personage almost peculiar to this country."[6] Although Strutt claims such figures were at one time also part of Christmas tradition in other parts of Europe, he emphasizes that foreign visitors saw the lord of misrule as peculiarly English; he adds, "even with us his government has been extinct for many years, and his name and his offices are nearly forgotten" (Strutt, 298–99). On the basis of a passage from John Stow's *Survey of London*, Strutt concludes Christmas pastimes associated with "holidays" were calculated from "All-Hallows Eve to the day after Candlemas-Day," which would be October 31 to February 3. The implication is that medieval Christmas not simply

---

[6]   Joseph Strutt, *Glig-gamena angel-deod, Or, The Sports and Pastimes of the People of England*, 2nd edition (London: Bentley, 1810), xxxv; The quotation is from Polydore Virgil, *De Rerum Invent. Lib v. cap 2.*

a religious celebration, but a season in itself for everyone. Stow certainly states that the King had a "Lord of Misrule" in residence and that gambling took place, and one may suspect that the length of the Christmas period was to avoid other religious injunctions restricting pastimes such as gaming.[7] By the nineteenth century, however, while the Church might recognize Advent and the wealthy might still have a "Christmas season" of social activity consisting of at least the period from Christmas Eve to Twelfth Night, for most working people Christmas had been curtailed to no more than a day or two.

Washington Irving's seasonal episodes in *The Sketch Book* and *Bracebridge Hall, Or, The Humorists* therefore perform the task of recreating a time when Christmas was a "season" for more than the rich. The stories were supposedly created to inform American readers who had limited traditions of their own, but the book was a major success in Britain also. Possibly we might imagine a slightly different response from British and American readers. Whereas residents of the United States of America might be interested in the history that their recently founded communities do not have, British readers might be prompted to rediscover their own – at least as represented by Strutt and filtered through Geoffrey Crayon – and come to the belief that present-day Christmas was only a shadow of the past.

The remaining Christmas chapters in *The Sketch Book* depict Geoffrey Crayon's visit to Bracebridge Hall for a multiple-day "Christmas season." In "The Stage-Coach" Crayon depicts himself on a coach taking people home for the Christmas holidays, something that only the more privileged members of society such as boarding school and university students would be able to do. Then he encounters Frank Bracebridge, who invites him to his family home promising him "a hearty welcome in something of the old fashioned style" (*Sketch Book* 2:28). Crayon presents his description of a country Christmas as ethnography: he himself witnesses the cultural practices, with Frank acting at least partly as his informant. Frank calls his father "a bigoted devotee of the old school" at a time when the figure of the "old English country gentleman" is fading away (2:30–31). Yet this is not entirely a "folk" culture, where traditions have been passed down orally. Frank tells Crayon that his father has "consulted old books for precedent and authority for each 'merrie disport'" (2:33). The house is both medieval (one wing is "evidently very ancient") and in the taste and style of Charles II, the "merry monarch" who, in popular tradition,

---

[7] Strutt xlv; quoted from Stow, *Survey of London*, 79. Stow writes, "at Christmasse, there was in the Kinges house wheresoever hee was lodged, a Lorde of misrule, or mayster of merrie disporters, and the like had ye in the house of every noble man, of honor, or good worshippe, were he spirituall, or temporall. Amongst the wich the Maior of London, and either of the shiriffes had their severall Lords of Misrule, ever contending without quarrel or offence, who should make the rarest pastimes to delight the beholders. These Lords beginning their rule at Alhollon Eve, continued the same till the morrow after the Feast of the Purification, commonly called Candlemas day. In all which space there were fine and subtile disguisings, Maskes, and Mummeries, with playing at Cardes, for Counters, Nayles, and poyntes, more for pastimes than for gaine." Fifteenth-century carols and even the seventeenth-century Robert Herrick mention Candlemas as a concluding point for Christmas (for example, Wright's 1847 carol collection, 24–25; Robert Herrick, *Complete Poems*, ed. Alexander Balloch Grosart, 3 vols [London: Chatto and Windus, 1876], 3:38), but I have not found other evidence that Christmas was considered to start on November 1.

restored Christmas festivities after they had been forbidden during the Common-wealth. While the servants are frolicking in truly antique style, playing games such as "hoodman blind, shoe the wild mare, hot cockles, steal the white loaf, bob apple and snap dragon," the family and their guests are playing cards and sitting by the "Yule clog," where, Crayon explains in the footnote to the reader, it is traditional to hold friendly conversation and tell tales.

Christmas Day itself is first a religious holiday, marked by carols and private and public services of worship. The medieval church, which contains the remains of multiple generations of the Bracebridge family, is decorated with greenery, but incorrectly with mistletoe.[8] The parson preaches a sermon on the appropriateness of celebrating Christmas that suggests to Crayon that he lives "but with times past," knowing little of the present (2:62). From the carol-singing to mumming, Christmas is, in fact, overdetermined and not quite authentic in a number of respects. Just as the attempt at traditional greenery is incorrect, so the carols sung are not truly ancient but apparently the arrangement of Master Simon. Simon functions as a Master of Ceremonies and even, Crayon later observes, as a medieval "Lord of Misrule" (2:85), but like the Squire he consults old books to learn the right thing to do. The local children cry "Ule, ule!" but whether this is a local tradition or an innovation of Squire Bracebridge is not quite clear. The Squire himself confesses that although he tried traditional hospitality of throwing open his home to all like the barons of old, "many uncouth circumstances occurred." He has thus moved to "distributing beef, and bread, and ale among the poor, that they might make merry in their own dwellings" (2:67). Nevertheless, the poor are apparently willing enough to indulge the Squire's whims, performing a "nearly extinct" Morris dance with cudgels in return for "brown and beef" (2:68–69).

After the Christmas dinner, replete with boar's head and simulated peacocks, the final ritual of the evening is "a burlesque imitation of an antique masque," which a footnote explains had been the practice in "old times" (2:90). Simon dresses as "Ancient Christmas" in a ruff and steeple hat, and is accompanied by "Dame Mince Pie," "Robin Hood" and "Maid Marian," plus other representations of festive food and drink, with the Oxford student who brought home the Boar's Head ritual as Lord of Misrule. Understandably, Crayon is confused as to what historical period or periods are being represented; he recognizes that some elements are derived from Ben Jonson's Christmas masque, but Robin Hood suggests the medieval period, as does the figure of the Bracebridges' supposed ancestor the Crusader, all the more mysterious since Crayon has already voiced the suspicion that none of the associated relics associated with him is authentic. Whatever Irving thought of this

---

[8]   This detail suggests that "Geoffrey Crayon" may have been reading Henry Ellis's 1813 edition of Brand's *Observations on Popular Antiquities*, which insists that "mistletoe" in churches is incorrect (1:409). A 1792 article in the *Gentleman's Magazine* by a correspondent known as "Robin Hood" mentions that holly and ivy are used in churches but not "missletoe," leaving him to conjecture that "our forefathers" were averse to "any token of antient Paganism, or object of Druidical veneration" in churches. *Gentleman's Magazine* 62 (April 1792), 332–33. "Robin Hood" mentions kissing under the mistletoe. He received a reply from "Antiquariolus" the following month who maintained that some churches at least used to use mistletoe in their Christmas decorations (432).

behavior, the fictional Crayon seems wistful for the idealized Christmases of the English past, especially the very un-American sense of feudal obligation. If in the present, that generosity of the local landowner towards his tenants does not quite work, it does not entirely negate the possibility that at some time in the very distant past, as Scott had suggested, Christmas was truly a time when class differences were temporarily forgotten.

William Hone also represents Christmas as a time of general celebration and subversion of hierarchies, and although Hone was known as a parodist, he seems more in earnest than Irving about the Christmas of the past. For historical accounts of Christmas, he was largely indebted to Strutt, whose works were reprinted many times. Hone also published his tribute to ancient Christmas in a variety of forms, including *The Every-Day Book*. He was never afraid to cut and paste from other texts, and the result is a compendious overview of Christmas customs with a special focus on the practices of the poorer members of society: he quotes a text lamenting the reduction of most people's Christmas to "at most a day or two"; and the decline of Christmas spirit and those Christian "feelings which should remind us of the equal rights of all" (*Every-Day Book* 1:1623).[9] Among the activities listed for the Christmas season are eating and drinking (especially mince-pies); carols; waits; and mumming. The second volume of the *Every-Day* Book includes even more medi-evalist detail: some practices are described as of pagan origin, such as the use of greenery; or Kentish "Hodening," a procession involving a horse's head "supposed to be an ancient relic of a festival ordained to commemorate our Saxon ancestors' landing" in Thanet (*Every-Day Book* 2:1642–43). Others claimed origins in the ancient times of Christianity, including the Glastonbury thorn that according to legend grew from the staff of Joseph of Arimathea and flowered at Christmas and Easter; Hone includes the observation that after the calendar reform in 1753, the thorn did not flower on the new Christmas Eve, but eleven days later (*Every-Day Book* 2:1641).

A similar view of Christmas is presented in Hone's *Ancient Mysteries Described*. Although Hone is aware that scripture-based dramas took place in summer, he ascribes their origin to ancient celebrations of the season of Christmas and the New Year. He provides many later examples from continental Europe, but reminds his readers that such practices were also part of the English Christmas: "During the period of gloom that succeeded the first ages of ecclesiastical power, we have seen the nature of the diversions it provided for the people on the continent: and that one of the them, the ceremony of the Boy Bishop, was practiced in the churches here" (*Ancient Mysteries*, 199). Hone therefore suggests that not merely the wealthy but also the working poor extended the Christmas season.

A few years later William Sandys prefaced his collection of Christmas carols with a lengthy survey of Christmas customs, starting from the creation of the world: pagan religions are, he suggests, a "corrupted" version of true spirituality after the Tower of Babel, and most pagan practices involved a festival "in honour of the return of the sun" around winter solstice. This survived in present-day Britain because after the introduction of Protestantism, some Catholic practices were "connived at, in

---

[9]   Quoting "The Literary Pocket-Book."

order to humour the uneducated part of the community, and festivals handed down, though with various alterations, from our Pagan ancestors, were preserved."[10] He depicts the Anglo-Saxons as both aware of the celebration of Yule and, after Christian conversion, keeping Christmas as "a solemn festival" (xiv). Sandys proceeds to describe the celebratory tone of medieval Christmas, noting that the "working classes" were "allowed greater privileges at Christmas than at any other part of the year" (xxv). Whether or not Sandys's intention was to prompt guilt in his readers at a time when Parliament was in the process of passing the Poor Law Amendment Act that would further divide rich and poor, he depicts Christmas as a time of generous spending. Perhaps because one source of information about medieval practice is account-books, most of his examples suggest that Christmas entertainment always involved large-scale expenditure. For Sandys, Christmas declined after it was forbidden during the Commonwealth: for example, the "amusements at Whitehall" do not "appear to have ever recovered their former splendor" (xliii). Sandys's story of Christmas, then, depicts medieval Christmas as a syncretistic festival marked by extravagant spending and community interactions over multiple days; post-Reformation Christmas as an attempt to keep the poor happy; and post-Restoration Christmas as never quite matching that of earlier times. Although he is only one of numerous collectors of the time interested in Christmas carols, he still regards Christmas as in decline, especially in forms of hospitality: "The Christmas feasts in the establishments of noblemen and gentlemen of wealth abated in splendor and hospitality more gradually than those of the royal household, and are still kept up in parts of the country, but each succeeding festival finds them fewer in number" (xlv).

Sandys was writing, however, in the era of the Christmas and New Year gift book, a new form of seasonal expenditure. The most expansive attempt to make a Christmas gift book actually about the season is *The Book of Christmas* (1836). As was the standard practice for illustrated gift books and annuals, the pictures were produced first, and then the text to accompany them. In 1835 the artist Robert Seymour produced three dozen lively etchings of Christmas customs old and new, but the writer Thomas Kibble Hervey, whose obituary describes him as "desultory and procrastinating,"[11] spent so long on the text that the book was not ready until the day after Christmas and thus missed the gift book market.[12] Given the disappointing sales, the initial plan for a series of "Holiday Books" mentioned in the Preface seems to have been abandoned (Seymour and Hervey, vi).

Hervey's Preface warns that to give a full account of Christmas traditions "it was necessary, at times, to go into more antiquarian details than may be approved of by the general reader" (v–vi). In the four hundred-odd pages, details are plenty, and

[10] William Sandys, *Christmas Carols, Ancient and Modern* (London: R. Beckley, 1833), xi. Sandys's introduction is 140 pages long. Subsequent references in text.
[11] "Thomas Kibble Hervey." *Gentleman's Magazine* 206 (1859), 432. The obituary makes no mention of *The Book of Christmas*.
[12] In a biographical note attached to reprints of Seymour's engravings, "Alfred Crowquill" (Alfred Henry Forrester) points out that for Christmas sales the book should have been ready a month before Christmas. *Seymour's Humorous Sketches*, 6. Tara Moore states that through reprints *The Book of Christmas* continued to have an influence well into the Victorian period. Tara Moore, *Victorian Christmas in Print* (New York: Palgrave Macmillan, 2009), 10–18.

many attempt to show how current practices derive from medieval times, when Christmas was still a "Season" – the title of the first section. The Book promises to provide readers with "a programme of some of the more important ceremonies observed by our ancestors on the occasion; and to give them some explanation of those observances which linger still" before they fade away to "extinction." The celebrations of King Arthur, King John, Queen Elizabeth, and Charles I are cited as instances of long-gone "high ceremonial" (26–27), no distinction being made between the legendary Arthur and rulers whose celebrations are documented through account-books. One of the earlier illustrations is the "Baronial Hall" (Fig. 6), showing a large throng of people in a Gothic banqueting hall about to share a massive joint of meat.

Hervey explains how these practices might have survived the Reformation. He detests Elizabeth I, calling her "a weak and worthless woman" with "the soul of a milliner, and no heart at all." But he credits Elizabeth's vanity with keeping alive many of the medieval Christmas rituals that Protestantism might have put aside, the difference being that devotion was directed to her than to the Virgin and Child: "The festival was preserved, and even embellished; but the saint, as far as the court was concerned, was changed." Yet "the example of festivity to the people was the same; and the land was a merry land" (52–53). Hervey includes an extensive discussion of the what he believes to the peculiarly English character of a Lord of Misrule who directed celebrations during the Christmas season – and then concedes that the season itself is ill-defined, being either the "Twelve Days" or the long season described by Stow (92). Even at the time of writing, "our days of less prominent and

Fig. 6.   "Baronial Hall." By Robert Seymour. From *The Book of Christmas* (1836), by Robert Seymour and Thomas Kibble Hervey.

Fig. 7. "Enjoying Christmas." By Robert Seymour. From *The Book of Christmas* (1836), by Robert Seymour and Thomas Kibble Hervey.

ceremonial rejoicing, the holiday-spirit of the season is by no means to be restrained within the narrower of those limits." (94). *The Book of Christmas* is a long read, and Seymour's illustration "Enjoying Christmas," which shows a Pickwick-like man sitting by his fireside reading it (Fig. 7), may be revealing: if Christmas is once again to be a season, some level of study is involved.

Christmas Carols

Irving's "Bracebridge Hall" stories involved enforced carol-singing as part of the seasonal celebration. In her edition of John Mason Neale's letters, his daughter recalled how in "Good Christian Men, Rejoice" the lines "Calls you one, and calls you all,/ To gain his everlasting Hall" reminded her of her childhood at Sackville College. The carol always:

> brings back to me the picture of the Hall with its oak wainscots and gallery, wreathed with shining ivy and holly, where the children stood to sing; of the old men in their clean smocks; of the old women in their granny bonnets, seated round the open hearth with its big log fire; of the smell of spiced elder wine; of the ruddy glow on the lined and wrinkled faces, and bent forms, of those whose old age had found a shelter in this harbour of refuge, and a friend to guide them to a better one.[13]

Mary Sackville Lawson was a child in the 1850s, and this nostalgic recollection of Christmas carol singing is ironic in more than one respect. First, she remembers contented poor pensioners in the almshouse that her father supervised, whereas her own record suggests that at least at times other than Christmas they complained about their conditions and especially about Neale's insistence on involving them in the practice of church ritual. Second, the fondly remembered "traditions" at Sackville College were largely the product of her father's medievalist invention.

By Neale's time, carols were gaining a new respectability. Like other Christmas traditions, carol-singing seemed a dying practice in the early years of the nineteenth century. William Hone, who amassed a collection of broadside ballads of Christmas carols, lamented that these "ditties which now exclusively enliven the industrious servant maid and the humble labourer, gladdened the festivity of royalty in ancient times" (*Ancient Mysteries*, 100). Hone's phrase "the festivity of royalty in ancient times" suggests that at some distant point in the national past, even the monarchy participated in carols as an integral part of Christmas. Multiple medieval English lyrics celebrating the birth of Christ have survived; Thomas G. Duncan notes that about 500 Middle English carols are extant, mainly from after 1400.[14] Nineteenth-century antiquarians were aware of some of these, and also knew that

[13] *The Letters of John Mason Neale, D.D.*, edited by his daughter (Mary Sackville Lawton) (London: Longman, 1910), 282.
[14] Thomas G. Duncan, ed., *Medieval English Lyrics and Carols* (Cambridge: D.S. Brewer, 2013), 25.

Christmas carols were printed as early as the sixteenth century.[15] Their examples of "ancient" carols, however, tend to be of much later date. Thomas Warton describes medieval carols as "enlivening the merriments of the Christmas celebrity," to be later suppressed by Puritan "enemies of innocent and useful mirth"; he provides the Boar's Head Carol in a sixteenth-century version and one scrap of a Middle English and Latin Nativity carol but no more.[16] Joseph Ritson printed some selections from a manuscript in the British Museum, Sloane 2593, in the 1790s;[17] Thomas Wright reproduced more of the carols from this source in a medieval-looking black-letter text in 1836,[18] and was later to edit all the carols in another fifteenth-century manuscript now in the Bodleian.[19] Yet most carols described as "ancient" do not appear medieval in source or language. Although Hone, for example, has just provided a historical overview of carols, the song that he recalls having heard in his youth is the post-medieval "God rest you merry, Gentlemen," which fills him with nostalgia for "the shivering carolist's evening chaunt" (*Ancient Mysteries*, 106).

Hone was perhaps the first to collect and catalogue individual printed Christmas carols, but around the same time antiquarians began to transcribe regional carols from oral tradition. Davies Gilbert collected words and tunes of carols sung in the west of England "up to the latter part of last century," noting that they were sung both private homes on Christmas Eve and in church on Christmas Day.[20] Gilbert believes that "shadows of the customs" of celebrating Christmas from before the Reformation have been "until lately, preserved in the Protestant West of England" – with the implication that they are now extinct. Even the anonymous editor of a collection of new carols published in 1833 by J.W. Parker for the Society for Promoting Christian Knowledge agrees that "before the era of the Reformation the singing of 'Christmas Carols' was very commonly practiced in this country, as well as in other countries in Christendom." The new carols are an attempt to reclaim the carol-singing tradition for the "festival of our Lord's nativity."[21]

An even more significant contribution to the preservation of Christmas carols is William Sandys's *Christmas Carols, Ancient and Modern* (1833), which again focused on carols from the west of England. I have already mentioned the expansive introduction, possibly the longest antiquarian discussion of Christmas before

[15]   On early printing of Christmas carols, see Edward Bliss Reed, *Christmas Carols Printed in the Sixteenth Century* (Cambridge, MA: Harvard University Press, 1932). Reed repeats the point that for the carol writers the Christmas season lasted from "Christmas" to February 2.

[16]   Thomas Warton, *History of English Poetry*, 4 vols (London: Dodsley, 1774–81), 3:143.

[17]   Joseph Ritson, ed., *Ancient Songs, from the Time of King Henry the Third, to the Revolution* (London: J. Johnson, 1790). The book contains additional carols from other manuscript sources.

[18]   Thomas Wright, *Songs and Carols Printed from a Manuscript in the Sloane Collection* (London: W. Pickering, 1836). Wright published an even more extensive selection from Sloane 2593 in modern typeface twenty years later as *Songs and Carols from a Manuscript in the British Museum of the Fifteenth Century* (London: T. Richards, 1856).

[19]   Thomas Wright, *Songs and Carols; Now First Printed from a Manuscript of the Fifteenth Century* (London: Percy Society, 1847).

[20]   Davies Gilbert, *Some Ancient Christmas Carols, with the Tunes to which they were sung in the West of England*, 2nd edition (London: J. Nichols, 1823), iii.

[21]   *Christmas Carols; Or. Sacred Songs suited to the festival of our Lord's Nativity* (London: J.W. Parker, 1833), 8.

Hervey and Seymour's ill-fated work in 1836 – which at points, relies heavily on Sandys's researches. Sandys is aware that carols were among the first works printed by Wynken de Worde in 1521 (Sandys, cxxviii). Even, though, if many early carols celebrated the season, some of them at least may not have been restricted to Christmas. Multiple Middle English carols begin by celebrating Christ's birth but also allude to his death, paralleling the baby in his mother's lap with the dead Christ in Mary's arms.[22] Those derived from play cycles such as the "Coventry Carol" and the shepherds' songs would have been sung in summer, when the plays were performed. Christmas carols are frequently in the present tense, reminding singers that "Christ is born" (rather than was born). Yet rather than celebrating the Nativity the year round, the new interest in Christmas carols limits it to the Christmas season.

Even if now restricted to a particular time of year, attempts to revive the Christmas carol were largely successful and reinforced by the official Anglican publication *Hymns Ancient and Modern* (from 1861), which included a number of carols that Neale and others had adapted from medieval Latin texts.[23] An article published in *Once A Week* on Boxing Day 1863 remarks,

> Some twenty or thirty years ago we should scarcely have dared to predict the resuscitation of the Christmas Carol. At that time the custom of singing carols had become little better than a respectable scheme for raising money, the miserable street-singer drawling out, in lamentable and tuneless strains (in hope of pecuniary recompense), the "good tidings" that "our Saviour he was born On Christmas Day in the morning." In villages and quiet places, it is true, carols in some form or other have never been allowed to die out, and appear to have been cherished with no little reverence as one of the rarest delights of the "blessed Christmas Tide."[24]

The author, Edmund Sedding, evidently believes in the medieval origins of English Christmas Carol singing, since he shows awareness of Hone's *Ancient Mysteries Described*; provides a useful overview of Christmas carol scholarship; and concludes with a modern poem written as a medieval Christmas carol, William Morris's "Masters in This Hall." He is optimistic that "the Christmas carol bids fair to be re-instated with full honours to its orthodox position among the festivities of Yule Tide."

Deep and Crisp and Even

I turn now to one of the oddest but most influential of Victorian Christmas carols, "Good King Wenceslas." This is not "medieval," but decidedly "medievalist." The words were another example of the work of John Mason Neale. In 1853 the British ambassador to Stockholm gave Neale one of the handful of surviving copies of *Piae Cantiones*. Compiled in 1582 by the Finnish scholar Theodoricus Petri, *Piae*

---

[22] For example, in Duncan's collection "That lovely lady sat and song," "This endrys nyght" and "A baby ys borne us blys to brying" all connect Christ's birth and death (Duncan, 236–40); all were printed by Wright in 1847.

[23] Examples include "Creator of the Starry Height" (Hymn 31), "O Come, O Come, Emmanuel" (Hymn 36) and "Of the Father's Love Begotten" (Hymn 46).

[24] Edward Sedding, "Christmas Carols." *Once A Week*, December 26, 1863, 10–13.

Cantiones records the words and music of over seventy hymns and songs, many of which originated before the Reformation. Neale saw in these songs the potential for a revived hymn tradition in England that would rival the emphasis on personal subjectivity seen in the works of non-conformist hymn-writers such as Charles Wesley. Working with music arranger Thomas Helmore, Neale published *Carols for Christmas-Tide, Set to Ancient Melodies* in 1854. The title itself disclaims authenticity: while some of the words are translations, others are very free adaptations, and two are Neale's poems set to tunes from *Piae Cantiones*.

An example of an adaptation is Neale's "Good Christian Men, Rejoice." *Piae Cantiones* gives the text of this song in Latin and German as:

> In dulci jubilo,
> Nun singet und seid froh!
> Unsers Herzens Wonne
> Leit in praesepio,
> Und leuchtet als die Sonne
> Matris in gremio,
> Alpha es et O, Alpha es et O![25]

The song is attributed to the fourteenth-century Heinrich Suso.[26] Neale's adaptation reads:

> Good Christian Men, rejoice,
> With heart, and soul, and voice;
> Give ye heed to what we say:
> News! News!
> Jesus Christ is born today:
> Ox and ass before him bow,
> And he is the manger now.
> Christ is born today! Christ is born today![27]

This version retains the general idea of rejoicing (although limiting it to Christian men), but removes the reference to Mary's lap: in medieval carols Mary is often given as much if not more attention than the Christ Child, but Neale had already come under scrutiny from the Anglican hierarchy for his supposedly Roman Catholic leanings,[28] and he probably wanted to avoid any accusation of Mariolatry. He adds, though, more detail to the stable scene. Possibly the reference to alpha and

---

[25]   In sweet rejoicing, let's sing and be happy; Our heart's desire lies in a manger; and shines like the sun in Mary's lap; You are Alpha and Omega.

[26]   See the multiple versions of the carol collected in Douglas D. Anderson and Richard Jordan's comprehensive www.hymnsandcarolsofchristmas.com.

[27]   J.M. Neale and Thomas Helmore, *Carols for Christmas-Tide Set to Ancient Melodies, Vocal Score* (London: Novello, 1854), 20–21.

[28]   Eleanor Towle notes that as early as 1846, not long after Newman had joined the Roman Catholic communion, Neale was seen to possess a Vulgate Bible and a breviary and was accused of making the chapel he was building seem Roman Catholic. Eleanor A. Towle, *John Mason Neale D.D., A Memoir*, 2nd impression (London: Longmans, 1907), 156–59.

o(mega), the beginning and the end, suggested the reference to Ox and Ass, where Neale draws on an English tradition that animals kneel at midnight on Christmas Eve, the time of Christ's birth. Henry Ellis's 1813 edition of *Popular Antiquities* records a Devonshire claim that this still happens, but on Christmas Eve "old style" as before calendar reform (Ellis 1:355). As in the medieval original, two moments in time are drawn together: the birth of Christ, which for Neale is a historic event; and the present-day Christmas.

In the case of "Good King Wenceslas," the words bear no relation to those in *Piae Cantiones*: Neale borrowed the tune of a spring carol and gave it a snowy setting; piecing together a medieval legend, he composed a carol about a story he had written, then collaborated in setting it to an early melody. Neale's biographer Eleanor A. Towle laments that Neale did not appreciate Wordsworth's poetry, noting that "Though he readily recognized subtle forms of poetic beauty in quaint mediaeval attire, he was impatient of the vague sweetness of much modern poetry" and that he "strangely failed to appreciate either the deliberate majesty of Wordsworth's poems or the high dignity of the thoughts they enshrined."[29] Nevertheless, Neale's insistence on the use of ordinary language for his poems and translations recalls Wordsworth's adoption of "the language of common men" in *Lyrical Ballads*. Yet the debt may be more extensive. "Good King Wenceslas" is, I want to suggest, is in spirit a Victorian reworking of Wordsworth's Lyrical Ballad "Goody Blake and Harry Gill: A True Story."[30]

Rather than following the usual form of Christmas carols in celebrating the mystery of the incarnation, the song focuses on the benevolent action of a medieval saint. Neale had earlier written a story about Saint Wenceslaus in his collection of tales for children, *Deeds of Faith* (1849). Drawing on later medieval legends that describe the Bohemian king's benevolence to the poor, Neale's story tells how Wenceslaus sees from his castle window a poor man pulling sticks from bushes. He sends his page Otto to learn more about the man, who is revealed to be Rudolph the Swineherd.[31] Wenceslaus and Otto set out to deliver provisions and firewood, and when the cold night proves too much for the page, the King tells him, "Only tread in my footsteps, and you will proceed more easily." Otto obeys, with the result that he "felt not the wind; he heeded not the frost; the footprints glowed as with a holy fire."[32] In the carol, though, the story is pared down to the point where it becomes an inversion of what happens in "Goody Blake and Harry Gill." Both poems describe a poor person who while seeking firewood by moonlight encroaches on the property of a wealthier

[29] Towle, 209.
[30] Wordsworth announced in the Advertisement to *Lyrical Ballads* that the "true story" was "founded on a well-authenticated fact which happened in Warwickshire." The source is Erasmus Darwin's *Zoonomia* (1796), which Wordsworth borrowed in 1797. For the date and circumstances of composition, see R.L. Brett and A.R. Jones's edition of *Lyrical Ballads* (London: Methuen, 1963), 282.
[31] The spelling changes from "Wenceslaus" in the story to "Wenceslas" in the carol. In *Good King Wenceslas, The Real Story*, Jan Rejzl mentions a late Czech legend in which Duke Wenceslaus and his page Podevin deliver "wood, food, and money" to those in need; the page "did not feel any cold when following Wenceslas in his footsteps on these missions of mercy." Jan Rejzl, *Good King Wenceslas, The Real Story* (Norwich: 1st Choice Publishing, 1995), 14.
[32] J.M. Neale, *Deeds of Faith* (1849), 2nd edition (London: Mozley, 1860), 135.

man. The reactions of the wealthier men, however, are directly opposite, as are the ambiguously supernatural consequences of their choices.

In Wordsworth's poem, Goody Blake dwells alone, and to keep herself warm in winter she is dependent on gathering firewood; usually she collects "rotten boughs" brought down by the wind, but she is unable to keep "A pile beforehand, wood or stick,/ Enough to warm her for three days."[33] When the weather is particularly cold, she goes out under the cover of darkness and takes sticks from Harry Gill's hedge. A similar quest for firewood is central to Neale's "Good King Wenceslas." King Wenceslas looks out and sees a "poor man … gathering winter fuel" in the snow by moonlight (*Carols for Christmas-Tide*, 37). Usually, night-time in winter is not the best way to collect wood. Goody Blake collects firewood by moonlight both because she is desperately cold and because she is aware that she is committing a "trespass." Although "Good King Wenceslas," which is less than half the length of Wordsworth's poem, gives less detail, the "peasant" is presumably similarly desperate. He apparently has no woodcutting skills since he lives "right against the forest fence" – the boundary between the cultivated and the wild – but has no firewood and has walked a "good league" (three miles) through the snow to find some. If the snow is "deep and crisp and even," he would have great difficulty picking up deadwood from the ground. Most likely, then, the poor man is, as in Neale's earlier story, pulling wood from trees or hedges close to the royal residence. He is seemingly close enough for the king's page to be able to identify immediately from the window – within a stanza and with no pause – precisely who the fuel-gatherer (a departure from the earlier story when Otto goes outside and inquires). Even if the poor man is not taking the king's own wood, he is certainly gathering wood very close to the king's home.

In Wordsworth's poem, Harry Gill's response to the "trespass" is to spring upon Goody Blake in the act of theft and to cry "I've caught you then at last!" King Wenceslas's response to the peasant's encroachment is precisely the opposite. Once his page has told him where the poor man lives, he orders food, wine, and "pine-logs,"[34] then the two set out to deliver them to the peasant's home and to "see him dine." The peasant is seen only from a distance and never has the opportunity to speak. Goody Blake, in contrast, speaks when Harry Gill lays hold of her, and the result is a curse, prayed with "the cold, cold moon above her head":

> She prayed, her withered hand uprearing,
> While Harry held her by the arm:
> "God, who art never out of hearing –
> Oh may he never more be warm!"

Harry Gill hears "what she had said," and turns away "icy cold." As Harry turns, so does the focus of the poem; the rest of the poem describes the effect of the curse on him as he can never be warm again. Goody Blake is only mentioned in the narrator's

---

[33]   William Wordsworth, "Good Blake and Harry Gill." *Lyrical Ballads* (London: J. and A. Arch, 1798), 88.

[34]   Pine logs would probably not be the best option for a long-lasting fire; possibly they provide an indirect reference to traditional Christmas evergreens.

concluding address to the reader, where she becomes representative of the poor in general: "Now think, ye farmers all, I pray,/ Of Goody Blake and Harry Gill" (*Lyrical Ballads*, 93).

Whereas Harry Blake is cursed with being cold for his lack of compassion for the poor, kind King Wenceslas and his page are blessed with being warm. Wordsworth's poem makes no clear distinction between the natural and supernatural world – Goody Blake appears to be able to pray simultaneously to God and to the moon – but in "Good King Wenceslas" God is not mentioned at all. The will of God, though, appears to be in opposition to a hostile nature. The page remarks that the "night goes darker" and the "wind grows stronger" as he travels with the king on their errand of charity. The King tells the page to tread "boldly" in his footsteps, because "Thou wilt find the winter's rage/Freeze thy blood less coldly." The page discovers that "Heat was in the very sod/ Which the saint had printed." Like "Goody Blake and Harry Gill," the last lines of the poem turn the message to the reader:

> Therefore, Christian men, be sure
> Wealth or rank possessing,
> Ye who now will bless the poor,
> Shall yourselves find blessing.
>
> (*Carols for Christmas-Tide*, 40)

The concluding focus is hence, as in "Goody Blake and Harry Gill," not on the recipient or non-recipient of charity but on the effect on the one who had the opportunity for charity.

"Good King Wenceslas" presumably takes place in the Saint's kingdom of Bohemia, a potentially snowier place than England. Yet it is part of a fairly new trend in English Christmas traditions in emphasizing snow, and suggesting that the Christmas season has its own weather. Robert Herrick's "Christmas Caroll," quoted by Irving in *The Sketch Book*, suggests that the Nativity symbolically makes December turn "to May," the winter weather being less important than the wonder of Christmas.[35] In nineteenth-century envisionings of Christmas, in contrast, cold weather plays a significant role. This is strange since while England may have experienced some very cold winters in the eighteenth century, snow and solid ice at Christmas seem to have been relatively rare in the 1800s. The first London readers of *A Christmas Carol* in December 1843 would have had to imagine its snowy scenes, since it was one of the warmest Decembers of the century.

Martin Rowley, who has compiled historical meteorological data for Britain, concludes that 1810–19 was the coldest period in England since the 1690s, generally explained by the volcanic activity that caused 1816 to have gone down in literary history as "the year without a summer." Rowley states that "It is generally thought that the works of Charles Dickens take the character of the weather from this less than perfect period, e.g. the often-quoted snow/frost in such as 'A Christmas Carol' & 'The Pickwick Papers'."[36] He notes of 1828 that it was a "wet summer," some-

---

[35] Robert Herrick, "A Christmas Caroll, Sung to the King in the Presence at White-hall." *Complete Poems* 3:159.
[36] http://booty.org.uk/booty.weather/climate/histclimat.htm (Martin Rowley).

what borne out by the *Pickwick Papers*, but the snowy Christmas and ice-skating on Christmas Day 1827 seem improbable, even in Dingley Dell. Of the winters of 1842 and 1843, the time of *A Christmas Carol*, "For two years running, these Decembers were remarkably mild, with CET [that's Central England Temperature] values respectively 7.2 & 7.4degC (about 45 degrees Fahrenheit): these values represent an anomaly on the all-series mean of at least +3C, and on the modern-era mean of at least +2C." In December 1842 Elizabeth Barrett expressed to Mary Russell Mitford a hope that the "lovely, unduly warm weather, this Christmas June, may last"; while on Boxing Day 1843 she jests to another friend, "This is such a lovely May day, day I am afraid of breaking the spell by writing down Christmas wishes" (*Brownings' Correspondence* 6:227; 8:108). Incidentally, she may have picked up on the cold imagery, since after giving *A Christmas Carol* a mixed review on December 27, 1843, she concludes her letter to Mitford, "Wishes warm as the Yule log are with you at Christmastime & always" (*Brownings' Correspondence* 8:113). Exactly when Scrooge has his encounter with spirits is not entirely clear, but Scrooge's references to workhouses, prisons, and treadmills suggest that it is the 1830s at earliest, and most likely the balmy 1840s: his neighborhood is lit by gaslights.

Yet cold is clearly part of Dickens's purpose. The constant emphasis on combating the cold provides a clue as to a practical way in which the rich can help the poor. The Ghost conveys to Scrooge that if the "shadows remain unaltered by the Future," Tim Cratchit will die.[37] If Tiny Tim has a specific ailment, from rickets to tuberculosis, Scrooge's intervention will be unlikely to make much difference. But significantly, Tim's contribution to the Christmas festivities is a song "about a lost child travelling in the snow" (*Christmas Carol*, 84).[38] In very literal terms, the Cratchits, although by no means the poorest of the poor in London, need warmth and healthy food. Apparently, none of them owns an overcoat (Martha arrives in a shawl and bonnet), and within their four rooms they have no cooking stove, not uncommon in apartment-dwelling of the time. They do have a fireplace where family members can warm themselves and cook potatoes, assuming that they can afford both fuel and potatoes; John Leech's illustrations of Scrooge's room show that his fireplace contains a metal grate with side plates where kettles and saucepans can be boiled (Fig. 23), and the Cratchits would presumably have a similar arrangement. But the pudding is being boiled in the washhouse copper, and the goose is being roasted at the baker's oven. Scrooge himself is aware of the problem of cooking food at a time when some Christians were proposing that stores including bakers' shops should be closed on Sundays (86), so it seems a misplaced example of feudal benevolence to give the Cratchits a giant turkey that they will have great difficulties in cooking (113). All the same, if Scrooge becomes a "second father" to Tim and provides the family with sufficient income to afford coal, warm clothing and nourishing food, Tim might not succumb to one of the many childhood illnesses that might kill him.

---

[37]   Charles Dickens, *A Christmas Carol* (1843); quoted from Michael Slater's edition of *A Christmas Carol and Other Christmas Writings* (London: Penguin, 2003), 94. Subsequent quotations follow this edition.

[38]   The description does not match any specific Christmas song; a broadside ballad from around this period titled "The Pauper's Child" has been suggested. See https://musicb3. wordpress.com/2018/12/21/the-song-of-tiny-tim/ (accessed May 2, 2020).

Dickens's work was likely a contributory factor towards the increased references to snow in sung carols. The date of Christ's birth, and hence of Christmas, is a convention adopted by the early Christian church, roughly aligning of the coming of the Son with the winter solstice,[39] which gave English celebrants of Christmas scope for imagining that Christmas was cold. Snow, however, seems to have entered into Christmas carols relatively late. Edith Rickert's *Ancient Christmas Carols 1400–1700*, published in 1900, is a useful overview of the English Christmas Carol tradition, revealing that although carols refer from time to time to winter, they rarely mention snow.[40] The tradition that Christmas Eve was cold is found in many early texts. For example, in *The Second Shepherd's Play* in the Towneley manuscript, the three shepherds complain about the cold and stormy weather; they also note that they have to look after their sheep in all conditions, including snow and sleet. On this particular night, though, there is apparently no snow, and it is reasonable to assume that in snowy conditions the sheep would be in a fold rather than on a hillside.

The thirty pages of Rickert's appendices contain more references to snow than the 270 pages of the main collection. The first appendix features what Rickert calls "Christmas Hymns and Other Lyrics," creating a category separate from the mainly anonymous Christmas carols. These do include a very few references to snow in devotional poems, not Christmas carols. In Robert Southwell's poem "The Burning Babe," the speaker describes himself as having "in hoary winter's night stood shivering in the snow."[41] The speaker sees a Christmas Day vision of a "pretty Babe all burning bright" who will use his flames to purify "men's defiled souls." A second poem by Southwell does not refer specifically to snow but asks the hearers to "Behold a silly tender Babe/ In freezing winter night." An additional appendix is titled "Modern Poems in the Medieval Manner." William Morris's "Masters in this Hall" is spoken in the voice of a singer who asks those in the hall to "Hear ye news to-day,/ Brought from over sea,/ And ever I you pray." The chorus of "Nowell" connects with medieval French and English carols, concluding in lines that recall both the Magnificat and Morris's own class consciousness: "God to-day hath poor folks raised,/ And cast a-down the proud" (289). Taking the immediacy of Christmas carols to the extreme, the singer describes himself as "Going over the hills,/ Through the milk-white snow," and encountering shepherds leaving for "Bethlem." He goes with the shepherds and sees Mary and her child, along with the kneeling ox and ass. In bringing together a medieval setting and the immediacy of the Nativity story, Morris pays his own tribute to medieval drama.

If "Masters in this Hall" uses snow in an imaginative retelling of the nativity story, the winter snow is a constant presence in Rickert's other selection from Morris's works, "Outlanders, Whence Come ye Last?" In this poem "The snow in the street and the wind on the door" is a refrain, paired with "Minstrels and maids, stand forth

[39] Mark Forsyth sets out the reasons for the date of Christmas in *A Christmas Cornucopia* (London: Viking, 2016), 1–19.

[40] "The First Nowell," admittedly, imagines the shepherds of the Nativity "a-keeping their sheep/ On a cold winter's night that was so deep." Since shepherding in deep snow would be nigh impossible, I assume that the cold and perhaps the dark are deep, rather than snow.

[41] Quoted from Edith Rickert, *Ancient English Christmas Carols MCCCC to MDCC* (London: Chatto and Windus, 1914), 270. Subsequent references in text by page number.

on the floor." In "stand forth on the floor," Morris may possibly be referring to the antiquarian belief that "carols" were initially "round dances"; Rickert notes that "In French it is usually regularly, as early as the twelfth century, to describe the song-dance of spring and love" (xiv). But this is now an image of winter, as Morris has found a way to combine the Christmas story with images of snow, and the medieval world provides a bridge between the first Christmas and the present.

Christina Rossetti's Christmas Carols

Among Rickert's collection of "Modern Poems in the Medieval Manner" is Christina Rossetti's "A Christmas Carol," which has become known by its first line, "In the bleak mid-winter." In selecting this as a poem in the "medieval manner," Rickert may have been thinking of vocabulary such as "In her maiden bliss," yet Rossetti's poems reflect the carol tradition in other respects. In *The Poetical Works of Christina Rossetti* several poems are identified as "Christmas carols."[42] They follow tradition in using simple, childlike language; in being in the most part singable – many of them have been set to music multiple times –; in being written from a present narrative perspective; and being emphatic in their connection of Christmas with winter. Her brother and editor William Michael Rossetti observes that frequently her "poems about festivals of the Church, or about seasons of the year, were written at dates by no means corresponding."[43] This may be true, but imaginatively, or perhaps meditatively, Rossetti is able to enter the moment of Christmas. In "A Christmas Carol," dated 7 March, 1849,[44] the narrator and other worshippers are kneeling in Church as Christmas Eve becomes Christmas Day:

> Thank God, thank God, we do believe:
> Thank God that this is Christmas Eve.
> Even as we kneel upon this day,
> Even so, the ancient legends say,
> Nearly two thousand years ago
> The stalled ox knelt, and even so
> The ass knelt full of praise, which they
> Could not express, while we can pray.
> Thank God, thank God, for Christmas was born
> Ages ago, as on this morn.
> In the snow-season undefiled
> God came to earth a little child:
> He put his ancient glory by
> To live for us and then to die. (117)

---

[42]   I am being cautious here because although Rossetti used the title in her collected poems of 1892 for "In the Bleak Midwinter" and the three-carol "chimes" sequence, her editor may have supplied some of the titles of posthumously published poems.

[43]   *The Poetical Works of Christina Georgina Rossetti*, ed. William Michael Rossetti (London: Macmillan, 1904), 472. Unless otherwise stated, subsequent references to Rossetti's poetry are to this edition, by page number.

[44]   Robert Browning identified this as St Perpetua's Day, as did Christina Rossetti many years later in *Time Flies*.

In this single stanza, the narrator links the present moment of the kneeling faithful with the medieval tradition that the ox and ass kneel at midnight as they knelt at Christ's birth; the moment of the Incarnation itself "nearly two thousand years ago"; and eternity, God's "ancient glory" put aside at that moment.

Even in this poem written when she was nineteen, Rossetti associates Christmas with the "snow-season" of winter. In another poem titled "A Christmas Carol" dated August 26, 1859, Christ is born "Before the paling of the stars,/ Before the winter morn." The speaker imagines how "Saint and Angel, ox and ass,/ Kept a watch together,/ Before the Christmas daybreak/ In the winter weather" (217). Although Christ's birth is here described in the past tense, in the concluding lines the speaker and addressees are included in the scene: "Let us kneel with Mary Maid,/ With Joseph bent and hoary,/ With Saint and Angel, ox and ass,/ To hail the King of Glory." A series of three carols from around 1887 draw inspiration from the chiming of Christmas bells to visualize the scene of Christ's birth. Even the angels marvel at the God of Glory – described in Part 3 as "Lord of storm and snow,/ Angel and star" – becoming a baby in such chilly and humble surroundings:

> The cave is cold and strait
> To hold the angelic state:
> More strait it is, more cold,
> To foster and infold
> Its Maker one hour old.

The reference to place of Christ's birth, described in the King James Bible as a "stable," as a cave draws on ancient and medieval tradition in imagining the stable as a cave, and thus paralleling the tomb in which Christ was laid after his death. Most memorably, however, in yet another poem titled "A Christmas Carol," Rossetti depicts a truly frosty world:

> In the bleak mid-winter
>   Frosty wind made moan,
> Earth stood hard as iron,
>   Water like a stone;
> Snow had fallen, snow on snow,
>   Snow on snow,
> In the bleak mid-winter
>   Long ago. (264)[45]

Rossetti doubtless understood, as may some of the anonymous writers of earlier carols, that December snow in England is comparatively rare and hardly ever in the category of "snow on snow"; and that such a happening would be even rarer in Roman-occupied Bethlehem in the eastern Mediterranean. Winter functions as a representation of the unredeemed world before the Incarnation – but with extra emphasis on details of the weather. Read collectively, Rossetti's poems indicate that she really disliked winter. For many poets, winter is a metaphor for death, but

---

[45]   Dated by William Michael Rossetti before 1872.

Rossetti, who had a very literal understanding of heaven and hell,[46] does not seem to dislike the idea of death nearly as much as she hates "all-lack Winter" (366). In contrast, "Seasons," dated December 7, 1853, pleads with summer, "Stay awhile," but orders winter,

> Dreary Winter come at last:
> Come quickly, to be quickly past:
> Dull and sluggish Winter, wane
> Till Spring and sunlight dawn again. (310)

Winter sometimes has connotations of age: in the sonnet "If Only," the speaker begins, "If only I might love my God and die! –/ But now He bids me love Him and live on" (274). The speaker, who self-identifies as having passed "the second half of life, has passed spring and summer and is moving through autumn to a winter that may not pass a weary while." Winter, then, is not death as much as age, sin, and sadness.

But Christmas can, her poems suggest, overcome winter:

> Christmas hath a darkness
> Brighter than the blazing noon,
> Christmas hath a chillness
> Warmer than the heat of June,
> Christmas hath a beauty
> Lovelier than the world can show:
> For Christmas bringeth Jesus,
> Brought for us so low. (158)

Just as Rossetti adds to the Christmas carol tradition through her depiction of winter, she also adds to the spirit of the season by her emphasis on gifts. As early as the "Christmas Carol" of 1849, the speaker asks "How shall we thank God?" and "What presents will he take from us?" In this poem the answer is that Christ himself is "the gift we must bring," drawing on the concept of Christ as the sacrificial Lamb. In most of the poems, however, the answer is love (117). The child speaker in "A Christmas Carol (For my Godchildren)" identifies with the Shepherds and Wise Men of the Christmas story, but asks, "shall I give no gift to God?" Answering his or her own question, the child concludes, "Lord, I will give my love to Thee" (188). The speaker in "A Christmas Carol: In the Bleak Midwinter" seems less sure that he or she can be a shepherd or a Wise Man, but concludes, "what I can I give Him,/ Give my heart" (247).

In the "Christmastide" poem from *Time Flies* that begins "Love came down at Christmas," the speaker represents Christ as the embodiment of divine love. The most difficult line of this seemingly simple poem is "But wherewith for sacred sign?" Since the previous lines have been about worship, "wherewith" seems to stand here for "What shall we use for the sign of true worship?" Again answering the question

---

[46] For example, a poem under the text "All flesh is Grass" begins, "So brief a life, and then an endless life/ Or endless death" (200).

he or she has raised, the speaker concludes, "Love shall be our token,/ Love be yours and love be mine,/ Love to God and all men,/ Love for plea and gift and sign" (*Time Flies*, 159). "Love to God and all men" suggests that although Christ, the Love who "came down at Christmas" is the Christian's "plea," the sacrificial substitute, humans also need to make a "gift and sign" by showing love.

Boxing Day

The second respect in which "Good King Wenceslas" is innovatory is in giving a medieval context to Boxing Day. In the early years of Queen Victoria's reign Britons were well aware that some Christmas practices were new. Although evergreen decorations were part of British tradition at least since the 1500s, Prince Albert is credited with introducing the Christmas tree, and by the 1840s "Christmas tree parties" for children with dancing and presents grew fashionable among the wealthy.[47] Very likely, the Christmas tree celebration helped cement Christmas, rather than New Year, as the time to give and receive gifts. The introduction of the penny post was an impetus to the development of printed Christmas cards: Henry Cole, who worked for the Post Office, commissioned the first mass-produced card, designed by John Horsley. Although the start of a new tradition, it takes the medieval form of a triptych (Fig. 8), where a festive gathering is flanked by figures clothing and feeding the poor. "Good King Wenceslas," however, helped medievalize the giving associated with Boxing Day.

Unlike the version in *Deeds of Faith*, where the story is set in Advent, the action of "Good King Wenceslas" takes place the night after Christmas, on "the feast of Stephen," or December 26. The carol associates the "feast of Stephen" with giving. A few instances of St Stephen's Day carols can be found in the English tradition, such as "St Stephen was an Holy Man," but, like the account in the Book of Acts, they emphasize Stephen's willingness to preach, rather than acts of giving. In nineteenth-century England, the custom was that on this day those who had performed services such as servants and tradespeople, and under certain circumstances the poor, could request a gratuity known as a "Christmas Box." It is difficult to trace this tradition back much further, but antiquarians once again theorized that it was medieval. In *Medii aevi kalendarium* R.T. Hampson observes that "the custom of giving *Christmas Boxes*, or presents, although falling into disuse, is still a serious tax on large families and establishments." This would suggest that tradespeople were demanding tips, but Hampson also mentions that official recipients of "charity" such as parish schoolchildren might also ask for money, to the extent that in London the day has become known as "Boxing Day": "Parish boys and children in London, still carry about the specimens of writing, asking for their Christmas Box" (Hampson, 106).

---

[47] Dickens calls the Christmas tree "that pretty German toy." See Michael Slater's note to "A Christmas Tree" in his edition of *A Christmas Carol and Other Christmas Writings*, 230, 283; also, Forsyth, 31. Thomas Kibble Hervey's wife Eleonora L. Hervey brought together Christmas trees, the first Christmas, and the medieval tradition of kneeling ox and ass in her poem "The Christmas Tree," published in the Christmas supplement to the *Illustrated London News*, December 25, 1852 (574).

Fig. 8. "Henry Cole's Christmas Card." The first mass-produced Christmas card, designed by John Horsley (1843)

Hampson's confused account theorizes that the practice might be derived from a medieval custom of putting money in a box to pray to saints for safe travel or for remission of sins; or from Roman New Year gift-giving; or from the solstice practices of "our ancestors" (Hampson, 107). The idea that a Christmas box might be a kind of medieval insurance policy for bad Christmas behavior may derive from John Brand, who says that the "Christmass Box" was "*Money* gathered against that time, that *Masses* might be made by the Priests to the Saints to *forgive* the *People* the *Debaucheries of that Time*" (Brand, 183). A *Punch* article of December 1849 remarks that "Christmas-Boxes have for ages ranked among the festivities of the season, though the festivity must come home more to those who have to receive them, than those who have to pay them" (*Punch* 17 [1849], 248). An accompanying poem, "Christmas is not what it ought to be," shows regret that "all the old customs are banished!" but expresses relief that "The butcher, the baker, the sweep,/ Employing their men as their proxies,/ No longer a harvest can reap/ By a cool application for boxes." Still, the poem ends by reminding readers that:

> At Christmas the hand should be free
> Not numbed by the coldness of caution.
> Of beef, of plum pudding, of beer,
> Permit not the neediest short to be:
> To all here's a happy new year,
> Whose Christmas has been what it ought to be.

Pantomime Season

By the 1840s, the Christmas season had also become pantomime season. Before the 1820s, theatres mainly treated the pantomime as a supporting program to other dramas. In the eighteenth century, pantomimes were usually true mimes in having no dialogue, a convenient means of circumventing theatre licensing and censorship laws. Pantomimes indicated their debt to Italian *commedia dell'arte* tradition by including the word "Harlequin" in the title or subtitle; at the pantomime's end the main characters appeared in the dress of Harlequin and Columbine, sometimes with Pantaloon and "the Clown."[48] The extensive lists of productions in Allardyce Nicoll's *History of English Drama* indicate that by the 1820s, new pantomimes had become a Christmas tradition and generally opened in December.[49]

The relationship between pantomime and the older mumming tradition was obscure. Nineteenth-century writers use the term "mumming" in three different ways. Strutt quotes Bourne's "Vulgar Antiquities" on cross-dressing mumming "practiced in the North," which was another form of wassailing or waits, going from house to house to share festivities (Strutt, *Sports*, 243). Even in Ellis's revision of Bourne's *Antiquitates Vulgares*, "mumming" is defined as cross-dressing (Ellis, 354), which would connect it with the English version of pantomime, where the Principal Boy is played by a female and the Dame by a male. The term "mumming," though, is also used in medieval and Tudor account books for Christmas court entertainments. Largely from information supplied by John Stow, Strutt traces elaborately staged Christmas plays at least back to the reign of Edward III.[50] Claiming that in "the middle ages, mummings were very common," he explains that Henry VIII forbade such practices (Strutt, *Sports*, 233); nevertheless "masques" continued or revived in Stuart times, and in the royal context "mummings" appears synonymous with "masques." The final use of the term "mumming" is for local community plays and dances, traditionally involving some version of the play of St George and the Dragon, and sometimes people dancing as characters from the Robin Hood stories. William Sandys, whose Christmas Carol study includes the text of a St George play, notes that "Christmas plays, however puerile they seem at present, are of a remote origin, and supposed by many to be as old as the Crusades" (Sandys, cvii). Like Scott, whose Christmas description detects in mumming "traces of ancient mystery," Sandys believes the play of St George is descended from medieval community drama, although he does not explain how it moved from summer to winter.[51]

---

[48] A shadow of this is retained in most present-day pantomimes, where in the finale the Principal Boy and Principal Girl take their bow last, in spectacular outfits. Maureen Hughes notes in *A History of Pantomime* (Barnsley: Pen and Sword History, 2013) that rather than the star of the show (in today's pantomime usually the Dame or the Clown) the Principal Boy and Principal Girl "walk down" last (29).

[49] Allardyce Nicoll provides a list of "Harlequin" pantomimes in *A History of English Drama 1660–1900*, 2nd edition, volume 4 (Cambridge: Cambridge University Press, 1963), 470–76.

[50] Strutt, *Sports*, 145; see also Sandys, xviii.

[51] Ronald Hutton states that "no trace of" the mummers' play of St George has been found before 1738 (*Merry England*, 8).

Ironically, the mummer's play was a form of Christmas celebration that faded during the Victorian period, in many instances unlamented. An 1849 *Illustrated London News* article on Christmas customs – by Thomas Miller, who elsewhere regrets the loss of local community – states:

> There is no more to deplore in the absence of *Friar Tuck*, *Maid Marian*, *Robin Hood*, with all his merry men, the huge dragon, and the hobby-horse, than there is in the extinction of the old moralities, whose places are now supplied by the plays of Shakespeare, and others which have appeared since he first wrote. Christmas has outlived all antique mummery, and is all the better for having shaken off his ancient and faded trappings.[52]

Mumming plays declined, although towards the end of the Victorian period, when J.G. Frazer had sparked new interest in what he believed to be fertility rituals, some were revived.[53] In 1881 Leopold Wagner detected the origins of English pantomime in "the Mysteries, the Moralities, the old Comedies, the Opera, and lastly, the Puppet Shows" of the past.[54] In the earlier years of the nineteenth century, though, pantomime became an urban substitute for other kinds of community performance, and especially associated with Boxing Day.

As the true "Christmas pantomime" became a seasonal event in its own right, two of the relatively few stories that became pantomime standards, *Dick Whittington and His Cat* and *The Babes in the Wood*, derive from medieval sources, one historical and one very questionable. *Dick Whittington* claims inspiration from a historical Lord Mayor of London, Richard Whittington. Whittington, who died in 1423, served three or four times as Lord Mayor; he was a merchant who bequeathed money to a number of charitable institutions, and the Mercers' Guild claimed him as one of their own. As early as the seventeenth century, chapbooks and ballads started to tell his story in a standard way. In the storybooks Dick Whittington is a poor boy who has come to London to seek his fortune. Having nothing else to invest, Dick sends off his cat on his employer Fitzwarren's merchant ship the *Unicorn*, and it saves the kingdom of the Barbary Coast from a plague of rats. The King of the Barbary Coast rewards the cat's owner with fabulous wealth, and he is able to marry Fitzwarren's daughter Alice.[55]

The story departs from fairytale conventions in some significant respects. Dick Whittington is a poor boy, not a prince in disguise. He does not win his bride through feats of courage, skill, or cunning, but earns the fortune that enables him to marry through an extremely speculative investment. The only supernatural aspect is the prophecy that Dick hears in the bells of Bow Church foretelling that he will

[52]   Thomas Miller, "Christmas in Town and Country." *Illustrated London News*, Christmas 1849, 418.

[53]   Frazer discussed Whitsuntide mumming as a relic of human sacrifice in *The Golden Bough* 3: 207–13. Reginald Tiddy argued in his study of the English mumming play written the early 1900s that it "bears distinct traces of a ritual origin." R.J.E. Tiddy, *The Mummer's Play, With a Memoir* (Oxford: Clarendon, 1923), 70.

[54]   Leopold Wagner, *The Pantomimes and All About Them* (London: John Haywood, 1881), 27.

[55]   *The Famous and Remarkable History of Sir Richard Whittington* (London, 1656).

become Lord Mayor of London. Nineteenth-century interpretations vary in their approach to the medieval aspects of the story: for example, an illustrated chapbook from around 1820 concludes cheerfully: "Sir Richard was Sheriff of London in 1340, and was three times Mayor of London; and King Henry V. in Whittington's last mayoralty knighted him." This would make Dick's career last over a hundred years by the time of his death in 1423.[56] Yet other texts also choose to tie in Whittington's story to historic events, noting that he must have lived through the people's rising led by Wat Tyler. The 1811 *Life of Sir Richard Whittington* retells the "cat" story unquestioningly but also imagines "Sir Richard" advising Wat Tyler and the "misguided populace to represent the cause of their complaints with coolness and candour," to no avail.[57] The anonymous novel *The Life and Times of Dick Whittington: An Historical Romance* (1841) imagines Dick encountering Lollards, the mistress of Edward III, and other historical figures such as "the abandoned miscreant Wat Tyler," together with topographical descriptions of medieval London.[58]

Beyond dressing Dick in a jerkin and hose, however, pantomimes largely ignored the medieval context.[59] Since pantomime was a visual spectacle, pantomime adapters added more magic to the story; even in one of the earliest Christmas pantomime versions, *Harlequin Whittington; Or, Lord Mayor of London* (1814), a fairy named Busybea ensures that Dick's destiny is fulfilled.[60] As in the prose tradition, Dick himself does not accompany his cat on the voyage to what is here said to be the "East Indies," but in later pantomimes Dick himself travels with the Cat, usually to an exotic locale. In every pantomime version Dick is reminded that one day he will be "Lord Mayor of London," and he has a cat, the pantomimes leaving it to historians to argue whether in fact the historic Whittington ever had a cat. In the most earnestly antiquarian version of this discussion, *The Model Merchant of the Middle Ages, Exemplified in the Story of Whittington and His Cat* (1860), Samuel Lysons spends thirty pages arguing that cats were historically of high value, and that the association of the real-life Whittington with a cat is plausible. Despite his researches, Lysons does not entirely embrace the Middle Ages, representing Whittington as "a man of enlightenment in the midst of darkness."[61]

---

[56] *The History of Dick Whittington, Lord Mayor of London; With the Adventures of his Cat.* (Banbury, J.G. Rusher, n.d.), 15.

[57] *Life of Sir Richard Whittington, compiled from authentic documents by the author of memoirs of George Barnwell* (London: M. Jones, 1811), 47–48. On diverse opinions of Wat Tyler, see Chapter 7.

[58] *The Life and Times of Dick Whittington, An Historical Romance* (London: H. Cunningham, 1841), 275.

[59] Modern-day productions of *Dick Whittington* still usually dress Dick (played both by men and women) in a quasi-Robin Hood outfit, but other characters are seldom medievally attired.

[60] *Harlequin Whittington; or, Lord Mayor of London.* Adam Matthew, Marlborough, Eighteenth Century Drama, www.eighteenthcenturydrama.amdigital.co.uk.proxy.lib.ohio-state.edu/Documents/Details/HL_LA_mssLA1835 (accessed May 2, 2020).

[61] Samuel Lysons, *The model merchant of the Middle Ages, exemplified in the story of Whittington and his cat* (London: Hamilton, Adams, and co., 1860), 9. Lysons was especially incensed by the comparative mythologist Thomas Keightley's dismissal of the Dick Whittington story in *Tales and Popular Fictions* (London: Whittaker, 1834) as containing "not one single word of truth" beyond his marriage to Alice Fitzwarren (246).

In the pantomime tradition, however, Dick, often played by a woman, earns his good fortune through his good nature rather than through his reasoning power, and is hardly a "model merchant."

A more persistently medievalist pantomime is an adaptation of a post-medieval ballad variously known as "The Norfolk Tragedy," "The Children in the Wood," or, most familiarly for modern audiences, "The Babes in the Wood." The original story contains no romance, while the young children at the center of the story die, as do the people who victimize them.

In the late eighteenth and early nineteenth century, antiquarians frequently claimed that ballads were, to use Thomas Percy's phrase, "reliques of ancient English poetry," the study of ballads being an important example of how Britons were beginning to think more positively about the Middle Ages. Collections such as Walter Scott's *Minstrelsy of the Scottish Border* emphasized that ballads had been passed down through oral culture and that part of their value was as a window into the thinking and values of earlier times. This is simply not true of the ballad of the "Babes in the Wood," although when Percy reprinted it in 1767 he suggested that it was derived from a lost Elizabethan stage tragedy.[62] In 1595, Thomas Millington of Norwich published "The Norfolk Tragedy," and the story was reprinted without major variation for over two hundred years. Although it contains folklore elements, the story is explicitly tied not to oral but to written culture and proclaims its own modernity.

First, the narrative claims to describe not an event of "long ago," as in many ballads, but a "true Relation" that happened "of late." Moreover, the plot hinges on a will and a trust fund that seems to be invested. A Norfolk gentleman and his wife die, leaving "two Babes behind" who are due to receive substantial inheritances.[63] Although the children's uncle has vowed to look after the children, within a year he recruits "two Ruffians" to "slay them in a Wood." The two ruffians disagree over whether to kill the children and "he that was of mildest Mood,/ Did slay the other there." The surviving man goes to find food and fails to return; the children wander until "Death did end their Grief," and their only burial comes from "Robin Redbreast" covering them with leaves.[64] The Ruffian who abandoned the children is hanged for robbery and the uncle's sons are lost on a trip to Portugal, while the uncle himself, having lost all his property, dies in debtor's prison. The final lines point the moral example:

---

[62]   Thomas Percy, *Reliques of Ancient English Poetry*, new edition (London: J. Dodsley, 1767), 3:172.

[63]   Charles Kent makes the point that the legal matters, and even the name Jane, are not medieval in *The Land of the Babes in the Wood* (London: Jerrold, 1910?), 15. He ties the story to local gossip in the Elizabethan period about a Catholic uncle whose Protestant nephew died suddenly.

[64]   The original ballad mentions "Robin red-breast" (singular), but this could be one robin functioning metonymically for many. A later song, "Poor Babes in the Wood," says that the story took place "a long time ago." In this nursery rhyme/folksong, although the children may, according to some versions, have been "stolen away" (in some they are simply lost), the focus is on the children and their fate. The song adds the detail that many robins cover the dead children with strawberry leaves. I am not focusing on this song because it probably post-dates the pantomime versions.

> All you that be Executors made,
>   And Overseers eke,
> Of Children that be fatherless,
>   And Infants mild and meek,
> Take you Example by this Thing,
>   And yield to each his Right,
> Lest God with such like Misery,
>   Your wicked Minds requite.

Despite this moral warning directed not at children but at adults, readers seem to have admired the ballad for its simple emotional appeal. Joseph Addison describes it in *Spectator* 85 (1711) as "one of the darling Songs of the common People, and has been the Delight of most Englishmen in some Part of their Age."[65] Almost a century later, William Wordsworth, contrasting it with a parodic ballad stanza by Samuel Johnson, quoted some lines in his 1800 Preface to *Lyrical Ballads*:

> These pretty babes with hand in hand
> Went wandering up and down;
> But never more they saw the Man
> Approaching from the Town.

For Wordsworth the difference in merit between the two is due not to language or form but to "the *matter* expressed."[66] He assumes that the reader is familiar with the ballad and would understand that unless the second Ruffian returns from the town with food the children are facing death.

Wordsworth focuses on "feeling" prompted by the story, yet the representation of the natural and divine as working together – the robin or robins and "the Wrath of God" unite in their outrage at the children's treatment – was probably appealing to the Romantics. It recalls works where nature helps to bring about justice such as Wordsworth's "Goody Blake and Harry Gill," Mary Robinson's "The Poor Singing Dame" and Coleridge's "Rime of the Ancient Mariner." Even at this time, however, the cosmic justice that avenges the children may have seemed inadequate. Thomas Morton wrote an opera, *The Children in the Wood* (1794), in which the children are saved through the assistance of Walter, a carpenter in love with their nurse Josephine.[67] The children's parents prove to be still alive and when their uncle Sir Rowland appears with a second pair of Ruffians to dispatch them Walter fights them and saves the family. It is unclear from text whether the play is staged in contemporary dress, but in an interesting reference to the story's ballad origins, at a moment when Walter believes he has failed the children and they are dead, Josephine (rather insensitively) sings him an old ballad "bought of the old blind peddler … entitled and called The Norfolk Tragedy …" It is not the original ballad but tells how a Yeoman who had murdered a babe "By reason of its large estate" is haunted by the child's ghost. Fortunately, Lord and Lady Alford arrive at this moment with

---

[65] Joseph Addison, *The Spectator* 85 (June 7, 1711).
[66] William Wordsworth, Preface to *Lyrical Ballads*, 2nd edition, ed. Brett and Jones, 269.
[67] Thomas Morton, *The Children in the Wood, An Opera*, 3rd edition (London, 1794).

the children whom they found in what must have been a fairly small wood, and for the virtuous characters all ends well.

Yet for some with an audience of children in mind this may not have been didactic enough. Around 1801 "Clara English" retold the ballad in prose as *The Affecting History of the Children in the Wood*.[68] In this moral story, illustrated by figures in Romantic-era dress, the wicked receive the same fate as in the original ballad but when abandoned in the wood, the children "cry" rather than "die" and are almost immediately rescued by an old woman. She places them in a model workhouse where they grow up learning useful skills, and they are able to reclaim their inheritance after the gallows confession of the second Ruffian. The ballad, with references to children's death excised, is reprinted at the end of the prose tale.

While Romantic-era writers clearly had problems with the death of innocent children, in the Victorian age, the idea that nature and heaven might combine to achieve a cosmic justice seems to have been even less convincing. One solution was to increase the distance between story and reader. In some printed versions for children, the text remains the same but the images represent the story not as a product of the Elizabethan era but as drawing on a more distant past: in other words, a printed story becomes an oral history of the Middle Ages. Some of these illustrations therefore suggest not cheap printed ballads, but illuminated medieval manuscripts. For example, a full-color version printed in London in 1861 in the Pre-Raphaelite style depicts the characters in medieval costume framed by decorative borders (Fig. 9).

On the stage, where the lack of comedic character was more obvious, the story underwent similar transformations. The short plot suited the pantomime form of second-piece plays in length, but not content. An 1856 pantomime attributed to John Baldwin Buckstone, *The Babes in the Wood; or, Harlequin* follows Morton's version in introducing a love-story element. Although the children die, they ascend into heaven surrounded by cherubs and Lubin the romantic hero is transformed into Harlequin. The first pantomime (as opposed to opera) that I have found where the children actually live is the prolific Henry James Byron's *Babes in the Wood and the Good Little Fairy-Birds* (1859?). The simultaneously oily and Macbeth-like aunt and uncle of the two children, Sir Rowland and Lady Macassar (both played by women in the original production),[69] follow the ballad in hiring two "Ruffians" to murder them, but one of the Ruffians is actually the children's father in disguise, who has been assumed lost at sea; he saves the children and reunites the family. A similar plot device is found in an anonymous pantomime performed at the Standard Theatre, Bishopsgate and Shoreditch, probably in the 1892–93 season.[70] Aided by robins, a Fairy places the children in suspended animation for six months, to

---

[68]   Clara English, *The Affecting History of the Children in the Wood* (c. 1801). I have been unable to discover anything about "Clara English." The *Affecting History*, sometimes abridged, appeared in at least twenty-six editions in Britain and America.

[69]   The name is a spoof both of Thomas Morton's Sir Rowland and the hair product Rowland's Macassar Oil.

[70]   H.J. Byron, *The Babes in the Wood, and the Good Little Fairy-Birds*; reprinted in H.J. Byron's *Select Plays*, edited by Jim Davis (Cambridge: Cambridge University Press, 1986), 41–69.

He bargain'd with two ruffians strong,
  Which were of furious mood,
That they should take these children young
    And slay them in a wood.

He told his wife an artful tale,
  He would the children send
To be brought up in fair London
  With one that was his friend.

Away then went those pretty babes,
  Rejoicing at that tide,
Rejoicing with a merry mind,
  They should on cock-horse ride.

They prate and prattle pleasantly,
  As they ride on the way,
To those that should their butchers be,
  And work their lives' decay;

Fig. 9. *Babes in the Wood: The Ruffians* (London: Low, 1861).

produce them on their father's reappearance; even the dead Robber proves to have been only wounded and lives to repent.

Yet as the story changed into true seasonal pantomime, a significant difficulty was that the characters do not match up well with the traditional Harlequinade. In nineteenth-century English pantomime, a fairy or some other magical process transforms the characters of the main story into the masked Harlequin, his lady-friend Columbine, her father or guardian Pantaloon, and a couple of comic servants. None of this works well with the plot of *The Babes in the Wood*, but an intriguing medievalist solution developed. The original story is, of course, set in a wood and also involves at least one robin. The full medievalizing of the story comes with the introduction of Robin Hood, which suggests some very loose association of ideas (wood – robin – Robin Hood?), and perhaps some awareness of the mumming tradition in which Robin Hood and his associates often played a part. Such a solution necessitates moving the story into the Middle Ages. Although there is disagreement among traditional sources as to when the Robin Hood tales take place, ranging from the late twelfth century to the mid-fourteenth century, he is definitely a medieval figure. The greenwood is to Robin Hood and his followers a refuge from unjust laws and a place where traditional barriers between rich and poor break down.

A significant early example is the medievally named Gilbert Arthur A'Beckett's *Babes in the Wood; or, Harlequin Robin Hood and his Merry Men*, first performed on Boxing Day, 1867. A medieval Baron not merely covets the wealth of his nephew and niece (both played by males) but is also exasperated by their horseplay. He hires "the Villian" [*sic*] to take them to the forest and kill them, to the horror of their nurse Maid Marian. Marian's lover Robin Hood (played by a woman) claims to know "every inch" of the forest and sets off in pursuit. The children are lost and exhausted, but as they lie down the Good Fairy Brilliantina – another reference to hair-oil – puts the audience's minds at rest. Even though the audience may think they know the ballad, they can have Robins without a tragedy. The Fairy explains:

> So far, so good, yet as the story goes
> One well might think it drawing to its close.
> You see our aim is not to nurture grief,
> And yet we can't let Robin drop the leaf;
> But he shall come in his accustomed place,
> To vindicate the honor of his race,
> And prove himself no less a constant friend,
> So Robins all! Your hoppings this way bend.[71]

A combination of children, robins, Merry Men (all played by women) and the repentant Villain thwart the Baron, and the fairies transform Robin Hood into Harlequin, Marian into Columbine, the Villain into Pantaloon and the Baron, whose guilty dreams have been disturbed by dumb-show horrors, into the Clown. While the jokes are topical rather than medieval, the costumes appear to have been in

---

[71]   Gilbert A. A'Beckett, *The Babes in the Wood; Or Harlequin Robin Hood and his Merry Men* (London: J. Miles, 1867), 16.

medieval style and Robin Hood proclaims the forest a place where "Our ways, our thoughts, our actions, all are free" (12).

By the end of the Victorian period, *The Babes in the Wood* is characterized by medieval costume, the Robin Hood subplot, and a deliberate undercutting of potential danger to children: Jimmy Glover, writing in 1913, recalls typical stage behavior by the actors playing the pair of Ruffians in "Boxing-Night" pantomimes:

> The Babes are lost;
> This is our chance
> To do our popular
> Song and dance.[72]

Despite, then, its origin in the early modern period, the pantomime version of *The Babes in the Wood* as developed by the turn of the twentieth century performs the medievalist maneuver of representing the past as a time when Robin Hood righted wrongs, yet still reminding the audience of the present through references to topical events and even consumer products such as hair oil. Admittedly, an audience is not going to become deeply imbued in medieval culture and values by seeing a buxom young woman dressed as Robin Hood. But that the Middle Ages are represented in pantomime as more picturesque, more romantic, more magical, and perhaps even more free than the present suggests just how much medievalism had helped reform the Christmas season.

---

[72] *Jimmy Glover and His Friends* (London: Chatto and Windus, 1913), 51. "Lost" refers both to the plot of the play – the Ruffians have lost the children – and to the fact that the comedians playing the parts have forgotten their lines.

4

Winter Love: St Agnes and St Valentine

J OHN KEATS'S 1820 poem "The Eve of Saint Agnes" is a medievalist's dream, not the product of the Middle Ages but a Romantic-era vision filtered through read-ings of Spenser and Shakespeare – the very version of the past that seems most patently inauthentic.[1] As the countless works published yearly based on research into a more accurate picture of the Middle Ages testify, the authentic – the "real" – still has an allure. Even in an artificially medieval poem, the reader is tempted to identify some germ of the actual Middle Ages. If there is an authentic medieval el-ement in "The Eve of St Agnes," it would appear to be the Saint Agnes ritual, which suggests that the poem recalls pre-Reformation times and beliefs passed down through oral tradition. The kinds of evidence used to establish authenticity, howev-er, such as contemporary written records and artifacts, do not help much in the case of a practice transmitted from person to person. In the case of the St Agnes charm, most literary representations can be traced back through a single thread; Valentine's Day practices, in contrast, suggest a patchy survival in popular culture from the Middle Ages.

From the English perspective any rituals associated with Saint Agnes might ini-tially seem to date back at least to medieval times. Saint Agnes's feast day prompted no official celebration by the English Church in Keats's time. Early versions of the Church of England's *Book of Common Prayer* omitted St Agnes entirely, although she and other saints were reinserted in the calendar in the 1600s. This would seem to be a fragment of something authentically medieval, yet problems immediately arise. Where and when is Keats's poem set? The easy answer is that St Agnes's feast day is January 21, and the poem takes place the preceding day and night, but which January 21, and where, are harder to determine.

The poem's form, Spenserian stanza, invoking the Protestant yet chivalric epic *The Faerie Queene*, simultaneously suggests medievalism and Englishness, but the setting is immediately made alien. The opening stanza takes the reader into a Roman Catholic world,[2] where a beadsman, whose task is to say prayers for the dead, is

---

[1]   See Pam Clements on "Authenticity," in *Medievalism: Key Critical Terms*, ed. Elizabeth Emery and Richard Utz (Cambridge: D.S. Brewer, 2014), 19–21. An early version of this section appeared in *Studies in Medievalism* XXVII (2018), 23–33.

[2]   Katharine Garvin explores the poem's use of Catholicism and what she calls "not vaguely Christian, but positively Catholic allusions" in "The Christianity of St Agnes' Eve: Keats' Catholic Inspiration." *Dublin Review* 234 (Winter 1960–61), 356–64.

repeating the rosary in front of an image of the Virgin.[3] "The Eve of St Agnes" has been the subject of much critical scrutiny,[4] but while critics recognize both the language choices and the temporal setting of the poem as vaguely medieval, they seem unconcerned as to where the story is supposed to take place.[5] References to time – the last stanza describes the characters as "gone – aye, ages long ago" (XLII) – suggest that the poem takes place in some part of Europe several hundred years ago, but the few names given do not help locate the story in any recognizable space. The story's resemblance to *Romeo and Juliet*[6] and Catholic setting may have prompted associations with Italy, echoed in Pre-Raphaelite artists' imagining of the story. John Millais, Arthur Hughes, and William Holman Hunt all painted scenes from the poem, using vaguely medieval costuming. The poem appeared in an illustrated edition with drawings by Edward H. Wehnert in 1856; again, the costumes are generically medieval, as in the banquet scene in a hall with early medieval arches (Fig. 10). Wehnert removes the ambiguity of the ending—do they live happily ever after or not?-- by concluding his illustrations with a picture of Porphyro and Madeline with two children and a dog (Fig. 11).

Yet the weather is not Italian. It is a Catholic world but with a very wintery location:

> ST AGNES' Eve – Ah, bitter chill it was!
> The owl, for all his feathers, was a-cold;
> The hare limp'd trembling through the frozen grass,
> And silent was the flock in woolly fold:
> Numb were the Beadsman's fingers, while he told
> His rosary, and while his frosted breath,
> Like pious incense from a censer old,
> Seem'd taking flight for heaven, without a death,
> Past the sweet Virgin's picture, while his prayer he saith. (I)

The eclectic choice of character names does not help. "Angela," the name of Madeline's nurse – ironic since she is a failure as a guardian angel – could be an Italian name, but "Madeline" is a French version of (Mary) Magdalene, who in Christian tradition, possibly conflating women in the Gospel narratives, is a repentant but previously sexually active follower of Christ. Keats was clearly conscious of this,

---

[3]   John Keats, *Lamia, Isabella, The Eve of St Agnes, and Other Poems* (London: Taylor and Hessey, 1820). Correspondence indicates that the poem was composed in early 1819. Quotations from the poem are identified in the text by stanza number in Roman numerals, following Keats's practice.

[4]   See, for example, Jack Stillinger, *Reading the Eve of St Agnes: The Multiples of Complex Literary Transaction* (New York: Oxford University Press, 1999).

[5]   Robert Gittings points out Keats's debt to the French romance *Pierre de Provence et La Belle Maguelone*. From this, and from Porphyro's Provençal lute-playing, he concludes that Porphyro is from Provence. Even accepting this, it does not solve the problem of where Madeline lives. Gittings, "Rich Antiquity," in *Twentieth-Century Interpretations of "The Eve of St Agnes,"* ed. Allan Danzig (Englewood Cliffs, NJ: Prentice-Hall, 1971), 86–98.

[6]   The Romeo and Juliet connection appears, for example, in *The Norton Anthology of English Literature*, 9th edition (New York: Norton, 2012), 912; and Herbert J. Wright (in Danzig, 14).

Fig. 10. "Argent Revelry." From *Keats's Eve of St Agnes*, illustrated by Edgar G. Wehnert (1859).

since one manuscript version of the poem contains the idea that a maiden who dreams the St Agnes dream will "wake again/ Warm in the virgin morn, no weeping Magdalen" (Stillinger, 134). "Porphyro" is Greek for "purple": in Keats's time, purple would have been associated with power and wealth; unlike Madeline and Angela, it is not a saint's name.[7] The two additional names given, Hildebrand and Maurice,

---

[7]   Anna Comnena, for example, notes that the royal family of Byzantium were called "Porphyrogenitus/a," which she explains as born in the purple room of the Palace (Anna Comnena, *Alexias*, Paris, 1651). While Marcia Gilbreath's quest for a source in her essay "The Etymology of Porphyro's name in Keats's 'Eve of St Agnes'" (*Keats Shelley Journal* 37 [1988], 20–25) does not entirely convince me, she at least draws attention to Porphyro's

XLII.

And they are gone : ay, ages long ago
These lovers fled away into the storm.
That night the Baron dreamt of many a woe,
And all his warrior-guests, with shade and form
Of witch, and demon, and large coffin-worm,
Were long be-nightmared.   Angela the old
Died palsy-twitch'd, with meagre face deform ;
The Beadsman, after thousand aves told,
For aye unsought-for slept among his ashes cold.

Fig. 11.   "Aye, Long Ago." From *Keats's Eve of St Agnes*, illustrated by Edgar G. Wehnert (1859).

are warlike, but not Italian.[8] Furthermore, Porphyro, noting that he has a home for Madeline "o'er the southern moors," describes her household as "Drown'd all in Rhenish and the sleepy mead," which do not sound like Italian beverages (XXXIX). Given the range of what Porphyro has delivered to Madeline earlier – "candied apple, quince, and plum, and gourd,/ With jellies soother than the creamy curd" (XXX), we either have to assume the castle has an international market within easy reach, or to understand that for Keats the Middle Ages functions both as time and place, and that he participates in the wonder that the medieval connotes for so many nineteenth-century writers.

The poem centers around two hopeful young people, Porphyro and Madeline, separated by a Romeo and Juliet-type family feud: Porphyro thinks of Madeline's kin as "barbarian hordes" (X). Madeline has no interest in the "argent revelry" of her wealthy relatives but has "brooded, all that wintry day,/ On love, and wing'd St Agnes' saintly care,/ As she had heard old dames full many times declare" (V). Associated with this particular day is a ritual through which young women can obtain a magical glimpse of their future lovers. According to this tradition, specifically stated to be passed down orally among women,[9] if a young girl completes a specific ritual, usually involving fasting, and lies "supine" in her bed without looking behind her, she will see "visions of delight" that identify her future lover. Madeline sighs "for Agnes' dreams, the sweetest of the year" (VII).

Before Madeline goes to bed, however, she has an almost-encounter with Porphyro, "with heart on fire/ For Madeline" (IX). Citing the feud between their families, Madeline's nurse Angela ushers him away; although she identifies the evening as among "holy days," she attributes Porphyro's decision to venture into the palace to magic: "Thou must hold water in a witch's sieve,/ And be liege-lord of all the Elves and Fays" (XIV).

The reference to holy days and magic together is appropriate, since after spying on Madeline Porphyro has a syncretistic idea. If it is the Eve of Saint Agnes, then he might hide in Madeline's bedchamber and "win perhaps that night a peerless bride,/ While legioned fairies paced the coverlet,/ And pale enchantment held her sleepy-eyed." The stanza concludes, "Never on such a night have lovers met,/ Since Merlin paid his Demon all the monstrous debt" (XIX). Although it is a saint's day, the moonlit night is again associated with ancient enchantment, charms, and faerie lore.[10] The depiction of Merlin as a lover who pays a "monstrous debt" suggests that his "Demon" is the damsel of the Lake who enchants the enchanter to such an

---

"cavalier attitude toward religion" (23). James Twitchell's ingenious connection of Porphyro with disease and vampirism through resemblance to the term "porphyria" does not work historically, since porphyria was not identified as a disease until the 1870s. James Twitchell, *The Living Dead: A Study of the Vampire in Romantic Literature* (Durham, NC: Duke University Press, 1981), 100.

[8]   St Maurice was a Roman soldier and is the patron saint of infantrymen; "Hildebrand" means war-sword in Old German and was the given name of Pope Gregory VII.

[9]   Jack Stillinger's useful overview of the poem's development, however, reveals that the stanza on oral transmission was not part of the original conception but added in the poem's second draft (Stillinger, 26).

[10]   Basil Blackstone draws attention to the moon in his essay on "The Eve of St Agnes" reprinted in Danzig, pp. 45–46.

extent that he reveals a charm to her.[11] In Malory's version of the story, Merlin shows Nenyve "many wondyrs," but always is desiring "to have hir maydynhode" (Malory IV.2). She fears him as a "devyls son." When Merlin shows her a "wonder" in the form of an enchantment involving a "grete stone," she induces him to go under it "to latte hir wete of the mervayles there, but she wrought so there for hym that he come never oute for all the craufte he coude do." In this story, the man is the sexual aggressor, and the woman uses a charm to avoid sexuality. The parallel with "The Eve of St Agnes" is suggestive but inexact, since Madeline, inspired by sensual imagination if not exactly sexual desire, tries to use a charm, but it is actually the male lover who succeeds in charming, although through careful planning rather than by supernatural power.

Madeline herself seeks supernatural insight. When she retires, she carries out the ritual, kneeling to pray, then going "supperless to bed" (VI) without looking behind her; she goes so far as to fancy "Fair St Agnes in her bed." For St Agnes to become the patron of a ritual of desire seems odd, since according to legend Agnes committed her life to purity. Agnes was a Christian child around the end of the second century. She was ordered to marry, but chose to maintain her purity and devotion to Christ. Roman authorities sent her to a brothel, attempted to expose her naked in public, and to burn her at the stake, but in all of these Agnes's purity was miraculously preserved. She achieved martyrdom when the Romans beheaded her, and her bones and skull are still said to be preserved in Rome.[12] Agnes's name suggests "Agnus," Latin for lamb, and her personal sacrifice is associated both with the Lamb of God and with a festival in Rome involving lambs, mentioned briefly in the eighth stanza. The legend of Saint Agnes thus seems in conflict with her association with a ritual that assumes sexual desire on the part of young women, and that they are eager to find out who their future lovers might be.

It would be tempting to believe that Keats knew of this ritual through oral tradition that might have survived from before the English Reformation – in other words, that even in this Italian-influenced setting he is shaping his story around a practice known in medieval England. More likely, he was aware of it through a couple of written sources. A version of the story appears in Sir Henry Ellis's 1813 edition of *Observations on Popular Antiquities*. Bourne's original *Antiquitates Vulgares* does not mention the St Agnes charm but claims that attempting to foretell the future is un-Christian: "The Observation of Omens, such as the falling of Salt, a Hare crossing the way, of the Dead-Watch, or Crickets, &c. are sinful and diabolical: They are the invention of the Devil, to draw Men from a due Trust in GOD, and

---

[11]   Because of the specific reference to "lovers" I would hence agree with Karen Harvey that the "demon" referred to here is not Merlin's incubus father but the damsel of the Lake who traps him under a rock. See Karen Harvey, "The Trouble About Merlin: The Theme of Enchantment in 'The Eve of St Agnes,'" *Keats-Shelley Journal* 34 (1985): 83-94. Stefan Hawlin, assuming that Keats might have had access to one of the editions of Malory issued in 1816–17, suggests a parallel with the story of Merlin, Uther, and Igraine, yet that implies a fruitful outcome (Arthur) and the ending to Keats's poem is ambiguous. "Merlin's Debt in Keats's 'The Eve of St. Agnes,'" *Notes and Queries* 66 (2019), 273–78.

[12]   See, for example, William Carew Hazlitt's revision of *Popular Antiquities*, *Dictionary of Faiths and Folk-Lore*, 3 vols (London: Reeves and Turner, 1905), 1:3–4.

make them his own vassals" (Bourne, 75). When John Brand republished Bourne's book with far more sympathetic additions in 1777, he made two brief mentions of St Agnes rituals, including sleeping with cheese under one's pillow (Brand, 387). Ellis's 1813 edition, though, is the first to quote John Aubrey's 1694 *Miscellanies* (Ellis 1:27).[13] Aubrey mentions seeing young women finding the necessary components to dream of their lovers on "the Day of St John Baptist" the previous summer, that is, 1693. He goes on to remark that similar rituals are associated with St Agnes:

> The Women have several Magical Secrets handed down to them by Tradition, for this purpose, as on St. *Agnes* Night, 21 Day of January, take a Row of Pins, and pull out every one, one after another, saying a *Pater Noster*, or (*Our Father*), sticking a Pin in your Sleeve, and you will dream of Him, or Her, and you shall Marry. *Ben Johnson* in one of his Masques makes some mention of this.

> *And on sweet Saint* Agnes *Night*
> *Please you with the promised Sight,*
> *Some of Husbands, some of Lovers,*
> *Which an empty Dream discovers.*[14]

All of the subsequent versions of *Popular Antiquities* that I have found, including William Carew Hazlitt's 1905 *Dictionary of Faiths and Folk-lore*, quote Aubrey on the St Agnes ritual, including the lines from Ben Jonson. The problem is that Jonson does not mention St Agnes at all. An "Elfe" speaks these lines as part of a tribute to Mab, Queen of the Fairies in Jonson's *Particular Entertainment of the Queen and Prince Their Highnesses at Althrop*, a masque performed on June 25, 1603 and published the following year.[15] In all the versions that I have been able to locate that were published before Aubrey's death, the "Elfe" names St Ann, not St Agnes. This problem was noted in the first printing of Aubrey's *Miscellanies*, where a marginal note states "'Tis printed St *Ann*'s Night falsely," but this note does not appear in later editions. Jonson's choice of "St Ann's Night" may be a tribute to Anne of Denmark in whose honor the "entertainment" was written; or to match the season of summer, not winter (St Anne's Day is July 26); or perhaps both.[16] Thus, some summer ritual associated with identifying one's future partner was known to Ben Jonson in the early 1600s; John Aubrey states that he observed girls carrying out a ritual in midsummer in the very late 1600s, and connects this with other traditions of the winter St Agnes' Eve with a misquotation.[17]

Keats may have consulted Ellis's edition of Brand, but equally possibly he derived ideas directly from Aubrey. This becomes more apparent when Aubrey goes on to

---

[13] This version reverses the quotation and charm as presented by Aubrey.

[14] John Aubrey, *Miscellanies Upon the Following Subjects...* (London, 1694), 103–04.

[15] *A Particular Entertainment of the Queen and Prince Their Highness at Althrop* [i.e. Althorp], No publication information. http://hollowaypages.com/jonson1692queen.htm (accessed September 29, 2016).

[16] Hazlitt remarks that in Cornwall, Anne is the saint associated with the ritual, not Agnes (3).

[17] From his references to St John's Night, I am assuming that by "Night" Aubrey means the night before the feast day.

mention another of the "Magical Secrets" that enable women to see their future husbands on "St Agnes Night": "Accordingly in your Dream you will see him; if a Musician with a Lute or other instrument; if a Schollar with a Book or Papers" (Aubrey, 104). Porphyro has brought to Madeline's chamber not only a large quantity of food – she has, after all, gone "supperless to bed" – but he also takes up "her hollow lute," with which he plays medieval music in the form of "an ancient ditty, long since mute,/ In Provence call'd, 'La belle dame sans mercy'" (XXXIII).[18] The intertextual references are thick here: Keats's reference to a lute recalls Aubrey, but the song played recalls another medieval imitation of his own, a poem where a man is enchanted by a woman.

But can these rituals be traced back any further? A slightly different ritual even more clearly overlaid with magic is found in *Aristotle's Last Legacy*, an early eighteenth-century fortune-telling book:

> On St Agnes *Day.*
> Take a Sprigg of Rosemary, and another of Time, sprinkle them with Urine thrice; and in the Evening of this Day, put one into one Shooe, and the other into the other; place your Shooes on each side your Beads-head, and going to Bed, say softly to your self:
>
>> St Agnes, *that's to Lovers kind,*
>> *Come ease the Troubles of my Mind.*
>
> Then take your Rest, having said your Prayers; when you are asleep, you will dream of your Lover, and fancy you hear him talk to you of Love; looking into your Shooes, and attempting to put them on your Feet, with much Kindness; If two are desirous of you, they will both appear, and strive who shall do you the best Offices, and the Party who overcomes in this, is your Lot; for you will perceive the other quickly vanish, sighing, and much displeased.[19]

Whether the young ladies need to use their own urine is not entirely clear, but it presumably would take a major curiosity to know one's future lover to put urine-splashed items in one's shoes. The version in *Aristotle's Last Legacy* uses "Time" (thyme) as a charm to see future time, and rosemary, presumably, for remembrance.

Aristotle's Last Legacy demonstrates that even if Keats's knowledge of the ritual is derived from his reading, around 1700, people in England do seem to have known about the St Agnes charm, and one of them connected it with the English medieval past. Less well remembered but quite possibly also known to Keats is John Gay's 1713 stage-play *The Wife of Bath*, a comedy that explicitly links the ritual to the English Middle Ages, although with an overlay of eighteenth-century rationalism. The character of Alison, the Wife of Bath in Chaucer's *Canterbury Tales*, is the inspiration for the play, but not much in the drama is indebted to Chaucer.

---

[18] Laura Wells Betts discusses the language used for the food in "Keats and the Charm of Words: Making Sense of the Eve of St Agnes," *Studies in Romanticism* 47:3 (2008), 299–319.
[19] "On St Agnes Day." *Aristotle's Last Legacy; Or, His Golden Cabinet of Secrets opened, for Youth's Delightful Pastime* (London, 1710), 50.

The scene is an "Inn, lying in the Road between London and Canterbury."[20] Here are staying not just Chaucer himself and the Wife of Bath, but also, among other characters, the Lady Myrtilla. Myrtilla is (at least from the eighteenth-century perspective) a very medievally minded woman: she is a devout believer in fortune-telling who has resolved to become a nun because she has no prognostications of a future husband. She has, she tells Alison the Wife of Bath, "try'd three Midsummer Eves successively; and there hath been not so much as a shadow of a Man" (4). Alison is more pragmatic: she points out, "What signifies the Shadow, when your Ladyship hath Youth and Beauty enough at any time to command the Substance?" (4). Having specifically identified herself as not superstitious, Alison reads, or pretends to read, Myrtilla's fortune in her palm and advises her to go to bed "and dream of a Husband." Myrtilla has apparently already made the experiment with some "Bride-Cake" under her pillow, but since it is "St *Agnes's* Night" she resolves "to try the Experiment of the Dumb-Cake" (7). A couple of points should be made here. The dumb-cake would be either a piece of dough marked with a name that the spirit-lover would touch; or some kind of cake made in silence. Secondly, the play echoes the confusion over the time of year common in accounts of the ritual. Is it January, or the pilgrimage season of April as specified in the *Canterbury Tales*?

Such details do not seem to matter in this play. When Chaucer learns of the plan to carry out the ritual from Myrtilla's companion Busie, who describes her mistress as "as superstitious as an ignorant Abbot," the poet, who has been pursuing Myrtilla to no avail, determines to take on the role of the "Apparition" (8). When Myrtilla carries out the St Agnes ceremony, she apparently has no problem with the apparition (actually Chaucer) addressing her and explaining that "you see Destiny will have it so"; but when he attempts to approach she "shrieks" and runs away (24). When Alison advises Myrtilla to try more fortune-telling, Chaucer borrows necromancer's garb from Dr Astrolabe, including his false beard, and is thus able to assure her, "The Gentleman, that at this time, seems your Aversion – will – make you happy" (37). After a brief interruption from Alison, he contrives to appear as himself in the "Necromantic Mirror." At his next opportunity, Chaucer tells Myrtilla he dreamed of her and that he "is now convinced that the Presages of Dreams are not to be ridicul'd" (42). After more complications brought about by tricks of the Wife of Bath, Chaucer again proposes and is accepted.

This marriage, and others in the play, are clearly not the work of destiny but of human contrivance: Alison jests that "The Pilgrim's here have made *Hymen's* the Shrine of their Devotion, instead of St *Thomas's*" (170).[21] In Chaucer and the Wife of Bath, then, Gay uses actual and fictional medieval people to turn the Middle Ages inside out. Neither character accepts the superstition of their contemporaries, but each uses it to personal advantage. Yet in effect the two have created a self-fulfilling

[20]   *The Wife of Bath, A Comedy* (performed 1713). John Gay, *Dramatic Works*, ed. John Fuller, 2 vols (Oxford: Clarendon, 1983), 107. Subsequent references cited by page number in text.
[21]   Continuing her lack of reverence towards the medieval, she also jokingly tells another character that his new wife's "Great Grandfather was killed at the Battle of *Cressy*; and her Great Uncle, in the Fifty Ninth degree, was Groom of the Privy Stool to *William* the Conqueror – ha, ha, ha" (Act V; 169).

prophecy in their manipulation of the St Agnes charm: Myrtilla, after all, really does see her future husband. Just how happy the rationalist Chaucer will be with the credulous Myrtilla is a question that the play does not try to answer.

The Wife of Bath is important because it directly connects the St Agnes charm with the Middle Ages. An indication that Keats may have known of it is that Porphyro tries a variation of the trick that works for Gay's Chaucer. Porphyro takes his role as a dream-vision further, since after appealing to Madeline's sleeping senses with exotic food and music, he melts "into her dream," shortly before the time that "St Agnes' moon hath set" (XXXVI). Although critics are divided as to whether to pass judgment on this not-consciously consensual sexual moment, the phrase "St Agnes' moon hath set" marks the end of the eve, and, we must assume, the end of virgin dreams.

The dream-sex connects Porphyro with the medieval concept of the incubus, the widespread belief that demons could have sexual encounters with mortal women. The association between Porphyro and Merlin continues, as Merlin's "devil" father is defined by Geoffrey of Monmouth as an incubus.[22] Yet Keats would also have known the real Chaucer's wry rationalizing joke when the Wife of Bath says that there used to be elves and fairies, but the prayers of the "lymytour" have driven them away, so that "Wommen may go saufly up and doun;/ In every bussh or under every tree/ Ther is noon oother incubus but he."[23] When Porphyro and Madeline finally converse, the narrative describes the weather as "an elfin-storm from faery land,/ Of haggard seeming, but a boon indeed" (XXXIX).

In an interesting reversal of the literary and folkloric, on January 21, 1835, *Leigh Hunt's London Journal* announced, "*To-day* is the Eve of St Agnes, and we thought we could not take a better opportunity of increasing the public acquaintance with this exquisite production, which is founded on the popular superstition connected with the day."[24] (It was actually not the eve, but St Agnes's feast-day, but very clearly, authenticity is less important to Hunt than winning Keats the recognition he deserves.) Hunt retells the legend of St Agnes and explains, "In the Catholic church formerly the nuns used to bring a couple of lambs to her altar during mass. The superstition is (for we believe it is still to be found) that by taking certain measures of divination, damsels may get a sight of their future husbands in a dream." He then cites Aubrey, quoted from Ellis's 1813 *Popular Antiquities*. Just in case the readers may have missed the medievalism, Hunt draws attention to "the legends of the season" and goes so far as to claim that the line "Its little smoke, in pallid moonshine, died" (XXIII) is "a verse in the taste of Chaucer, full of minute grace and truth."[25] Hunt has thus united the Catholic and folk practices, triangulating them through Keats's poem, which he prints in its entirety, marking Keats as a true poetic successor to Chaucer.

---

[22] Geoffrey of Monmouth, *History of the Kings of Britain* Book 6, chapter 18.

[23] "The Wife of Bath's Tale," 878–800; *Riverside Chaucer*, 3rd edition, ed. F.N. Robinson and Larry D. Benson (Boston, MA: Houghton Mifflin, 1987), 117. A "lymytour" is glossed as a friar who confined his wandering to a particular area.

[24] *Leigh Hunt's London Journal*, ed. Leigh Hunt (issue 42, January 21, 1835), 17–20.

[25] Some commentators have misinterpreted Hunt here: the source is not Brand, but Aubrey as quoted by Ellis in his edition of Brand.

Early Victorians and Saint Agnes

For the Victorians, one of the multiple functions of medievalism is that medieval examples provide a way of talking about sexual relations at a time when polite literature generally left such matters unsaid. Although Victorian prudishness was probably exaggerated by the more rebellious generation that followed, mainstream Victorian literature and art is certainly more reticent about bodily functions than Chaucer had been, while writers idealize the "pure" states of childhood and maidenhood. After the Reformation, the English Church had allowed, indeed encouraged, priests to marry, but Victorian art shows a fascination with virginal images in somewhat awkward juxtaposition with the cultural assumption (both articulated and challenged in the Surplus Woman debates of the 1850s) that the fulfillment of a woman's role in life was to marry and have children.[26]

Victorian references to Saint Agnes and related beliefs show a continued tension between an idealized virginity and sexual desire. Tennyson was to ascribe virginity to his "blameless King" Arthur, but his "St Agnes" poem – and the "May Queen," to which I shall turn later – raise the question of whether physical chastity is synonymous with purity of soul. Tennyson admired Keats and undoubtedly knew "The Eve of St Agnes," but also around this time made use of William Hone's *Every-Day Book*, which gives particulars of the St Agnes Eve rituals. The *Every-Day Book* notes that "Formerly this was a night of great importance to maidens who desired to know who they were to marry. Of such it was required, that they should not eat on this day." Ben Jonson and Aubrey are then quoted. With the observation that "Little is remembered about these homely ways for knowing 'all about sweethearts,'" the Book then credits "the sweetest of our modern poets" – that is, Keats – with keeping the ritual in readers' minds, quoting multiple stanzas (*Every-Day Book* 1:136–37).[27]

Tennyson thus had a ready source for the Saint Agnes tradition, and he first used it in an unpublished poem written around 1830. In "Amy," the speaker says of his beloved,

> St Agnes on St Agnes' Eve, who leadeth
>> Over the snowy hill
> Her snowwhite lambs and with hushed footstep treadeth,
>> Is not so chaste and still
> In the cold moon, e'er yet the crocus flamy
>> Or snowdrop burst to life;
> Yet with a human love I love thee, Amy,
>> And woo thee for my wife.[28]

---

[26]   Gerry Holloway has discussed Victorian anxieties about the role of women following the discovery in the 1851 Census that "as many as 30 per cent of all English women between the ages of twenty and forty were unmarried," in *Women and Work in Britain since 1840* (Abingdon: Routledge, 2005), 36–51.

[27]   Christopher Ricks mentions Hallam Tennyson and W.C. DeVane on "St Simeon Stylites" and "St Agnes," who note the poems as derived from Hone; see *The Poems of Tennyson*, 542, 553.

[28]   "Amy" lines 13–20, quoted from *The Poems of Tennyson*, ed. Christopher Ricks, 260.

St Agnes is here associated with winter, with chastity, and the moon, remote and (through the association with Diana) virginal. She leads her namesake lambs, usually a symbol of spring's fertility, but her day is before even the first flowers bloom. In this instance, as far as can be told, sexual desire is limited to the male speaker, while Amy loves him only "with that love which St Cecilia/ Did love Valerian," Cecilia and Valerian's marriage being unconsummated in accordance with divine revelation.[29] The speaker admires Amy's virtue, but also feels sexual frustration.

A similar tension is seen in "Saint Agnes," which Tennyson first published in *The Keepsake* in 1837. As may have been apparent to readers of an annual intended as a gift for Christmas and the New Year, the title refers to the day as much as to the saint that it commemorates; in editions after 1855 Tennyson changed the title to "Saint Agnes' Eve," which both makes the scenario clearer and reminds the reader of Keats's poem.[30] The speaker is a nun in a wintry convent, and like Keats's poem the time-period and nation are indistinct; in the 1830s, though, a nun does not belong in the British present. She is wishing for her soul's release to heaven:

> Deep on the convent-roof the snows
>   Are sparkling to the moon:
> My breath to heaven like vapour goes:
>   May my soul follow soon!

Unlike in "Amy," when St Agnes' Eve is before the snowdrops, here the "first snowdrop of the year" is in flower. Yet just after the speaker prays, "Make Thou my spirit pure and clear/ As are the frosty skies," she mentions that the first snowdrop "in my bosom lies."[31] This could be an image of hoped-for purity – or alternatively a love-token that she cannot yet surrender. Readers aware of the love-rituals associated with the Eve of St Agnes might wonder, especially since in *The Keepsake* the poem is preceded by a story of doomed love and followed by a love-poem.[32] Tennyson's own comments suggest an explicit connection with the St Agnes ritual: Ricks quotes Hallam Tennyson's note that his father said "Here the legend is told by a nun" (*Poems of Tennyson*, 552). One possibility is that at some point she tried the ritual, since in the second stanza the speaker connects her white robes that appear "soiled and dark" in comparison with the frosty ground with the state of her "soul before the Lamb." Whatever desire may have been in her past, she now longs for a sight of her future spouse, Christ. The St Agnes ritual should reveal one's future husband,

---

[29] Cecilia and Valerian are mentioned in Hone's *Every-Day Book* but Tennyson seems to have had another source for this specific anecdote.

[30] Ricks's note, *Poems of Tennyson*, 552.

[31] A notebook contains an alternative line 10 and 12; line 12 states that the snowdrop was "plucked today," hence not a lover's token. See Ricks, 552.

[32] Richard Monckton Milnes joked to Tennyson, who was sensitive about having agreed to publish in *The Keepsake*, "Your St Agnes looks funny between Lord Londonderry and Lord W. Lennox, God her aid!" Hallam Tennyson, *Alfred, Lord Tennyson, A Memoir*, 2 vols (London: Macmillan, 1897), 1:157. Even though he was uncomfortable about being associated with these titled authors, Tennyson's poem was not actually placed between their work. *The Keepsake for MDCCCXXXVII*, ed. Lady Emmeline Stuart Wortley (London: Longman, 1837), 228–49.

and looking at the winter world from the convent, she believes she sees "the Heavenly Bridegroom" who will make her "pure of sin."

The meter of "St Agnes" (tetrameter and trimeter arranged in twelve-line stanzas rhyming ababcdcdefef) resembles that of Tennyson's explicitly medieval poem "Sir Galahad," the difference being that the last four lines of each stanza in "Sir Galahad" are all tetrameters. Around the time of composition Tennyson told a friend that that the depiction was "intended for something of a male counterpart to St Agnes," which in effect queers the knight by placing him in the role of a maiden.[33] Hallam Tennyson also describes "St Agnes" as "a pendant to Sir Galahad."[34] In the 1842 *Poems in Two Volumes* "Sir Galahad" immediately follows "St Agnes." The hidden object Sir Galahad desires to see is not a human lover: although he fights to save ladies "from shame and thrall," he has "never felt the kiss of love,/ Nor maiden's hand in mine."[35] He describes himself as "a maiden knight" whose goal is to "find the holy Grail." He has his own version of the St Agnes ritual when from time to time "on lonely mountain-meres" he finds a "magic bark," from which he has a "blessed vision" of the Grail, held not by female Grail-maidens but by genderless angels.[36] The St Agnes ritual is associated with winter, as is Sir Galahad's story: when he rides through "dreaming towns … The cock crows ere the Christmas morn,/ The streets are dumb with snow." The cock crow and the "glory" that spreads through the wintry world closely link Galahad with the Christ he continues to seek: he is seeking one like himself.

The association of "St Agnes" with "Sir Galahad" medievalizes the former, but I would suggest that if the two poems are read together, the nun may also be part of the Arthurian story, since she resembles Tennyson's future characterization of Sir Percivale's sister in "The Holy Grail." As we have seen, Tennyson departed from Malory in depicting the initial inspiration for the Grail quest as coming from a reported vision of Percivale's sister, a "pale nun" who at midnight hears music, and then, she tells her brother:

> Streamed through my cell a cold and silver beam
> And down the long beam stole the Holy Grail,
> Rose-red with beatings in it, as if alive …
>
> ("Holy Grail," 115–18)

Later, Galahad reports that he saw the Grail, but Percivale, who is telling the story, states explicitly that although he saw a mystical illumination of the Knights of the Round Table, he did not. The possibility thus arises that the quest for the Holy Grail starts from the delusion of an enthusiast, or paired enthusiasts in the nun and Galahad. The nun shows her desire both for holy mysteries and for Galahad when, as in Malory, she creates him a sword-belt from her hair, and tells him:

---

[33] Hallam Tennyson, *Alfred, Lord Tennyson, A Memoir*, 1:142 (letter dated 1834).

[34] Hallam Tennyson, ed., *The Works of Tennyson, Annotated*. 9 vols (London: Macmillan, 1907–08), 2:347.

[35] Alfred Tennyson, *Poems in Two Volumes* (London: Moxon, 1842), 2:177.

[36] Many years later, Tennyson answered a criticism that a "magic bark" was out of keeping with the Christian tone of the poem by replying "'magic' includes 'mystic.'" H. Tennyson, *Memoir*, 2:378.

"My knight, my love, my knight of heaven,
O thou, my love, whose love is one with mine,
I, maiden, round thee, maiden, bind my belt.
Go forth, for thou shalt see what I have seen,
And break through all, till one will crown thee king
Far in the spiritual city:" and as she spake
She sent the deathless passion in her eyes
Through him, and made him hers, and laid her mind
On him, and he believed in her belief.

("Holy Grail," 155–65)

In Malory's account, Percivale's sister accompanies him and Galahad on the quest, and eventually sacrifices her own life to save a lady stricken with leprosy.[37] In Tennyson's *Idylls*, in contrast, she does not join the quest she has inspired, but is, like the speaker in "St Agnes' Eve," associated with whiteness and pallor: morally she has an "all but utter whiteness" (84), while physically she is a "pale nun" (129). The St Agnes charm is associated with visions of one's future love; if, as he himself stated, Tennyson from the outset linked together this speaker and Sir Galahad, she may be a first working through of his ideas about Percivale's sister, and another entry into the medieval world.

Valentines New and Old

Whereas the St Agnes charm provides an excuse for medievalism derived from a questionable source, Valentine's Day is much more plausibly a popular memory of the Middle Ages. Shakespeare, after all, had referred to Valentine's Day in one of Ophelia's songs in *Hamlet*, although Thomas Bowdler's 1818 *Family Shakespeare* omitted the last four lines of "Tomorrow is Saint Valentine's Day" that suggest that Valentine's Day activities lead to the end of being a "maid."[38] Yet perhaps for the very reason that Valentine's Day traditions were a genuine oral survival among working Britons, nineteenth-century medievalists seem to have found less need to reimagine it. An element of class snobbishness may be involved here: the landowning classes may have wished to ensure that workers remembered old Christmas customs, but the working poor themselves maintained the custom of valentines. Hence some commentators seem almost embarrassed to mention a tradition not merely preserved in picturesque rural backwaters but flourishing in urban communities, and accounts of Valentine's Day tend to involve mockery, if not of others then of oneself.

St Valentine's Day was inscribed in the Anglican calendar on February 14, but antiquarians were in doubt as to whether any such person existed. Bourne mentions

---

[37]   On the role of Percivale's sister as told by Malory and others see Martin B. Schichtman, "Percival's Sister: Genealogy, Virginity, and Blood," *Arthuriana* 9:2 (1999), 11–20.

[38]   Thomas Bowdler, *The Family Shakespeare in Ten Volumes; In which nothing is added to the original text; but those words and expressions are omitted which cannot with propriety be read aloud in a family* (London: Longman, 1818), 10:201. Despite the insistence on not changing Shakespeare's wording, Bowdler's four-line version of the song begins "Good morrow, 'tis Saint Valentine's Day."

disapprovingly the "*Ceremony*, never omitted among the Vulgar, to draw lots, which they term *Valentines*, on the Eve before *Valentine-day.*" Although this "is look'd upon as a good Omen of their being Man and Wife afterwards," Bourne suspects that similar attempts to discover one's mate by lot may have led to "great Inconveniences and Misfortunes, with Uneasiness to Families, with Scandal, and sometimes with Ruin" (Bourne, 175–77). Almost a century later, Ellis's edition of the same text mentions a number of ancient traditions, such as choosing one's Valentine by lot, or one's Valentine being the first person of the opposite sex encountered on Valentine's Day (Ellis 1:47–53). Hone's *Every-Day Book* gives the same information as most sources:

> Of this saint, so celebrated among young persons, little is known, except that he was a priest of Rome, and martyred there about 270. It was a custom with the ancient Roman youth to draw the names of girls in honour of their goddess Februata-Juno on the 15th of February, in exchange for which certain Roman catholic pastors substituted the names of saints in billets given the day before, namely, on the 14th of February. (*Every-Day Book* 1:216)

The assumption is a common one among antiquarians: that in the early Christian period, a pagan custom was reinvented as a saint's day.

Although the supposed origins of Valentine's Day may be the product of antiquarian speculation, Valentine's Day seems to have been an English tradition that survived in the popular consciousness at least in some regions from medieval times. The idea that on St Valentine's Day the birds choose their mates is central to Chaucer's *Parliament of Fowls*, where Nature states that the birds "knowe wel" that this is the day for mating.[39] Larry D. Benson notes that there is "no basis for the old theory that he drew on some folk tradition, no association of love in previous literature, and little in the saint's legend to suggest such an association,"[40] but Hone and his contemporaries saw in this and later medieval references to Valentine's Day a popular tradition. Quoting this passage from Chaucer, the *Every-Day Book* adds that:

> It is recorded as a rural tradition, that on St Valentine's day each bird of the air chooses its mate; and hence it is presumed, that our homely ancestors, in their lusty youth, adopted a practice which we still find peculiar to a season when nature bursts its imprisonments for the coming pleasures of the cheerful Spring. (*Every-Day Book* 1:223)

Valentine's Day is thus part of the natural cycle of love and fertility, but by the later eighteenth century it is almost unique among medievalist celebrations in having become as much an urban as a rural tradition.

Oddly for a practice traced back to birds choosing their mates, Valentine's Day, like the St Agnes rituals, assumes a preordained universe in which individuals are destined for each other. Lovers could, however, help bring about their own destinies by anonymous declarations of love. A "valentine" (small v) was a note or card sent to one's loved one, a practice that substantially predates the sending of commercially

---

[39]   Chaucer, *The Parliament of Fowls*, lines 309–10; 386–87.
[40]   Robinson and Benson, *The Riverside Chaucer*, 383.

produced Christmas cards. Valentine's Day might recall the "natural" world of the Middle Ages, but by the early 1800s it was, perhaps even before Christmas, a commercial opportunity.

Amelia Opie's 1816 novel *Valentine's Eve* has a plot twist dependent on early nineteenth-century Valentine's Day customs and the exchange of cards. After the saintly Catherine Shirley marries her cousin Lord Shirley, the latter's persistent insecurities are exploited by a plot between their rejected admirers John Melvyn and Sophia Clermont, who even forge a note in Catherine's handwriting to persuade Lord Shirley that her affections are elsewhere. Implicitly, Melvyn and Sophia are also having an affair, so when they both decide to marry others they agree to exchange any incriminating letters. Destiny, however, intervenes in the form of Valentine's Eve. Melvyn receives back and destroys his letters to Sophia on "the 12th of February, 1809,"[41] but when on February 13 he entrusts Sophia's correspondence in a thrice-sealed white envelope to the same messenger, along with a long letter detailing their plot against the Shirleys, the messenger makes the mistake of delegating the delivery to a footboy. The footboy is spotted by:

> A group of boys on the watch, as boys always are on Valentine's night, to snatch valentines: and this packet looked so like a valentine, or valentines, that its fate, especially as it was only guarded by a boy, was soon decided upon; and in a twinkling of an eye the parcel disappeared out of the hand of its holder, and the boy who stole it vanished speedily out of sight.

In an otherwise noteless book, Opie appends a footnote explaining that "Should this incident be thought improbable, I must beg leave to say it is a *true* one" (Opie 3:193–94). It actually occurred to her friend, who was carrying "letters from a most admirable mother to as admirable children" through "the streets of Norwich on *St Valentine's Eve*, when a boy suddenly snatched it and ran away with it." The significant difference between the two incidents, however, is that the real-life, innocent valentines were never seen again, whereas those guilty letters proving lust rather than love snatched by the boys in the novel show the work of Providence: they end up in the hands of Catherine Shirley's faithful servant, who uses them to demonstrate to Catherine's distinctly unworthy husband her innocence of all offenses against their love.

Valentine-snatching, if it was ever really a practice, would be dependent on the hand-delivery of cards. The expansion of the postal service in the nineteenth century enabled Britons to send their loved ones near and far letters and cards. P.G. Patmore's *Mirror of Months* states that in the 1820s, "Two hundred thousand letters beyond the usual daily average, annually pass through the twopenny post-office in London on St. Valentine's Day."[42] In the *Pickwick Papers*, when after Christmas Mr Pickwick receives a summons to appear in court in his breach of promise case "on the fourteenth of next month," Sam Weller immediately notes the "remarkable coincidence" of the date. The elderly bachelor Mr Pickwick still does not see the point until Sam points out that it will be "Walentine's day" (337). In the February

[41]   Amelia Opie, *Valentine's Eve*, 3 vols (London: Longman, 1816), 3:187.
[42]   P.G. Patmore, *The Mirror of the Months*, 31.

1837 episode, Sam is passing "a small stationer's and print-seller's window," where an image arrests him. The description of the valentine is a spectacular example of Dickensian defamiliarization: it is:

> A highly coloured representation of a couple of human hearts skewered together with an arrow, cooking before a cheerful fire, while a male and female cannibal in modern attire, the gentleman being clad in a blue coat and white trousers, and the lady in a deep red pelisse with a parasol of the same, were approaching the meal with hungry eyes, up a serpentine gravel path leading thereunto. A decidedly indelicate young gentleman, in a pair of wings and nothing else, was depicted as superintending the cooking; a representation of the spire of the church in Langham Place,[43] appeared in the distance; and the whole formed a "valentine," of which, as a written inscription in the window testified, there was a large assortment within, which the shopkeeper pledged himself to dispose of to his countrymen generally, at the reduced rate of one and sixpence each. (403–05)

One and sixpence would be a substantial investment for Sam, who instead buys "a sheet of the best gilt-edged letter-paper, and a hard-nibbed pen which could be warranted not to splutter." With input from his father, who reminds him that "Poetry's unnat'ral," Sam pens a letter to Mary, a housemaid he met on their travels; signs it "Your love-sick/ Pickwick"; and prepares to send it through the "General Post." Whether the valentine addressed to "Mary, Housemaid, at Mr Nupkins's Mayor's, Ipswich, Suffolk" reaches its addressee is unclear, although Sam later marries her, which suggests that it does. The twopenny post required the recipient to pay the fee, and perhaps many valentines were never paid for. The introduction of penny post in 1840, paid by sender with a stamp, prompted a major increase in numbers: "Just one year after the uniform Penny Postage, 400,000 valentines were posted throughout England. By 1871, 1.2 million cards were processed by the General Post Office in London."[44]

Earlier valentines needed to be on sheets that could be folded in order to post them. After the introduction of envelope manufacturing machines in the later 1840s, larger and more elaborate valentines could be sent through the post. By the 1860s, lovers could buy valentines readymade or assemble their own from stationers' supplies such as embossed paper, paper lace, and die-cut scraps; more elaborate valentines might have fabric flowers, ribbons, and scent sachets. Standard iconography included cupids, flowers, doves, and hearts, although the last appear with less regularity than on present-day cards. In the language of flowers, roses – the most common identifiable flower – suggest true love.[45] Also frequently featured is the pansy (representative of thoughts); violet (associated with modesty, as in "blushing

---

[43]   All Souls' Church, Langham Place, has a narrow spire supported by classical columns; it would have been very new in the 1820s, when the novel is supposed to take place.

[44]   "Valentine's Day in the Victorian Era." www.sociallearningcommunity.org/Victorian-valentine (accessed October 20, 2018). This article showcases the Laura Seddon Collection of cards at Manchester Metropolitan University.

[45]   Most of the roses depicted on mid-Victorian valentines that I have seen look pink rather than red, possibly due to the difficulty of color lithography.

violet"); and the forget-me-not (self-evidently representative of memory and rhyming conveniently with "rustic cot" and "happy lot").

As Sam Weller's attempt at romance shows, Valentine's Day was in the English tradition associated with poetry, or at least with verses. For example, Richard Cobbold, writing his own Valentine verses in the 1820s, recalled that his mother Elizabeth Cobbold, also a poet, would hold Valentine's Day parties and write verses on cards for her guests.[46] By this time, before February 14, would-be admirers could buy booklets of verses to choose lines appropriate for the loved ones. That these verses very often involved humor and sometimes even double-entendres suggests a certain degree of self-consciousness about the day. For example, *The Whimsical Valentine-Writer*, with a frontispiece of Cupid peeing on his bow and arrows, contains lines such as:

> As a lass loves to be trim.
> As a lawyer loves to sign;
> As a duck in ponds to swim,
> So I love my Valentine.

Or, in a slightly risqué verse addressed to "an Old Lady":

> An old maid is like a bad fire,
> Long after the coals have been caked,
> As you may the reason desire,
> It ought to've been well *raked*.
> Oh, there was no poker in hand,
> To keep up the fire, and to move;
> No, Valentine, pray, at command,
> To stir up the embers of love?[47]

In the early Victorian period, Valentine's Day is similarly treated with humor, marked by comic publications but largely ignored in all but ephemeral literature. The *Comic Almanack* for 1837 lists on its calendar for February 14, "VALENTINE. All Fool's Day," and follows it by a Valentine addressed to Harriet Martineau, which begins,

> "Come live with me, and be my love,"
> And we to all the world will prove,
> "That hill and valley, grove and field,"
> Are waste, if Nature's store they yield,
> While rustic joys, and simple swains
> Are nought compared with rich men's gains.
> We'll demonstrate to please the Tabbies,

[46] Richard Cobbold, *Valentine Verses; Or Lines of Truth, Love, and Virtue* (Ipswich: Shalders, 1829), Preface.

[47] *The Whimsical Valentine-Writer* (London: T. Hughes, n.d.); one date given is 1820, and verses refer to fads such as dandies and Gothic novels, so the date of publication is probably around 1821.

> That none but boobies will have babbies,
> And dose and diet all the nation,
> To check the growing population.[48]

The parody of Elizabethan poetry (Marlowe and Raleigh) suggests that the author has some knowledge of the literary tradition, presented in combination with the present's obsession with wealth. Even more explicitly medievalist is a Valentine poem for 1841, "Saint Valentine: Des Oiseaux," which parodies the "birds" tradition dating back at least to Chaucer:

> Sweet Valentine, thy praise is heard
>   In ev'ry grove so green-oh!
> And thousand birds press on to join
>   The *Concert Valentino.* (1:258)

In 1846, among "Things to be borne in mind in February," the *Almanack* suggests, "on the 14th, if there is any one you wish to insult, it can be done cheaply and anonymously by a valentine" (2:93–94). In 1848, noting that "Valentines have hitherto been sentimental," the *Almanack* advises that in "a nation of shopkeepers" lovers would be more receptive to a full financial statement (2:186).

Early issues of *Punch* also included funny Valentines. In the first almanack in 1842, February 14 does not name Valentine but is annotated, "General skewering of hearts. The Toxophilite Society give a public breakfast in honour of the Archer Boy. And Penny Postmen 'Cuss the heathen zoology."[49] In February, the paper announced "PUNCH'S VALENTINES!" In a parody of gift books such as *The Keepsake* and *Finden's Tableaux*, the spoof advertisement promises "Twelve Large Designs" from its leading artists and that "the dull and most stagnant affection will be rendered bright and palatable by a judicious use of our patent *philtre*" (*Punch* 2:62). The first page, "Young Loves to Sell" by Kenny Meadows, shows a gruesome image of Mr Punch hawking Cupids in a cage and hung up by their ankles, and pierced hearts (Fig. 12). With a slight nod to medievalism the verse beneath explains, "Though Loves of old were not sold for filthy gold, but a heart could buy one;/ The times are changed, and PUNCH has turn'd Love-huckster, so come and try one./ Buy my Loves! Prime young Loves!" The pictures and verses that follow represent irritating stock figures of the times, such as a "Drawing-Room Captain" who has never seen action (military or otherwise); a Lawyer; a "Literary Gentleman" – revealed as a Newgate novelist; and others. Largely the puns stay clean, although an "Adonis" of a footman is told, "I'd change into silver myself pretty soon,/ To be leather'd, *yes leather'd* – by thee as a spoon." A touch of pathos enters the description of a "Milliner" with dreams of "Lord Vapour," who is urged to settle for the writer of the Valentine: "Refuse not – lest forced to the Borough to go,/ With 'plain work done here' in thy window to show." The final Valentine, "The Politician," is written

---

[48]   *The Comic Almanack*, rpt, 2 vols (London: Chatto and Windus, n.d.), 1:79. References follow this edition.
[49]   *Punch* 2 (1842): almanack for February.

Fig. 12. "Young Loves to Sell." By Kenny Meadows. *Punch* 1842 (volume 2, page 63).

THE EARLY HISTORY OF VALENTINES.

Fig. 13.   "Early History of Valentines." *Punch* 1845 (volume 8, page 85).

in prose since "Turnstile" is "above the prettiness of poetry." At a time of "terrible distress," this politician is urged to "*have a heart.*"

Despite the opportunities for topical satire, *Punch* articles continue to refer back to the ancient origins of Valentine's Day. In 1845, "The Early History of Valentines" is illustrated by courting birds in hats and bonnets (Fig. 13). Of St Valentine the writer remarks, "He was martyred at Rome in the year 270, and were he alive now would have another martyrdom to endure in seeing the desecration to which he is subjected by the connection of his name with the vilest daubs and the most wretched poetry" (*Punch* 8:85). The writer notes the frequent subject for such cards is a girl by a country cottage, although the sender is probably a "seedy clerk who is compelled to walk into the heart of the city every day, and who has no more chance of being able to live out of town in the humble cot, than he has of taking up his quarters in the round tower of Windsor Castle."

As "The Early History of Valentines" suggests, the penny post era created increased demand for verses suitable for valentines. "Borrowed" verses from stage songs or poetry books would be printed on paper or fabric for centerpieces for commercial or home-assembled valentines.[50] A notable feature of verses on valentines is that they frequently rearrange poetic lines in order to create a verse that will fit in a central oval on the card. Printed on card and sometimes on fabric, they become "shape" poems. For example (Fig. 14):

[50]   In the Armstrong Browning Library's collection of valentines, for example, one poem is borrowed from Alfred Buss's opera *The Crusaders* (1846), and another garbles lines from the American poet Emeline S. Smith's "We've had Our Share of Bliss, Beloved," first published in 1847.

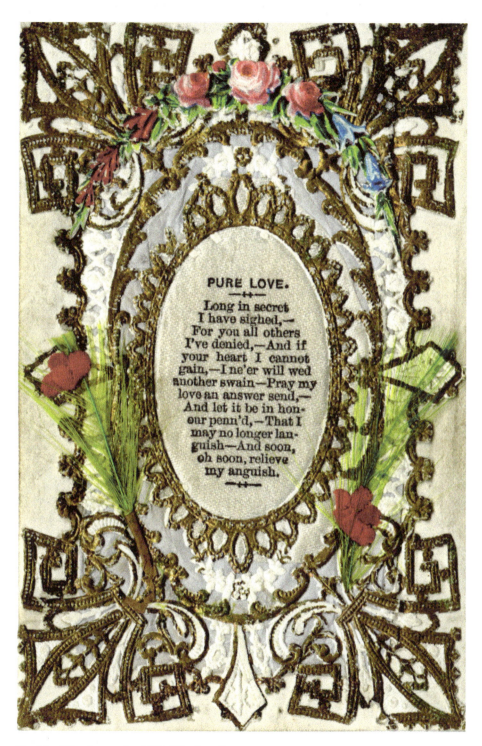

PURE LOVE.

Long in secret
I have sighed,—
For you all others
I've denied,—And if
your heart I cannot
gain,—I ne'er will wed
another swain—Pray my
love an answer send,—
And let it be in hon-
our penn'd,—That I
may no longer lan-
guish—And soon,
oh soon, relieve
my anguish.

Fig. 14. Valentine card, c. 1870. Mixed media.

PURE LOVE

—++—

Long in secret
I have sighed,—
For you all others
I've denied,—And if
your heart I cannot
gain,—I ne'er will wed
another swain—Pray my
love an answer send,—
And let it be in hon-
our penn'd,—That I
may no longer lan-
guish—And soon,
oh soon, relieve
my anguish.[51]

The wording is relatively unusual in being addressed from a woman to man. The first lines of this verse are ridiculed in a mock literary analysis of valentines, "Vox Populi as Represented in Valentines," published in the *Dublin University Magazine* in February 1871, where the title of the first quatrain (up to "swain") is given as "ONLY THINE." The review author notes of this poem, which he possesses in a "stuffed parallelogram," that "No marriage, from the female point of view, may mean a sisterhood, a nunnery, or a leap, *à la* Sappho, into the depths of the ocean wave."[52] Praising anonymity, and tongue firmly in cheek, the article exclaims: "Sweet – sweetest of all is it to receive or to scatter the uncertain and romantic tokens of affection as impersonally as the precocious mid-February violet just lifts up from the ground its tender bloom, and radiates its odours in the scented air" (185). The author goes even quotes the greatest of anonymous valentine verses: "The rose is red, the violet blue,/ Carnations sweet, *and so are you*" (188).

The two well-known Victorian poets I have found who admit to enjoying Valentine's Day are both women. In a rare example of a Victorian letter inscribed "Valentine's Day," Elizabeth Barrett wrote to Mary Russell Mitford on February 14, 1843 and signed it "Valentine EBB" (*Brownings' Correspondence* 6:323). Her affection for her friend is clear in this letter, as it is in all the other letters between the two. In a later letter, describing Mitford's letters as "delightful," she says, "For now, I will confess to you! – I like letters *per se* … & as letters! I like the abstract idea of a letter – I like the postman's rap at the door – I like the queen's head on the paper – and with a negation of queen's heads (which doesn't mean treason) I like the sealing wax under the seal and the postmark on the envelope… " (7:144).

---

[51]   Printed on fabric, possibly silk, on a card in the Armstrong Browning Library collection of Valentines. The poem was extant prior to 1871, and this card was probably made in the 1860s or 1870s.
[52]   "Vox Populi, as Represented in Valentines." *Dublin University Magazine* 77 (February 1871), 191. Subsequent references given in text.

It was left to Christina Rossetti, though, to unite the elements of Valentine's Day. She remarks in her *Time Flies* entry for February 14 that a Christian martyr was among the "various saints" named Valentine; and that:

> With St Valentine's Day stands popularly associated the interchange of "Valentines": this custom having its origin, we are informed, in a pagan ceremony wisely exchanged for a Christian observance.

> And thus our social habit, even if degenerate, assumes a certain dignity: we connect it not merely with mirth and love, but with sanctity and suffering.

She adds that "Never is interchange of affection more appropriate than on a holy day," but advises that such communications should be "pure as snowdrops."[53] Rossetti's "Valentines to my Mother" series show her sensitive awareness of the time of year and its contrast with eternity. According to her brother and editor William Michael Rossetti, "Christina left a penciled note about them thus: 'These Valentines had their origin from my dearest mother's remarking that she had never received one.'"[54] Rossetti wrote her mother a Valentine verse each February 14 from 1876 until her mother's death in 1886. Mostly addressed to "The Queen of Hearts," the poems collectively contrast eternal family relations with the cycle of the year. Some of these poems seem to imitate the "shape" poems of valentine cards of the time. Appropriately for love poetry, "1882" is a sonnet that recalls the poet's "blessed Mother dozing in her chair/ On Christmas Day," the passing from winter's holly to Spring's "paler and frailer snowdrops" marking the changing world in contrast with the speaker's "lifelong love." Valentine's Day is "before sweet Spring ... Sets all the throng of/Of birds a-wooing,/ Billing and cooing –" ("1879"). By mid-February,

> All the Robin Redbreasts
> Have lived the winter through,
> Jenny Wrens have pecked their fill
> And found a work to do;
> Families of sparrows
> Have weathered wind and storm
> With Rabbit on the stony hill
> And Hare upon her form. ("1885")

Just as animal families have to survive the winter, so humans need to be reminded that "Love has no winter hours." "1881" continues:

> If even in this world love is love
>   (This wintry world which felt the Fall),
> What must it be in heaven above
>   Where love to great and small
>   Is all in all?

[53] Christina Rossetti, *Times Flies*, 32.
[54] Christina Rossetti, *New Poems*, ed. William Michael Rossetti (London: Macmillan, 1896), 387. Subsequent poems are cited in text by year.

The valentine for 1877 is signed "C.G. for M.F.R.," which William Michael explains as giving voice to their lately deceased sister Maria Francesca. In short lines reminiscent of "Goblin Market," the poem addresses the mother:

> Own Mother dear,
>   We all rejoicing here
>   Wait for each other,
>   Daughter for Mother,
>   Sister for Brother,
> Till each dear face appear
> Transfigured by Love's flame
>   Yet still the same –

Divine Love transforms human love – yet in this vision of eternity, individual identities and family relationships remain after death. In the poem for 1878, the speaker hopes to be with the "singing Saints who, clad in white,/ Know no more of day or night/ Or death or any changeful thing." Yet in the world of nature, change is apparent: it is "A world of change and loss, a world of death" ("1883"), where the only constant is love, and where the valentine is an ancient symbol that unites not only woman with man but also past with present, and natural fertility with human commerce.

5

Rites of Spring: Imagining Origins

ASTER IS THE most sacred season in the Christian year, yet nineteenth-century Britons frequently traced the rites and traditions associated with Easter to the pre-Christian practices of their ancestors. Nineteenth-century poets were of course aware of the Prologue to the *Canterbury Tales* and many other medieval poems referencing the spring. As medieval poets themselves noted, the natural cycle of the year makes spring the time of fertility: crops begin to grow, and animals and birds mate and bear young. Still, most of the claims that British spring festivals, especially Easter and May-day, are relics of pagan practices transformed into something vaguely Christian during the Middle Ages require substantial leaps of the medievalist imagination.[1] Even matters widely accepted as fact can be hard to substantiate. For example, Bede, writing around 735, claims that the English word "Easter" derives from the name of a Saxon goddess Eostre, whose festival was in spring.[2] Long before the anthropological studies of the later nineteenth century elaborated on this idea, hints may be found in discussions of idolatry. For example, in John Keble's *Christian Year*, Poem LVIII, Eighth Sunday After Trinity, talks not just of "the heathen's wizard fires," but also of woodlands under moonlight,

> Where maidens to the Queen of Heaven
> Wove the gay dance round oak or palm,
>   Or breath'd their vows at even
>   In hymns as soft as balm.[3]

The *Oxford English Dictionary*, however, while not entirely dismissing the possibility that there may have been a goddess Eostre otherwise unmentioned in history, suggests that the word is derived from the Germanic word for "East." The commonly repeated fact, then, that when they were converted to Christianity the Anglo-Saxons also converted a pagan spring festival to a Christian one is far from proven. Ronald Hutton somewhat skeptically outlines later arguments that Eostre was derived from an Indo-European goddess of the dawn (Hutton, *Stations*, 180).[4] These were not,

---

[1] See particularly Hutton, *Stations*, 233–37.
[2] Bede, *De Temporum Rationae* XV.
[3] John Keble, *The Christian Year*, 2:31.
[4] In contrast, in *An Egg for Easter: A Folklore Study* (Bloomington, IN: Indiana University Press, 1971) Venetia Newell presents the arguments for "the Goddess Eastre" (384–86).

however, known to the enthusiasts who visualized pre-Christian Saxons eating hot cross buns, combining antiquarianism and imagination in some curious ways.

At the Reformation, the English either lost the carnival celebrations that marked the beginning of Lent, or they never had them. They did, however, have certain traditions involving food that may have originated in the popular memory of Lent. Whereas antiquarians were in general agreement that although feasting at Christmas was an ancient tradition, specific Christmas foods such as plum-pudding that required imported ingredients were post-medieval, they found much to say about the origins of foods of the Easter season. In the Roman Catholic church, Lent is a period of denial of bodily desires through fasting and repentance, yet oddly enough, by the late eighteenth century, the English treated the Easter period as one of distinctive foods and rest from labor.

In March 1790 a correspondent using the pseudonym "Antiquarius" wrote to the *Gentleman's* Magazine to ask,

> Whence originated the custom at Westminster school, of the under-clerk of the college entering on Shrove Tuesday into the school, and, preceded by the Beadle and the other officers, of throwing a large pancake over the bar, which divides the upper from the under school? Or, if this question is of such a local nature as to admit of an answer from no one – Whence originated the custom of eating pancakes on Shrove Tuesday?[5]

The reply communicated did not entirely solve the question of the Westminster School pancake, but implied a medieval origin to Shrove Tuesday practices. This second letter pointed out that English name for the day before the first day of Lent, Shrove Tuesday, derives from "shriving" one's soul, and that the word "shrive" was of Saxon origin, a point also made in John Brand's edition of *Popular Antiquities* (Brand, 333). The correspondent adds that some ancient Anglican churches ring bells on that day: in London it is called "the *Pancake-bell*; perhaps because, after the confession [before the Reformation], it was customary for the several persons to dine on *pancakes* or *fritters*."

Possibly in some communities Lent was strictly kept, and thus pancakes provided a means of using up ingredients such as eggs before the fast; antiquarians agreed that this was the case on the day before Shrove Tuesday, "Collop Monday," when the faithful would eat up "collops" of meat (Brand, 331). Brand sees the custom of making pancakes as one that "seems, if the present fashionable Contempt of old Customs continues, not likely to last another Century." John Brady, in contrast, explains pancakes as themselves a celebratory food: "After the people had made the confession, they were permitted to indulge in festive amusements, although not permitted to partake of any repast beyond the usual substitutes for flesh; and hence arose the custom yet preserved of eating *Pancakes* and *Fritters* at Shrovetide" (Brady 1:208). A character in Shakespeare's *All's Well That Ends Well* mentions "Pancakes for Shrove Tuesday," so the association of pancakes with this date is very plausibly a popular practice that survived the Reformation. Although

---

5   *Gentleman's Magazine* 60:1 (March 1790), 256.

commentators suggest that making the pancakes was a social occasion, usually involving tossing them, they do not mention pancake races, which now occur in a number of communities but that seem with one exception noted by Blackburn and Holford-Strevens to be fairly recent institutions.[6] One of *Punch*'s "sentiments" for Shrove Tuesday in February 1844 is "may we never want a pancake, nor an appetite to eat it!" (*Punch* 6 [1844]:2).[7]

Although they were convinced that medieval Shrove Tuesday had involved large-scale community merrymaking, nineteenth-century antiquarians were less sure how much they wished to maintain these activities. Possibly in some vague memory of carnival, Shrove Tuesday was a traditional time for ball-games, which implies that the day was still kept among some groups – apprentices and school-boys are mentioned – as a holiday (*Every-Day Book* 1:259).[8] Less happily, Shrove Tuesday was a time for cockfighting and with killing chickens by throwing sticks and other objects at them (*Every-Day Book* 1:247–58). Brady repeats a cautionary tale from the *Gentleman's Magazine* of a man who was cruel to a cock that had lost a fight and when he threatened those who wanted to interfere, *"fell down dead on the spot!"* (Brady 1:210). Both the treatment of Shrove Tuesday as a holiday or half-holiday and the abuse of chickens seem to have waned by the early Victorian period: in the 1860s, Chambers' *Book of Days* mentions "throwing at cocks" as an "inhumane sport" of "days not very long gone by" (*Book of Days* 1:238). The *Book of Days* nevertheless notes wistfully if not completely grammatically, "When Shrove Tuesday dawned, the bells were set a ringing, and everybody abandoned himself to amusement and good humour" (1:236).

Literature links pancakes with the beginning of the Easter season from the 1400s; the origins of other Easter season foods, the simnel cake of mid-Lent and the hot cross buns of Good Friday, were more contested. The simnel cake, usually a fruit cake with almond paste, was associated with the mid-Lent Mothering Sunday, a day to visit one's mother and give gifts. Robert Herrick mentions this custom in the seventeenth century: "To Dianeme," subtitled "A Ceremony in Gloucester," reads:

> Ile to thee a simnell bring,
> 'Gainst thou go'st a-mothering:
> So that when she blesseth thee,
> Half that blessing thou'lt give me.[9]

---

[6]   Bonnie Blackburn and Leofranc Holford-Strevens state that the all-women's pancake race in Olney "traces its origins back to 1445." See *The Oxford Companion to the Year*, 607. Olney does not suggest a completely continuous tradition, but claims some evidence that the race was run in the fifteenth century; it was certainly in existence some time before the Second World War and revived again after it. See http://olneypancakerace.org/pancake-race-history (accessed December 6, 2018).

[7]   "Want" here would imply lack rather than desire.

[8]   The examples provided are Scottish. John Brand notes that in his home town of Newcastle upon Tyne in the 1770s, the church bell was rung at noon on Shrove Tuesday and the rest of the day was regarded as a holiday, a "sort of little *Carnival* ensuing for the remaining Part of the Day" (Brand, 331).

[9]   Robert Herrick, *Complete Poems*, 2:224. Grosart provides a footnote explaining "simnell."

Nathan Bailey's *Dictionarium Britannicum* of 1730 defines "Mothering" as:

> A Custom still retained in many places of *England*, of visiting Parents on *Midlent-Sunday*; and it seems to be called *Mothering*, from the Respect in the old Time paid to the *Mother Church*. It being the Custom for People in old Popish Times to visit their Mother Church on *Midlent- Sunday*, and to make their Offerings at the High Altar.[10]

Bailey thus suggests a secularization of a medieval practice, so that people would offer gifts to their own mothers rather than to the church. In the eighteenth century, "Mothering" seems to have been a regional custom. Correspondents to the *Gentleman's Magazine* in the 1780s are very vague about this day, but believe it may have associations with food or drink. When "H.T." mentioned "furmety on Mothering-Sunday" in a 1783 communication, another correspondent claimed to be unfamiliar with Mothering Sunday, and observed that others probably were too. "J.M.", writing in January 1784, knew what "furmety" was – a kind of milk pudding – but thought "Mothering Sunday" was "some Sunday near Christmas," and had to be corrected by "Scrutator," who had consulted "Bailey's Dictionary."[11] "D.A.B." added that he had first heard of "Mothering" the previous year "near Chepstow in Monmouthshire."

Possibly, the correspondents to the *Gentleman's Magazine* did not know about Mothering Sunday and related foodstuffs because of class differences or regional practices. A generation later Hone's *Every-Day Book* remarks that it is "still" the practice for "servants and apprentices to carry cakes or some nice eatables or trinkets, as presents to their parents"; and that they might share a meal of furmity or cakes (*Every-Day Book* 1:359). In a children's story of the 1860s, *Copsley Annals Preserved in Proverbs*, an elderly lady who was once a household servant in western England recalls making a simnel cake for her mother, who had taught her the following rhyme:

> She who would a simnel make,
> Flour and saffron first must shake,
> Candy, spices, eggs must take,
> Chop and pound till arms do ache:
> Then must boil, and then must bake
> For a crust too hard to break.
>
> When at Mid-lent thou dost wake,
> To thy mother bear thy cake:
> She will prize it for thy sake.[12]

The story footnotes the dying Shropshire custom of "going a-mothering" and adds that "simnel cakes are still made and sold in some north-country neighborhoods

---

[10]   "Mothering." *Dictionarium Britannicum*, ed. Nathan Bailey and others (London: T. Cox, 1730). No page numbers.

[11]   *Gentleman's Magazine* 1783 (578, 928); 1784 (97–98).

[12]   Emily Elizabeth Steele Elliott, "Mrs. Blackett: Her Story." *Copsley Annals Preserved in Proverbs* (Boston, MA: Dutton, 1868), 126.

from Mid-lent to Easter." The author, Emily Elizabeth Steele Elliott, was a Sussex hymn-writer – perhaps from her south-eastern England origins she does not distinguish between Shropshire and the north. She may herself have originated the verse recipe; her other poetry shows that she was a committed member of the Reformed faith and would probably have been horrified at some of the proposed connections with medieval Catholicism.

Etymologists were divided as to whether the word "simnel" was derived from a Latin word for fine flour; from Lambert Simnel, who in the reign of Henry VII claimed to be one of the Princes who went missing in the Tower of London under the watch of their uncle Richard III;[13] or an affectionate old couple named Sim and Nell (*Book of Days* 1:336–37). Some believed that originally they would have featured images of the Mother of God, or perhaps symbolic representations of the Disciples.[14] Today's *Oxford English Dictionary* votes for the "fine flour" definition, but the story of Sim and Nell suggests that the origin of simnel cakes was mysterious to those who made them, hence the development of an explanatory story. Again, the *Book of Days* of the 1860s remarks on the festive moods of the past: "The harshness and general painfulness of life in old times must have been much relieved by certain simple and affectionate customs which modern people have learned to dispense with" (*Book of Days* 1:335). Ronald Hutton ascribes the revival of what is now also called "Mother's Day" to commercial opportunism in the mid-twentieth century, converting a regional practice of the working poor into a "nation-wide, and classless" event (Hutton, *Stations*, 177).

The decline in Shrove Tuesday pastimes and the representation of Mothering Sunday as a quaint regional custom gives some validity to the notion that people of the Middle Ages found more occasions for festivity than their nineteenth-century descendants: the humble hot cross bun, though, shows an instance where the medieval connection was largely fanciful. Whereas written evidence supported claims that pancakes and simnel cakes had existed at least by the Early Modern period, no writer mentions hot cross buns before the 1700s. Nevertheless, so prominent were theories as to the origin of the hot cross bun that in April 1867 Julia Goddard poked fun at them in a poem published in *Once a Week*. "Hot Cross Buns. – (After Pope.)" begins:

> Awake, my muse! Aside thy buskins fling,
> This day 'tis mine of hot cross buns to sing;
> Sure none but pedants would disdain the theme,
> The climax of the schoolboy's Lenten dream:
> Salt-fish with egg-sauce to its birth he owes,
> And hot cross buns await him at its close.
> Say to what god or goddess I shall bend,

[13]   Intriguingly, Simnel is associated with cookery; he is claimed to have been a baker's son and after his defeat he was sent to work in the royal kitchens.

[14]   Modern recipes for simnel cakes – usually described as an Easter cake, not a mid-Lent cake – suggest decorating with eleven marzipan balls to represent the twelve disciples minus Judas; I have found no mention of this in nineteenth-century accounts and suspect that it may be a later borrowing from other European traditions.

> Or Pallas wise, or Ceres, be my friend?
> *That* knowledge might impart, of *this* 'tis said
> That she taught man the art of making bread.
> Shall I o'er ponderous tome industrious pore
> To learn if hot cross buns were known of yore,
> Link them with "bouns" blessed by the heathen priest,
> Or sweet cakes at the Roman seed-time feast, –
> Find if from later Rome their fame they win
> Or to unleavened bread owe origin?
> Or to Queen Anne's or George's days draw nigh,
> When Chelsea Bun Houses held rivalry?[15]

The lines, while following Pope's form of heroic couplet and epic invocation, do not seem a close parody of a particular poem by Alexander Pope. Perhaps "After Pope" is also a joke, implying that Victoria's reign was so far after the pope's authority had been suppressed in England that memories of what came before were very vague.

The last possibility in Goddard's list of theories, that hot cross buns were an off-shoot of the eighteenth-century enthusiasm for buns, seems most likely. In early nineteenth-century London, on the morning of Good Friday, street-vendors would sell hot cross buns: Hone includes the lines preserved as a nursery rhyme, "One-a-penny, two-a-penny, hot cross buns!" Hone identifies them as "of the usual form of buns; though they are distinguished from them inwardly by a sweeter taste, and the flavor of all-spice." He (or his source) further claims that the "hot-cross-bun is the most popular symbol of the Roman catholic religion in England that the reformation has left" (*Every-Day Book* 1:403).[16] The attribution of hot cross buns to the medieval period seems to be on the basis of the cross – yet Good Friday buns would seem an inappropriate food for a day of fasting, and a generation later, Henry Mayhew's *London Labour and the London Poor* explicitly states that Irish Catholics do not eat hot cross buns, since the day is "a strict fast, and the eggs in the buns prevent their being used."[17] Given the necessary un-Lenten ingredients – not only flour, eggs, butter, and milk but also imported items such as dried fruit, sugar, and allspice – a medieval origin seems questionable.[18]

---

[15] "Hot Cross Buns – After Pope," signed Julia Goddard. *Once A Week*, April 1867, 68.

[16] In the sixteenth and seventeenth centuries, communities had many regulations as to who could bake breads, and when. Some restrictions were eased on holidays (Christmas and Good Friday). The *Court Leet Records of the Manor of Manchester* (Manchester: Henry Blackburn, 1884) quotes a 1638 Privy Council prohibition of "spiced bread… except for use at funerals, and on Good Friday and Christmas" (67). This may be a possible origin of what became hot cross buns, but it is not medieval.

[17] Henry Mayhew, ed., *London Labour and the London Poor*. 4 vols, 1861–62. Rpt (New York: Dover, 1968), 1:201.

[18] The most extreme medievalist claims about hot cross buns, such as that they are ancient Saxon, are frequently repeated in the internet age. See, for example, https://ireland-calling.com/lifestyle/the-hot-cross-bun-origins-and-superstitions/ (accessed December 6, 2018). They are contradicted by another modern theory, that Queen Elizabeth I permitted them, which seems to have arisen from the city ordinances about who was entitled to sell baked goods.

Nevertheless, more than one Victorian scholar tied them to pagan practices surviving in medieval culture. Ignoring the complete lack of historical records about the supposed goddess, Chambers's *Book of Days* asserts, "Our hot cross buns at Easter are only the pagan cakes which the pagan Saxons ate in honour of their goddess Eastre" (1:337). Even more bizarre is the claim made about hot cross buns in *The Worship of the Generative Powers During the Middle Ages of Western Europe* published in 1865 together with a reprint of Richard Payne Knight's *Discourse on the Worship of Priapus* (1786). I accept the usual attribution of this illustrated but anonymous work to the hard-working and usually astute antiquarian editor Thomas Wright. Wright (for I shall call the author such) believed that relics of ancient fertility practices could be seen in the art of the Middle Ages through the representation of both male and female "generative organs." Expanding Knight's work on the phallus, he also drew attention to medieval "Shelah-na-Gig Monuments." He explains the term as meaning "Julian the Giddy," since these gargoyle-like carvings, usually on column capitols or keystones in churches, represent "a female exposing herself to view in the most unequivocal manner."[19] Nobody knows why medieval people wanted these figures on their buildings. Perhaps they suggest the sin of lust, or perhaps they are meant to be funny. Thomas Wright, however, believed them both "protecting charms against the fascination of the evil eye" and derived from "the most ancient superstitions of the human race" (36–37). Wright saw relics of this worship in the practice of nailing up horseshoes for good luck, which he also saw as a representation of the vagina (48). A related claim is that hot cross buns are relics of this ancient worship of the body, and that since the Romans offered cakes to Venus, the same were presumably offered to her Teutonic counterpart, Eastre or Eostre. Wright may not have been the first to make this claim, since R.T. Hampson had earlier rejected the idea that the cross on the bun was a sexual symbol. Hampson knew that cakes found at Herculaneum were said to bear a cross symbolizing the phallus, but after a multi-page digression on the cross as a sacred medieval symbol, he had insisted that "the piety of the early Christians" marked the buns "with the symbol of a saviour's suffering" (Hampson, 187–99). According to Wright, though, "there is some reason for believing that, at least in some parts, the Easter-cakes had originally a different form – that of the phallus." Not content with this, he quotes a medieval source describing cakes depicting "the secret members of both sexes" (87–88). Yet even if nineteenth-century attempts to see references to the reproductive organs and a link to ancient fertility rituals in hot cross buns are highly questionable, revealing more about the Victorian mind than about the medieval one, they complicate Victorian medievalism in intriguing ways. Scholars such as Thomas Wright were looking for secret codes for what could not be otherwise expressed in polite society, reinforcing the idea of the medieval period as simultaneously superstitious, unrepressed, and fun-loving.

---

[19]   Richard Payne Knight and [Thomas Wright], *A Discourse on the Worship of Priapus and On the Worship of the Generative Powers* (1865; rpt, New York: Julian Press, 1957), 35–36. Wright's account of Sheela na gigs (to use the now-standard spelling) is important because his text contains illustrations of carvings that no longer exist due to the ravages of time, over-zealous collectors, and quite possibly, prudery. Subsequent references in text, by page number.

Anglican Easter Day was a low-key affair compared with that of Roman Catholic countries. At least in some regions, however, they shared the use of eggs as a symbol of resurrection. John Brand, who suggested that the practice derived from the Jewish Passover, mentions that children in his home Newcastle area often received presents of "Paste eggs," colored and sometimes decorated eggs. John Brady noted the use of eggs in the Jewish Passover, but noted that the custom of giving eggs as gifts "is generally supposed to have been introduced by the Monks, typically to express the Resurrection" (Brady 1:293). With an unusual unanimity, antiquarians agreed that the word "Paste" was derived from "Pasche," itself descending from the Latin word for Easter.[20] "J.B." sent Hone Cumberland methods for decorating eggs in March 1825 (*Every-Day Book* 1:426).[21] Companies such as Cadbury and Fry began making chocolate eggs in the 1870s, and by 1900 had developed what became the customary form of an English chocolate egg: a hollow egg-shape made of chocolate containing other sweets.[22]

An earlier attempt to commercialize Easter was Letitia Elizabeth Landon's gift book for Easter, *The Easter Gift: A Religious Offering*. Published in 1832 in an apparent experiment in expanding the fashion for annuals to be sold as Christmas and New Year gifts to Easter, *The Easter Gift* follows the practice of other gift books in featuring poems that illustrate engravings of paintings.[23] The book has an awkward disjunction between visual image and text. Landon's poetry is largely based on Bible scenes and is in some respects anti-medievalist. For example, a poem addressed to Mary the Mother of Christ calls her "Thrice blessed and thrice beautiful" but immediately insists that worshippers come to her without "vain prayers" of "false idolatry." The poem adds, "We have no need of pagan rites/ To join with christian prayer."[24] L.E.L. traces the reverence of Mary to the relics of ancient paganism, suggesting that Mary assumed the role of ancient goddesses:

> Thine altars where thy statues stood,
> Thy hymns and votive flowers,
> Were relics of another age,
> Another creed, than ours...

The poem is equally unenthusiastic about the Middle Ages: even after the introduction of Christianity,

> Old superstitions still remained,
> And priestcraft next stept in,
> To rule by human ignorance,
> And work by human sin.

---

[20]   For example, Brand, 310.

[21]   Both John Brand and John Brady had died well before 1825, so this is a different J.B.

[22]   www.chocolatetradingco.com/magazine/features/history-chocolate-easter-eggs (accessed December 13, 2018).

[23]   Few gift books claimed to be specifically intended for Easter. Fisher published no more but reissued L.E.L.'s book in 1834.

[24]   Laetitia Elizabeth Landon (L.E.L.), *The Easter Gift: A Religious Offering* (London: Fisher, 1832), 12.

But although the poem criticizes "idolatry," its accompanying illustration is a "Madonna and Child" by Murillo, and many of the other paintings reproduced in the volume are similarly from the European Roman Catholic tradition, some of which are more linked to medieval beliefs than to the Bible, such as the representation of the Child Jesus with flowers. L.E.L.'s envisioning of Easter both retells ancient Bible stories and points to their contemporary application. The poem accompanying a picture of the child St John in the wilderness (again not a story from the canonical Gospels) suggests that the world may have reached its end times. The poem first depicts the "infant St John" as a "herald" of the coming of Christ; then moves to the present state of the world; and finally transitions to a direct address to God and coming judgment:

> There is a wild confusion in the world,
> Like the vexed seas.
> And ancient thrones are from high places hurled,
> Yet man not free.
>
> And vain opinions seek to change all life,
> Yet yield no aid
> To all the sickness, want, the grief and strife
> Which now pervade.
>
> Are not these signs of that approaching time
> Of blood and tears,
> When thou shalt call to dread account the crime
> Of many years. (38)

The Preface draws attention to Britain's state at the time of publication, March 21, 1832, when "a whole nation is addressing its supplications to Heaven." Parliament voted in favor of the Reform Bill five days later, although the constitutional crisis was to continue for another few months.

In a period when the Higher Criticism and new scientific theories were causing many to question their religious faith, comparatively few Victorian writers seem to have chosen Easter as the occasion to express doubts about the resurrection. The speaker in Robert Browning's "Easter-Day" ultimately finds that the natural world does not contradict Christianity as some of his contemporaries were suggesting, but rather confirms the presence of God. In writing this poem Browning very likely made use of a detailed account of the Aurora Borealis by the scientist Sir John Herschel, which appeared in the *Athenaeum* in 1843. The poem's speaker describes how at moments "the fire would shrink," but again the earth would be lit up with flashes of flame "as if a dragon's nostril split/ And all his famished ire o'erflowed."[25] The Editors of the Oxford *Poetical Works* suggest that this scene was inspired by a damaging hailstorm of August 1, 1846 (4:400, note), but the description here is not of

---

[25] Robert Browning, *Christmas-Eve and Easter-Day, A Poem* (London: Chapman and Hall, 1850); lines 356-7. Line-numbers follow *Poetical Works*, ed. Ian Jack and Margaret Smith.

rain and hail descending to earth but of signs in the "dome of heaven," and later the speaker specifically mentions "the shock of that strange Northern Light" (line 1016). In *The Athenaeum* in May 1843, Herschel gave an account of the Northern Lights or Aurora Borealis, also as seen from Kent on May 7, Browning's birthday. If Browning did read this description in the *Athenaeum*, as I believe likely, given his sensitivity to dates he would probably have noticed this. Nothing of spiritual birth or rebirth, however, appears in Herschel's report.[26]

In contrast, Browning's speaker is inclined to think medievally. He recalls the scene from three years previously, when he was keeping the ancient tradition of an Easter vigil. Bourne mentions "a common Custom among the Vulgar and unedu-cated Part of the World, to rise before the *Sun* on *Easter-day*, and walk into the Fields: The Reason of which, is to see the Sun *Dance*; which they have been told, from an *old Tradition*, always dances upon that Day." Bourne questions the tradition as not based on the Bible, but recognizes that metaphorically, the Easter season brings "a seeming Smile over the face of Nature, and Heaven and Earth show Tokens of Joy." All the same, Bourne approves rising early at Easter as "an ancient and commenda-ble Custom" (Bourne, 188–89). Browning's speaker, despite his repeated statement of "How hard it is/ To be a Christian!" recalls how he saw a cosmic event that for a while made him think of Judgement Day, and, implicitly, the return of Christ:

> Suddenly all the midnight round
> One fire. The dome of heaven had stood
> As made up of a multitude
> Of handbreadth cloudlets, one vast rack
> Of ripples infinite and black,
> From sky to sky. Sudden there went,
> Like horror and astonishment,
> A fierce vindictive scribble of red
> Quick flame across, as if one said
> (The angry scribe of Judgment) "There –
> "Burn it!" And straight I was aware
> That the whole ribwork round, minute
> Cloud touching cloud beyond compute,
> Was tinted, each with its own spot
> Of burning at the core, till clot
> Jammed against clot, and spilt its fire
> Over all heaven ... (503–20)

Yet even though he could use science as an at least partial explanation of an event that would have seemed apocalyptic to medieval observers, the speaker experiences a new personal connection with God, and develops his own new tradition of keep-ing the ancient vigil.

Although the setting is English, Browning wrote the poems published as "Christ-mas-Eve and Easter-Day" in 1849 while he was living in Italy, which represented for

---

[26]   *Athenaeum* 811 (May 13, 1843), 465.

English travelers both classical civilization and the medieval Christian traditions of the Roman Empire: about the same time John Ruskin was working on *The Stones of Venice*. Arthur Hugh Clough subtitled his poem "Easter Day" "Naples 1849." The speaker in this case is on the "sinful streets of Naples" when his "brain is lightened" after his "tongue had said, 'Christ is not risen!'"[27] When Clough incorporated some of this poem into *Dipsychus* the given setting was Venice, but "Dipsychus" explains that he uttered these lines at Naples the previous year. Dispychus sits unnoticed close to the "barbaric portal of St Mark's" as revelers fill the Piazza (2:112). The Spirit who dialogs with Dipsychus (perhaps his second self) comments that Venetian architecture is "formed of Gothic and of Grecian/ A combination strange," but one in which he has chosen to make his "abode" (2:129). Both Browning and Clough, I would suggest, are responding to an increasing sense of the gulf between the unquestioning reenactment of medieval tradition in Italian religion and its absence in England.

Good Friday was not only a Christian festival but also a financial holiday in nineteenth-century England; until 1871 the day after Easter was not. Many workers, however, seem to have kept it as a holiday, either by negotiation with their employers or by simply not showing up to work. Bourne traces the cessation from work back to the early church's week-long celebration of the Resurrection, attributing the introduction of games such as hand-ball to the corrupt church of the Middle Ages (Bourne, 196–97). As late as the Chambers' *Book of Days*, some areas were apparently still practicing "Lifting" or "Heaving" – usually defined as the raising of a person on a chair or on the arms of the opposite sex – on Easter Monday and Tuesday.[28] In Warwickshire, a correspondent told Hone, on Easter Monday "it was customary for the men to heave and kiss the women, and on [Tuesday] for the women to retaliate upon the men." "L.S." recalls how:

> Many a time have I passed along the streets inhabited by the lower orders of people, and seen parties of jolly matrons assembled round tables on which stood a foaming tankard of ale. There they sat in all the pride of absolute sovereignty, and woe to the luckless man that dared to invade their prerogatives!

The alcohol consumption, widespread kissing, and gender power reversal involved in "Lifting" probably doomed it to oblivion, and it is a regional custom, that unlike many others, seems never to have become national. Still the tradition of taking off work after Easter prevailed. In east London, Greenwich Fair took place on Easter Monday and Tuesday.[29] In theory, although not necessarily in practice,[30] theatres

---

[27]   Arthur Hugh Clough, "Easter Day. Naples, 1849." *The Poems and Prose Remains of Arthur Hugh Clough*, 2 vols (London: Macmillan, 1869), 2:103. Subsequence references follow this edition in text, by volume and page number.

[28]   For example, *Every-Day Book* 1:425; *Book of Days* 1:425, where it is called a "ridiculous practice."

[29]   Interestingly, Greenwich is the site of a recent attempt to revive "Heaving"; see https://traditionalcustomsandceremonies.wordpress.com/2012/04/30/custom-revived-easter-heaving/ (accessed December 18, 2018).

[30]   *Punch* mentions in an article titled "Amusements of Passion Week" published in 1852, "All the theatres are supposed to be shut, and yet all the theatres are actually open" *Punch* 22, 148.

were closed the week before Easter, giving actors more time to rehearse; so Easter Monday, like Boxing Day, was a good time to introduce new plays. On the introduction of bank holidays in 1871, Easter Monday became a financial, and in effect a national, holiday again.

May Day Innocence

Hardly surprisingly, the antiquarian who detected a phallic symbol in the humble hot cross bun also found one in the maypole of May Day: "There appears to be sufficient reason," Wright remarks, "for supposing that, at a period which cannot now be ascertained, the maypole had taken the place of the phallus."[31] J.G. Frazer was later to make a similar claim,[32] but writers of the Early Modern period had already suggested it; Philip Stubbs notoriously called the maypole a "stinckyng idoll" in his 1583 *Anatomie of Abuses*, of which the third edition was reprinted by William Turnbull in 1836.[33] In the 1650s Thomas Hobbes noted the parallel between maypoles and the classical worship of Priapus, although he did not specifically state that the English practice is derived from the Roman one.[34] Nevertheless, collectors of folk traditions such as John Brand and Joseph Strutt traced the maypole to the Roman festival of Flora, which, according to Brand, "was observed with all Manner of Obscenity and Lewdness, and the undecent Sports and Postures of naked Women" (Brand, 256). Extending the pagan idea to ancient Britain, Strutt adds, "Some consider the May-pole as a relic of Druidism, but I cannot find any solid foundation for such an opinion."[35] Similarly, the story of the maypole at the American settlement of Merrymount, revived in Nathaniel Hawthorne's short story in the 1830s, shows a defiant rejection of Christian values. "The May-pole at Merrymount," in which neighboring Puritans condemn a May revel as worshipping an "idol" or a "Baal," was published around the same time as the first parts of Tennyson's "May Queen." (Hawthorne's name, of course, is a synonym for the May tree.)

Once again, all of this assumes a continuity between pre-Christian times and the practices of the Middle Ages that cannot be substantiated; Ronald Hutton notes that maypoles cannot be traced back further in England than the fourteenth century (Hutton, *Stations*, 233–37). May Day celebrations were not unique to the English tradition: for example, Stéphanie Félicité de Genlis's moral story for children *Les Veillées du Château* mentions a May Day celebration where the local peasantry erect "le mai" and decorate it with flowers.[36] The works of "Madame de Genlis" were very popular in England, and Thomas Holcroft's English translation of this work, *Tales of*

---

[31]   *The Worship of the Generative Powers*, 93.

[32]   Frazer discusses May Day practices, which he believes are relics of tree worship and the "fertilising power of the tree spirit," in *The Golden Bough*, 2:51–72.

[33]   Philip Stubbes, *Anatomie of Abuses*, 3rd ed., rpt by William B.D.D. Turnbull (London: Pickering, 1836), 172.

[34]   In *Leviathan* chapter XLV, "Of Demonology and other Relics of the Religions of the Gentiles," Hobbes states that the Romans "had their procession of Priapus, we our fetching in, erection and dancing about Maypoles."

[35]   Strutt, *Sports and Pastimes*, 351.

[36]   Stéphanie Félicité, comtesse de Genlis, *Les Veillées du Château, ou Cours de morale à l'usage des enfans* (1784; Paris: Maradan, 1803), 2:237–30.

the Castle, uses both the term "May-pole" and "May-bush" for "le mai."[37] The term "May-bush" appears in Spenser's *Shephearde's Calender*, in which "Palinode," having noted that decorating the church with "Hawthorne buds, and swete Eglantine" will please "holy Saints," regrets standing apart from the May Day festivities and not being with the group of revelers "To helpen the Ladys their Maybush beare."[38]

Even though the poem challenges the Popish remnants of May Day and reader is guided to agree with Piers, Palinode's fellow shepherd who chides him for wanting to leave his pastoral duties and join the May Day celebrations, Spenser's "Maye" helps confirm a historical awareness of May Day activities apparently surviving past the Reformation. Antiquarians were also once again indebted to Robert Herrick, whose poem "Corinna's going a-Maying" mentions streets and homes decorated with "white-thorn," otherwise known as hawthorn or May. Corinna is encouraged to:

> marke
> How each field turns a street; each street a Parke
>   Made green, and trimm'd with trees: see how
>   Devotion gives each House a Bough,
>   Or Branch: Each Porch, each doore, ere this,
>   An Arke a Tabernacle is
> Made up of white-thorn neatly enterwove;
> As if here were those cooler shades of love.
>   Can such delights be in the street,
>   And open fields, and we not see't?
>   Come, we'll abroad; and let's obay
>   The Proclamation made for May:
> And sin no more, as we have done, by staying;
> But my *Corinna*, come, let's goe a Maying.[39]

Rather than depicting May-Day celebrations as sin, Herrick's poem suggests that it might be a sin to stay away from such picturesque activities. In spite of the long-established association between maypoles, paganism, and sexuality, May Day at least as depicted in poems, plays, and stories created an imagined innocence embedded in the rural past.

Calendar reform, however, created a problem for May Day revels. In 1752, when England converted from the Julian to the Gregorian calendar systems, May Day became eleven days earlier in the solar year. As a result, the hawthorn or May blossom that formed a traditional part of the May Day celebrations was not yet blooming in some places. This memory of "Old May Day" seems to have survived into the nineteenth century, becoming part of the nostalgia for the rural way of life. Robert Bloomfield chose "Old May Day" as the setting for his 1822 poem *May Day with the Muses*. Bloomfield, who became a shoemaker, had worked as a farm-boy

---

[37] Stéphanie Félicité, comtesse de Genlis, *Tales of the Castle; or, Stories of Instruction and Delight*. Translated by Thomas Holcroft (London: G. Robinson, 1785), 2:23–25.

[38] Edmund Spenser, *The Shepheardes Calender* (London, 1579), "Maye" line 34.

[39] Robert Herrick, "Corinna's going a-Maying," *Complete Poems*, 1:117.

for a family connection in his youth and his idyllic pictures of rural life suggest that he retained fond memories of the experience. His *Farmer's Boy: A Rural Poem* (1800), describing the activities of a young farmer through the four seasons, was a strong seller, although Bloomfield himself seems not to have gained much financial reward. Part of the appeal of *The Farmer's Boy* was its presentation of rural activities as shaped by the seasons of the year but rich in ancient tradition. Jonathan Lawson suggests that Bloomfield's farming experience was working for a tenant farmer "in the open-field system of agriculture" dating back to medieval feudalism but by 1800 frequently replaced by enclosed fields. [40] Although strictly speaking "Giles" is working in fields and tending sheep not on commons but in fenced pastures, harvest, for example, is represented as a community experience, with local people welcome to glean and even to receive their share of the reaper's work:

> No rake takes here what Heaven to all bestows:
> Children of want, for you the bounty flows!
> And every cottage from the plenteous store
> Receives a burden nightly at the door. [41]

At a historical moment when, as noted in "Spring," farming had become less a form of yeomanly self-sufficiency than the means of supplying the "dependant, huge Metropolis" ("Spring," 16), *The Farmer's Boy* preserved the centuries-old practices of rural people, many of which readers would be able to recognize as not much changed from the herding and agriculture described in the Bible.

As a rite of spring, May Day was part of this rural world now available to many Britons only through the written word, and Bloomfield showed his enjoyment of May throughout his poetic career. According to Bloomfield's over-intrusive editor Capel Lofft,[42] Bloomfield's first known poem, written when he was sixteen, was "The Milk-Maid: The First of May." The poem is written from the milk-maid's point of view, as she anticipates dancing on May Day and exchanging lifelong vows with Colin. It will be, she muses, an experience that will remain with them: "the remembrance will be ever dear!/ At no time LOVE with INNOCENCE ceases to charm" (*Farmer's Boy*, 11). "Lucy, A Song" informs the addressee that "the May-bush and the Meadow-sweet/ Reserve their fragrance all for you," and invites her to "share the merry Holiday" of May (115–16).

May Day with the Muses was Bloomfield's last substantial publication and most explicitly medievalist. The May in question is not the current first of May but specifically identified as "Old May Day." In many rural communities, the quarterly dates for rent payments and sometimes for wages still followed the Julian calendar;[43] Old May Day, though, was not a usual rent-day. The eighty-year-old landowner Sir Ambrose Higham, having given up public life and retired to his country property

---

[40] Jonathan Lawson, *Robert Bloomfield* (Boston, MA: Twayne, 1980), 57, 135.

[41] Robert Bloomfield, *The Farmer's Boy; A Rural Poem*, 5th edition (London: Vernor and Hood, 1801), 35 ("Summer").

[42] Capel Lofft took on a role as Bloomfield's editor and promoter; after the first edition he added his own comments on the merits of Bloomfield's poems.

[43] This is mentioned as still the practice in Thomas Hardy's *Tess of the D'Urbervilles* (1891).

decides to indulge his love of "the Muses" and remit his tenants six month's rent –
presumably from midsummer to Christmas – provided that they "pay their rents
in rhyme."[44] The preface acknowledges Bloomfield's awareness that "many readers"
might object that "It is not the common practice of English baronets to remit half
a year's rent to their tenants for poetry, or for anything else." Bloomfield, however,
mentions a passionate collector in Samuel Johnson's *Rambler* who, following the
example of Alfred the Great who "received the tribute of the Welsh in wolves heads,"
accepted his rent in butterflies, insects, and other natural oddities. This is hardly an
example to emulate since the fictional collector's letter goes on to state that he has
now bankrupted himself, but Bloomfield's use of appeal to the example of Alfred
sets a medievalist tone.[45]

The poem starts in the heroic couplets Bloomfield had used in *The Farmer's Boy*
but Sir Ambrose's announcement of the terms and conditions of the poems-for-rent
contest is in faster tetrameter as used by Scott, Byron, and other contemporaries.
Sir Ambrose addresses those who live at Oakly manor not as tenants but as "neigh-
bours" and tells them:

> Let not a thought of winter's rent
> Destroy one evening's merriment;
> I ask not gold, but tribute found
> Abundant on Parnassian ground.

Participants should choose their own themes, but although Sir Ambrose is fond of
fairies – a shepherd is to oblige and tell of a vision of fairies – he specifically asks
them not to choose the Gothic:

> surely fancy need not brood
> O'er midnight darkness, crimes, and blood,
> In magic cave or monk's retreat
> Whilst the bright world is at her feet…

Emphasizing that the countryside is tied to the past but not haunted by Gothic
gloom, he concludes:

> Then bring me nature, bring me sense,
> And joy shall be your recompense:
> On Old May-day I hope to see
> All happy:–leave the rest to me.
> A general feast shall cheer us all
> Upon the lawn that fronts the hall,
> With tents for shelter, laurel boughs
> And wreaths of every flower that blows.
> The months are wending fast away;
> Farewell,–remember Old May-day.
>   (*May-Day with the Muses*, 8–9)

[44]   Robert Bloomfield, *May Day with the Muses*, 2nd edition (London: printed for author,
1822), 7. Subsequent references in text, by page number.
[45]   Samuel Johnson, *The Rambler* 82 (December 1750).

Sir Ambrose himself might be able to remember the time before the calendar change in 1752, and is keeping it in the minds of his tenants.

The community eats together with "freedom" and "joy," and then the poetry recitations follow. Among these, "The Forester" stands out as linking medievalism and the present. The Forester recalls his life of freedom and specifically a fallen oak tree that reminds him of "Alfred, a king by Heaven enthroned,/ His age's wonder, England's pride!" The Forester's political stance is independent, or perhaps inconsistent. He has praised the good king Alfred, but the fall of the oak tree reminds him that "A people's wrath can monarchs dash/From bigot throne or purple car," which would seem to justify the overthrow of bad kings. The very next lines mourn the loss of the heirs to the throne Princess Charlotte and her child at her Clermont residence in 1817:

> When Fate's dread bolt in Clermont's bowers
> > Provoked its million tears and sighs,
> A nation wept its fallen flowers,
> > Its blighted hopes, its darling prize ... (42–43)

The implication is that England needs a kind, generous ruler like Sir Ambrose.

As late as 1836, the *Comic Almanack* includes a poem titled "Old May Day" with the subtitle "By a Nonagenarian." The poem begins,

> When I was young and in my prime,
> > Then ev'rything look'd gay;
> And nothing was so merry as
> > The merry FIRST OF MAY ...

In keeping with the illustration by George Cruikshank, which shows dancers around a garlanded maypole and people removing their hats in respect to a man on horseback (Fig. 15), the speaker claims to recall:

> The lovely scene
> > As though I saw it still:–
> The mansion of a noble race
> > Was seated on a hill;
> And smilingly it seem'd to look
> > Upon the plain below,
> Where groups of happy villagers
> > Were sporting to and fro.
> The May-pole in the centre plac'd,
> > All deck'd with garlands gay,
> While lads and lasses danc'd around,
> > And footed it away.

The speaker goes on to reflect:

> Ah! those were times that memory
> > Is happy to retrace,

But chang'd, alas! And sad are those
   Which now supply their place.
An honest, healthy peasantry
   Then shar'd the farmer's board,
Who'd shrink from parish pauper pay,
   As from a thing abhorr'd:
The sons of "Merry England" now
   Are chang'd to Mammon's slaves,
And "peep about to find themselves
   Dishonourable graves."
The "labourer" no longer "reckon'd
   Worthy of his hire,"
No more partakes the farmer's board,
   Nor warms him at his fire–
(Comic Almanack [1836], 52)

At this point the supposed editor of the almanack interrupts, and "nonagenarian" stops "croaking," but the picture of an idealized society, in contrast to the "hard" present, remains. The rural past as represented here has class distinctions – the

MAY.——'Old May Day'

Fig. 15. "Old May Day." By George Cruikshank. *The Comic Almanack*, 1836.

speaker mentions peasants, farmers, a female inn-keeper, and the gentry – yet the "peasants" and farmers live side by side, the farmers proving sufficient support for the workers, and the workers proud to earn their livings. The phrase "shrink from parish pauper's pay" seems to blame those in the present who seek public assistance, yet at the same time "Mammon's slaves" surely refers to the work conditions brought about by the Industrial Revolution. The verse makes substantial use of quotations: the traditional May Day song "Come lasses and lads"; the Bible's reference to the "labourer" being "worthy of his hire";[46] and more unusually, Shakespeare's *Julius Caesar*. Of course, a person who was ninety in 1836 would have been six in 1752, and perhaps even the writer of this poem can only half believe in the innocent "Old May Day" festivities that brought everyone together.

Tennyson's May Queen Poems

Other poets also found ways of invoking the rural past through May Day celebrations. The maypole stands as a ghost of spring at the village "Wake" in Wordsworth's summer poem *The Excursion*:

> Like a mast
> Of gold, the Maypole shines; as if the rays
> Of morning, aided by exhaling dew,
> With gladsome influence could re-animate
> The faded garlands hanging from its sides.[47]

George Darley's *Sylvia, Or The May Queen, A Lyrical Drama* (1827) combines folklore and fantasy in a strange pastiche drawing on Shakespeare's *Midsummer Night's Dream*, pantomime, and fairy tale.[48] *Sylvia* is written as a drama but Darley's preface indicates that he investigated the possibility of writing a stage-play or opera but decided to construct it as a "*dramatic poem*,"[49] even though like the plays by Shakespeare and Beaumont and Fletcher that he so admired, portions are written in prose.

The scene is "Italy, amongst the Apennines," and the period is apparently the first half of the sixteenth century, since Sylvia's father fought and died among the forces of the Chevalier de Bayard (1473–1524), legendary as the knight "without fear and without reproach."[50] The noble youth Romanzo is lost in the mountains, where he

---

[46]   Luke 10.7.

[47]   William Wordsworth, *The Excursion, Being a Portion of the Recluse* (London: Longman, 1814), 57.

[48]   The Irish-born Darley's writings an edition of the plays of Beaumont and Fletcher and two more "Lyrical dramas" with medieval themes, *Thomas à Beckett* and *Ethelstan*.

[49]   George Darley, *Sylvia, Or The May Queen, A Lyrical Drama* (London: John Taylor, 1827), vi. Subsequent references given in text, by page number.

[50]   This is established at Romanzo's first meeting with Sylvia's mother (20). Agatha mentions Aost[a], and Romanzo takes this as a reference to the Battle of the Sesia (1524), in which Bayard died.

hears the heavenly voice of Sylvia;[51] the two immediately fall in love. As in panto-mimes of the period, good and evil forces interfere in human affairs; they are here represented by Morgana, Queen of the Fairies and her attendant elves and fairies; and Ararach, King of the Fiends, and his demons.[52] Complications are caused by Romanzo's servant Andrea, whom the demons turn into a satyr. Andrea serves as a link between Sylvia's fairy-protected glen; the haunt of the demons; and the peasants in a nearby village. As in pantomime, where characters in period costume frequently reference events outside of the time and space of the story, the peasants and Andrea, specifically stated to be the "Merry-Andrew" of this piece (91), mention English fairy tales such as *The Babes in the Wood* and *Red Riding Hood* (95); and topical matters such as the Carbonari. The peasants in the village are planning their May Day celebrations while Romanzo and Sylvia are loitering in a myrtle grove with roses, lilies, and sweet williams, so presumably Sylvia's glen is sufficiently magic to allow June flowers to bloom at the dawn of May. Also magic is the poetic imagination, which creates an English May Day celebration in the Apennines. Already set up is the "Maybush" on the "village-green," festooned with flowers; their songs describe it as both a hawthorn tree and a maypole. The peasants sing to welcome the time:

> When lasses and their lovers meet
> Beneath the early village-thorn,
> And to the sound of tabor sweet
> Bid welcome to the Maying-morn! (79–80)

Yet the peasants are not quite sure of their own traditions. They realize that they have forgotten to choose a May Queen, and first attempt to do so by drawing lots. Under the fiends' spell, however, Andrea brings them a magic wreath that will only fit the true May Queen. Sylvia, Cinderella-like, arrives late to the trial and is deemed May Queen both as the most beautiful and as chosen by destiny as the true recipient of the wreath. Despite her cottage life in the mountains, Sylvia is recognized by all as of a different social class from the peasants, and in keeping with her breeding she is too polite to refuse their honor. Also in the tradition of fairy-tale princesses, the magic wreath causes her to fall into a death-like slumber, but all ends happily. The very long five acts include many songs by fairies and elves, much admired by Darley's contemporaries: ironically enough given the supposed Italian setting, these verses even won the praise of Thomas Keightley in *Fairy Mythology* as authentic examples of British fairy traditions.[53]

---

[51]   The singing mountain maiden was a feature of Darley's well-received short story "Lilian of the Valley," which he published in the *London Magazine* under a pseudonym: in the Preface to *Sylvia* he is therefore claiming authorship of the story.

[52]   References to individual fiends as "Black Prince" (165) and "Hottentot" suggests that they are dark-skinned; Andrea's reference to the fiend Grumiel as a "Hottentot Granny-maid" may be a reference to the South African woman displayed in London as the "Hottentot Venus" some years previously. Since evil beings were often played by actors in blackface on the Romantic-era stage, the use of stage conventions here and elsewhere indicate that *Sylvia* was written for performance.

[53]   Keightley considered that Darley "displays the fairies in greater splendor than they have enjoyed since the days of Shakespeare and Drayton." *Fairy Mythology*, 2:158.

Whether Tennyson knew about May Day from oral tradition or from other writings such as *Sylvia* when he first wrote "The May Queen" around 1830 is uncertain. He could have had access to works such as the *Popular Antiquities* and Joseph Strutt's *Sports and Pastimes of the People of England*; William Hone revised and edited the latter and it was available in multiple editions throughout the nineteenth century. He may have witnessed some May Day celebrations in his boyhood in rural England; or perhaps he combined his memories of both his own experience and other texts. Tennyson's poem "The May Queen" represents the rural rituals associated with May Day from the viewpoint of a participant. The poem, or sequence of three poems representing three moments in a young girl's short life, struck a chord with Victorian readers, even such curmudgeonly ones as John Stuart Mill, who cited it as an example of "simple, genuine pathos";[54] and Thomas Carlyle, who at least according to Tennyson's son Hallam found it "tender and true."[55] Yet perhaps in reaction to the same pathos that Victorians admired in it, "The May Queen" has been largely ignored by modern commentators. Much as I admire Christopher Ricks's work on Tennyson, I would disagree with his characterization of the Alice of Part Two as "being Christianly happy about to die."[56] Instead, I would suggest that Part Two shows Tennyson's awareness of the supposed connection between May Day and fertility rituals, as shaped by memories, personal or from his reading, of May Day celebrations in rural England.

First published in 1832 and an early example of what was later to be known as a dramatic monologue, "The May Queen" opens with a young girl commanding her mother, "You must wake and call me early, call me early, mother dear."[57] In Part One, the first three lines of each stanza are loosely in iambic heptameter, and the last line "For I'm to be Queen o' the May, mother, I'm to be Queen o' the May" stands out both since it is repeated with slight variation throughout, and because of its rhythmic irregularity. Unlike in "Locksley Hall," where the long lines become a rant, in the first part of the poem, they imitate the young speaker's excitement: her words are almost traditional ballad stanzas run together. The speaker, who self-identifies as "little Alice," claims to be recognized as the fairest in "all the land," hence her election as May Queen. The reader learns that she has a younger sister Effie, and an admirer Robin, whom she claims to scorn, noting, "They call me cruel-hearted, but I care not what they say" (1:19) and "They say his heart is breaking, mother – what is that to me?/ There's many a bolder lad 'ill woo me any summer day" (1:22–23).

In Part One Alice is fully confident that "Tomorrow 'ill be the happiest time of all the glad New-year" (1:2; 42); the reference to May as part of the "new year" may suggest that in her part of the world, March is still seen as the beginning of the annual cycle, the year starting on Lady Day, March 25.[58] Alice's only anxiety is that she might not wake up early enough to "gather knots of flowers, and buds and

---

[54] John Stuart Mill, "Tennyson's Poems." *London Review* I (July, 1835); reprinted in *Collected Works of John Stuart Mill* (Toronto: University of Toronto Press, 1981), 1:401–03.

[55] Hallam Tennyson, *Alfred, Lord Tennyson, A Memoir by his Son*, 2: 233.

[56] Christopher Ricks, *Tennyson*, 44.

[57] "The May Queen." First published in 1832; revised and expanded 1842. Quoted by section and line number from *The Poems of Tennyson*, ed. Christopher Ricks, 418–22.

[58] E.G. Richards, *Mapping Time*, 251–56.

garlands gay" (1:11). Part Two, "New-Year's Eve," recalling the past spring in the following winter, moves at a more rhythmic and temperate speed in recalling the traditional rituals of the day:

> Last May we made a crown of flowers: we had a merry day;
> Beneath the hawthorn on the green they made me Queen of May;
> And we danced about the may-pole and in the hazel copse,
> Till Charles's Wain came out above the tall white chimney-tops. (2:9–12)

Tennyson seems to have been aware of the problem with obtaining May-tree blossoms after calendar reform that made May 1 eleven days earlier since he mentions "blackthorn blossom" rather than "hawthorn blossom" and according to Christopher Ricks explained: "The May was so late that there was only blackthorn in May."[59] Moreover, ironically given what is to follow, in the language of flowers, the hawthorn is associated with hope. In *The White Goddess*, Robert Graves, writing not only after Frazer but also after Freud, claims that in the language of trees, the hawthorn is both "the tree of enforced chastity" in ancient goddess worship, in which May 1 would be Beltane; and later associated with the "orgiastic" worship of Flora that gave rise to "the English mediaeval habit of riding out on May Morning to pluck flowering hawthorne boughs and dance around the maypole."[60] This works well for a reading of "The May Queen" – so much so that Tennyson's poem may be a source for the theory, rather than an example of it.

This second section of the poem starts not with a command, but a request:

> If you're waking call me early, call me early, mother dear,
> For I would see the sun rise upon the glad New-year.
> It is the last New-year that I shall ever see,
> Then you may lay me low i' the mould and think no more of me. (2:1–4)

It is winter, with snow on the ground, frost on the window, and snowdrops yet to come, so there is also a shift in the definition of "New-year" from spring to the winter solstice (it would appear to be December 31). The speaker emphasizes that she is dying, but the cause is not given. The traditional reading is that she has consumption – Mill, for example, describes her as "dying of a gradual decay"[61] – and that apparently she was not aware of it in May.[62] It might be possible to imagine a scenario where Alice's behavior has caused her death, but beyond Alice's acknowledgment that she has "been wild and wayward" (2:33), there are few clues as to how this might have come about. Alice would have died faster of typhoid, cholera, or most sorts of illnesses she might have contracted running about the fields or associating with others in the village, and more slowly of a sexually transmitted disease. I do not believe, though, that Alice's behavior and Alice's death should be directly

---

[59] Quoted in *Poems of Tennyson*, 420.

[60] Robert Graves, *The White Goddess* (New York: Creative Age Press, 1948), 145–46.

[61] Mill, *Tennyson*, 403.

[62] Only a few commentators are prepared to discuss what is ailing Alice. John Oates, in *The Teaching of Tennyson* (London: Elliott Stock, 1903), describes the Alice of Part 1 as "obviously a vain and selfish girl" who by Part 2 is "fast wasting away in consumption" (152).

linked. This is not the world of the realist novel, where actions have consequences; the fact that Alice is dying seems to have little to do with her high spirits of the previous May, but rather suggests a world of random chance, where the young and beautiful can be struck down by an unnamed disease.

Alice is acutely conscious of the cycle of the year and imagines herself as being buried "beneath the hawthorn shade" where she had been crowned Queen the previous May. She tells her mother, "I have been wild and wayward, but you'll forgive me now" (2:33), but this almost-confession is the closest Part Two comes to conventional religion. The folk beliefs represented in Part 1 carry through to Part 2. Part One had hinted at spirits when Alice recalls how she had startled Robin: "He thought I was a ghost, mother, for I was all in white,/ And I ran by him without speaking, like a flash of light" (1:17–18). Alice now hopes to be a ghost: "If I can I'll come again, mother, from out my resting-place" (2:35). The future Alice envisages is of her sister Effie being a "better child" to their mother "than I have ever been," and tending to Alice's garden.

"New-Year's Eve," this second part of "The May Queen," mentions neither Alice's admirer Robin nor God. Tennyson himself seems to have had second thoughts about this, since in the 1842 edition of his poems he added a more specifically Christian third part, "Conclusion." The formerly pagan Alice has lingered long enough to see the coming of the violet and lambing season (March) and to hear the words of an old clergyman. He has showed her "all the sin," and yet the sin again is not explained. I fully recognize that in most instances in nineteenth-century literature, women's unspecified sin is sexual transgression, but here I would suggest that if Alice has a sin at all, she shares the sin of others of Tennyson's female figures such as Amy of "Locksley Hall" and Maud, namely pride that rejects true love in search of social status.[63] The poem preceding "The May Queen" in the 1842 collection is "Lady Clara Vere de Vere," who is specifically described as proud. Alice now wishes that Robin should receive a "kind word," and be told "not to fret," distinct from her scorn in Part I and her failure to think of him in Part II. In the 1842 edition, Alice's admirer's name is given as "Robert," not Robin, which critics have failed to explain. In many May Day festivities, however, the May Queen is identified with Maid Marian, who is paired with Robin Hood, and since I am suggesting that Tennyson's 1842 revisions are inspired by what might be described as a "Christian panic," he may have wished to disassociate the poem from Robin and Marian dances – especially since Alice pointedly refuses to dance with her Robin.

Ironically, then, Alice's problem may not be sexual transgression but that she is not sexual enough: her "sin" has caused the failure of fertility and she will not wed Robin and continue the family. The Alice of Part 3 hears not the signs of imminent death of folk-belief, the "dog-howl" and the "death-watch beat" (3:21), but the "angels call" and "music on the wind" (3:23, 32). We are left to believe that Alice will be buried not under the May tree as she requested in Part 2 but in the shadow of the Church, and since "there's One will let me in," she will exchange her earthly body for a heavenly one.

---

[63]   Donald S. Hair makes the point that Alice is "motivated by pride." See *Domestic and Heroic in Tennyson's Poetry* (Toronto: University of Toronto Press, 1981), 80.

Like Bloomfield, Tennyson returned to the theme of May towards the end of his life. In "Locksley Hall Sixty Years After" the speaker, now an eighty-year-old grandfather, asks, "After all the stormy changes shall we find a changeless May?"[64] The drama *The Promise of May*, published in 1886 in the same volume as the Locksley Hall poem, uses May as a synonym for youthful rural innocence. The opening situation is similar to that in *May Day with the Muses*: a farmer is planning a community feast in May to celebrate his eightieth birthday. His daughter Dora sings the song "The Promise of May" seemingly with little awareness of its implications. The first verse shows an innocent rural scene:

> The town lay still in the low sun-light,
> The hen cluckt late by the white farm gate,
> The maid to her dairy came in from the cow,
> The stock-dove coo'd at the fall of night,
> The blossom had opened on every bough;
> > O joy for the promise of May, of May
> > O joy for the promise of May. (55–56)

Yet in the second stanza the hopeful world is disrupted by a cruel Nature:

> But a red fire woke in the heart of the town,
> And a fox from the glen ran away with the hen,
> And a cat to the cream, and a rat to the cheese,
> And the stock-dove coo'd, till a kite dropt down,
> And a salt wind burnt the blossoming trees;
> > O grief for the promise of May, of May,
> > O grief for the promise of May.

Dora herself is unsure of the song, remarking, "I don't know why I sing that song; I don't love it" – but it foreshadows the coming disruption to the community. While Dora's father is attempting to bring the villagers together, he and Dora are unaware that his other daughter Eva is having an affair with an outsider; the narrative makes it clear that they are meeting in her bedroom. This outsider, Philip Edgar, is of the "Squire" class; he is also an atheist who does not value tradition and sees no reason why human relationships should not follow the struggle for existence seen in Nature:

> If my pleasure breed another's pain,
> Well – is not that the course of Nature too,
> From the dim dawn of Being – her main law
> Whereby she grows in beauty – that her flies
> Must massacre each other? (69)

Yet although Philip sometimes provokes the villagers with statements like "The land belongs to the people!" (61) his sham communism will break up community. He

---

[64] Alfred, Lord Tennyson, *Locksley Hall Sixty Years After Etc.* (London: Macmillan, 1886), 22. Subsequent references given in text by page number.

has already lost his status as his father's heir by his addiction to inter-class sex, and he explicitly states that he will not further damage his claims to his uncle's property by marrying a farmer's daughter like Eva. Symbolically, Philip breaks off a branch of her father's apple blossom to give to Eva, and she recognizes that the blossom will now never become fruit. Act One ends with the May Day dance, Eva sitting apart under the apple tree.

Five years later, Philip, under a new name, returns to the village and almost succeeds in seducing Dora; the play ends with Eva dead, Philip prostrate, and no certainty that even Dora will fulfill the promise of May. Whereas tragedy in "The May Queen" seems inexplicable, *The Promise of May* reverts to archetype, replaying the primal fall in which Philip states that he does not believe as the Eve of the rural Paradise is tempted under the apple tree. Dora's admirer Dobson pointed out earlier, "They feyther eddicated his darters to marry gentlefoälk, and see what's coomed on it" (110). Perhaps Tennyson's message is that the primal innocence of rural society, marked by community May Day celebrations, is ultimately no escape from class divisions and contemporary cynicism. Both "The May-Queen" and *The Promise of May* nevertheless emphasize the centrality of festival to traditional ways of life, which we shall see in responses to another form of seasonal celebration, English religious plays of the Middle Ages.

6

Summer Festivals: Religion in Performance

Going to Oberammergau

O<small>N</small> M<small>AY</small> 17, 1875 *The Times* published a notice headed "MEDIAEVALISM VULGARIZED." In its entirety the paragraph reads:

> A correspondent informs us that Oberammergau Passion Play, which has hitherto been confined to the few persons who once in ten years have been able to secure places, is now brought within the reach of the million. Schneider, who takes the principal *rôle*, and a number of the other actors have for the first time resolved to star the Provinces, and after performing in Bavaria and Austria, they have repaired to Breslau, where they are drawing crowded houses, and whence they will traverse northern Germany. Our correspondent very properly concludes: – "It is to be feared that the play will thus lose much of its quaintness." (*Times*, May 17, 1875, 13)

The Oberammergau Passion Plays have a claimed origin not in the Middle Ages but in 1633, when the villagers are said to have vowed to perform them every ten years in thanksgiving for their preservation from the plague. The only religious play still to be permitted in the region, it underwent extensive revisions in the early nineteenth century.[1] During a revival in interest in English mystery plays, Britons saw in the Oberammergau plays a relic of their own lost summer plays of the Middle Ages. The words "vulgarized" and "quaintness" in this paragraph suggest that the unnamed "correspondent" – probably *The Times*'s authority on the plays Malcolm MacColl – follows the scholars of the English mystery plays in conceding that the plays were conceived and performed by ordinary people as "folk" performances, but that only the elite can truly appreciate them.

By the 1870s Britons were well informed about the Oberammergau passion plays, but this was not the case in 1841, when an article in the *Christian Teacher* described the writer's trek to see the plays and what he or she witnessed there. The title is pointedly medievalist: "On the Holy Plays or Mysteries of the Middle Ages, with an account of a Sacred Drama which was performed in the year 1840

---

[1]   According to Malcolm MacColl, permission to perform the play was nearly rescinded in 1810. Malcolm MacColl, *The Ober-Ammergau Passion Play*, new edition (London: Rivington, 1880), 25.

at Oberammergau in Upper Bavaria." The article begins with an overview of the history of European drama and credits the Roman Catholic church with preserving some "learning" when "the genius of Italy" was "obscured by barbarian ignorance and oppression."[2] The writer, however, does not entirely endorse the content of such plays, which often included "frivolity and gross obscenities." He or she is aware of the "Chester Mysteries" and apparently decided to visit Oberammergau on July 26, 1840 to see the form of drama with typological scriptural exposition that Protestants, and indeed most Roman Catholic communities, had long "discarded" (155). This was the second time that the play was performed in a theatre, rather than the churchyard. The writer and friends traveled to the village with some of the "better classes" and traditionally attired "peasants," around six thousand in all, and was generally impressed by the performance both of the Passion scenes and of the *tableaux* representing "types" of the story from the Old Testament, explained by a chorus of singers. He or she notes that many of those present were moved to "grief" by the play.

A decade later, Richard Raby, an Englishman living in Munich,[3] provided a full description of the plays in the Roman Catholic periodical *The Rambler*. Even by the late 1840s, when the medieval style was only just becoming fashionable, *The Rambler* was frequently using the word "mediaeval" and featuring articles supporting the kind of historical continuity between pre- and post-Reformation England that Newman had envisaged but did not entirely succeed in demonstrating. Raby was possibly also the author of a study of the "Miracle-Plays of the Middle Ages," pointing out both that they were a form of festival found in multiple Catholic nations, and that they confirmed medieval knowledge of the Bible. The author invites readers "in imagination" to "transport" themselves back in time to sit "among the vast crowd of spectators, all inspired by one intense feeling of faith in what they are assembled to see."[4] For the writer medieval drama embodies a community uniting faith and everyday life. The "broad comedy" in some of the plays is characterized as for the most part "harmless and absurd" (332) and the "revival of learning" and the turn towards morality plays is blamed for the "stronger admixture than ever of comic humour" (406).

"Miracle-Plays of the Middle Ages" provides context for Raby's detailed description of the Oberammergau play as he saw it in September, 1850. The experience causes him to lament the loss of community caused by the Reformation:

> I carried away from it a deeper conviction than ever of the unspeakable injury inflicted on the public life of nations by the Reformation, especially in the blighting in the bud

[2]   "On the Holy Plays or Mysteries of the Middle Ages, with an account of a Sacred Drama which was performed in the year 1840 at Oberammergau in Upper Bavaria." *Christian Teacher* 3 (1841), 151. In the early Victorian period, British scholars of the German language were often women, and quite possibly the unidentified author of this paper was female.

[3]   Richard Raby Jr (1816–81) was a member of a Roman Catholic family from Leicestershire who worked in Munich as an English language tutor and historical writer; given that the "Miracle-Plays" and the account of Oberammergau are presented in series, he may have been the author of both.

[4]   "The Miracle-Plays of the Middle Ages." *The Rambler* n.s. 4 (1855), 329. Subsequent page numbers given in text.

the Christian drama of the middle ages, and in substituting in its place the noxious and semi-heathen drama of the present day.[5]

Raby thus disrupts the narrative of progress by suggesting that the past was better, both artistically and morally, than the present.

Although Protestant Britons might have disagreed with Raby, even they found something to admire at Oberammergau. Anna Mary Howitt, daughter of William and Mary Howitt, provided another expansive English-language account of the 1850 performances, although her focus is more on spectacle than religion. According to Howitt, when she was an art student in Munich, she saw the play advertised and exclaimed, "a miracle-play now-a-days!"[6] A German mentor informed her of the origin of the plays and promised that "it would be difficult to meet with a more striking picture of a past age and mode of thought," so she and her friend undertook the slow but scenic fifty-mile omnibus-journey to "Ammergau." In 1850 Oberammergau was apparently still not an international tourist destination, since Howitt remarks that the two Englishwomen "in our Regent Street dresses, and with our Protestant hearts, seemed singularly out of place in a crowd of simple peasants on their way to a miracle-play" (1:54).[7] Using a letter of introduction from their mentor, they met the woodcarver Tobias Flunger who played Christ, and this encounter seems to have allayed her Protestant reservations about depicting Christ onstage. Howitt appreciated the drama's "earnest solemnity and simplicity." The description of the play is very similar to that in the *Christian Teacher* ten years earlier. Howitt, however, felt that the tableaux typologically connecting the Old Testament stories with the narrative of the Passion were "singularly inferior to the rest of the spectacle" and found the crucifixion scenes too gruesome (1:59–60).

A *Times* article of 1878 recalls that even in 1860 a traveler would have had to be in the right place at the right time to have learned of "the strange survival of middle-age custom to be witnessed on any Sunday during the summer in the obscure village of Oberammergau" (*Times*, October 28, 1878, 9). Such a visitor "would have had little difficulty in fancying himself suddenly transported into the very centre of the middle ages." Howitt's account makes clear that in 1850 the plays were well known in Munich, but by a generation later they were attracting an international clientele. Traveling had become easier and more accessible to the less wealthy. By 1870 British visitors could make the first half of the journey from Munich by train, and buy guidebooks describing the plays and how to find accommodation.

One of these guides, Henry Blackburn's *Art in the Mountains: The Story of the Passion Play* is unusual in claiming that the Oberammergau plays differ from medieval English drama:

[5] "The Mystery of the Passion at Ober-Ammergau." *The Rambler* 5 (1855), 133. *The Rambler* identifies the author as "Mr. Raby." Some of this material had also appeared in *The Rambler* (old series) in 1851. Raby later incorporated some of his description of Oberammergau into his reader for students of the English language.

[6] Anna Mary Howitt, *An Art-Student in Munich*. 2 vols (London: Longman, 1853), 1:45. Many of the chapters are based on earlier journal articles, including "The Miracle-Play at Ober-Ammergau." Subsequent references given in text, by volume and page number.

[7] The Howitts were at least nominally Quakers; they later became interested in spiritualism and Anna and her mother probably died Roman Catholics.

> Those who are familiar with the records of the religious plays of the middle ages, and who remember that in our own cathedrals of Chester and Coventry, "Mystery Plays" and "Moralities" of the coarsest and most irreverent kind were continually exhibited with the sanction of the Church, may not be disposed to listen with favour to this narrative.

> But the *Passionspiel* at Oberammergau, in 1870, is as different from the miracle play called the "Harrowing of Hell," performed in England in the reign of Edward II., as the noblest tragedy is from the commonest farce ...[8]

Blackburn nevertheless sees in the performers survivors of the simple peasantry of the rural past, apparently unaware that his own book is contributing to the commercialization of Oberammergau. He laments that 1870 may be "the culminating point of excellence at Oberammergau," since "the performers still retain their simplicity of character" that will disappear as "the sons and daughters of these peasants are being educated in cities, and will bring back with them too much knowledge of the world" (146).

Most British spectators, however, seem to have been more swayed by the Anglican clergyman Malcolm MacColl's insistence that the Oberammergau plays represent a survival of the kind of mysteries seen in England in the Middle Ages. In the introduction to the 1880 edition of his collected accounts of the 1870 plays, MacColl admits his ambivalence about publicizing the festival, noting his "fear lest I might be helping thereby to vulgarize and profane the most striking and solemn relic left to us of the religious drama of the Middle Ages."[9] The Middle Ages is clearly important to *The Times*'s correspondent as he travels past medieval monasteries on his way to a Whitsuntide performance, even remarking a "tall May-pole" outside the monastery of Ettal. Having obtained the very best seats, MacColl mentions enjoying almost everything about the performance. He is less sure about the scenes after the Crucifixion, but reminds his readers that "this striking religious drama is intended for the edification of a simple people who have warm hearts and lively imaginations, but are not much given to abstract reasoning." Yet although MacColl initially distinguishes his own response from that of the "simple people," he himself finally shares their emotions: he has "never seen so affecting a spectacle, or one more calculated to bring out the best and purest feelings of the heart" (75–77).

By the time of MacColl's travels to Oberammergau but also back to the Middle Ages, medievalism itself had become fashionable. Such was the interest in this supposed relic of medieval times that touring companies performed the plays in other European cities. The Royal Aquarium in London announced performances of the "Oberammergau Passion Plays" in October 1878. Known for the performances of such artists as Zazel, a tightrope-walker who was shot out of a cannon twice daily, the Aquarium described the play as "a monster mystery, the last of its kind

---

[8]   Henry Blackburn, *Art in the Mountains: The Story of the Passion Play* (London: Sampson Low, Son, and Marston, 1870), 144–5. He records that the 1870 season was cut short by the Franco-Prussian War.

[9]   Malcolm MacColl, *The Ober-Ammergau Passion Play*, v. The book is based on articles originally appearing in *The Times*.

in Europe."[10] *The Times* received a number of letters protesting the performance. Blomfield Jackson, who taught at King's College, London, thought the performance would "give a great shock to English religious sentiments." He continues,

> Of at least doubtful propriety on its own Arcadian stage their performance could only be reconciled with reverence and decency by a remoteness of place which was almost equivalent to a remoteness of time, and gave the exhibition a quasi-archaeological interest, by the unsophisticated earnestness of piety of the performers, by the association of the spectacle less with amusement than with worship. (*Times*, October 19, 1879)

Jackson scornfully wondered how the Passion story would be fitted around the current sensational acts for which the Aquarium was known. The Roman Catholic Cardinal of Westminster (where the Aquarium was located) also voiced his objections, but the performances were only canceled when the theatre owner discovered that the actors were not, as he claimed to have been told, the original performers from Oberammergau, a fact confirmed by the town's Burgomeister.

The only opportunity to see the plays, then, was to make the once-a-decade visit to Oberammergau. All British accounts of the Oberammergau plays remark on the crowds of people from comparatively nearby in attendance, and their emotional involvement in the drama. Moreover, almost all speculate that English scripture plays of the Middle Ages must have had a similar impact on their communities: the author of the *Rambler* articles on "Miracle Plays," for example, claims that such dramas were "acted regularly in every town and village in England."[11] I am using the term "scripture play" even though some of the segments were based on apocryphal writings because other terminology was then, as now, in dispute.[12] Unlike the Oberammergau play, that focused on Christ's Passion and other Bible stories connected typologically, the English sequences or cycles of which we have knowledge spanned human history from Creation to the Last Judgment. Although many English towns and villages still had fairs, and in fewer and fewer places mumming survived at Christmas, they had lost most of the celebrations associated with summer, such as midsummer watches and these community performances. What nineteenth-century Britons knew about these plays, which was even less than the scant evidence now available to scholars, inspired in them a sense of difference from their medieval forebears. Some interpreted this difference as progress: modern-day Britons had a more civilized degree of modesty and piety. Yet others saw in the production of such dramas a festive community whose celebration of summer was now lost.

---

[10]   Advertisement in *The Times*, October 19, 1878. The Aquarium featured spectacle on a large scale. At the same time, the Aquarium Theatre was featuring a dramatized version of *Uncle Tom's Cabin* with one hundred "genuine freed slaves" as singers.

[11]   "The Miracle-Plays of the Middle Ages," 330.

[12]   Some, like the *Rambler* author, liked the term "miracle plays"; others, like Toulmin Smith and Hone, liked the term "mystery," although opinions differed on what "mystery" meant.

Mysteries Described

Quoting at length the *Proclamacio* announcing the York Plays, which urges the citizens to keep the peace, and directs the players to be ready at 4.30am, Lucy Toulmin Smith remarks: "The picture of these good folks up at half-past four on a summer morning ready to act their parts one after another reminds us of Ober-Ammergau, in strong contrast to the habits of the modern stage."[13] Whereas theatre in Smith's time usually took place in the evening, the scripture play cycles required all-day attendance by enthusiastic actors and spectators on long summer days. In England, these "pageants" were particularly associated with Whitsun and Corpus Christi in the optimistic belief that May or June was a good time of year for outdoor performance. English play cycles based on scripture and spanning the history of the world from Creation to Doomsday were performed as early as the thirteenth century, when the pope introduced the feast of Corpus Christi; they did not disappear at the Reformation but seem to have faded away by the late 1500s. Smith is aware that the Oberammergau performances began in 1633 but alludes to them later as a "relic" of earlier cycles in her survey of "religious drama" in other nations (*York Plays*, xlv).

When Smith published her edition of the York Plays in 1885, all the surviving English cycles of scripture plays were finally in print.[14] James Heywood Markland had printed two plays from the Chester cycle for the Roxburghe Club in 1818, and Thomas Wright published the complete cycle for the Shakespeare Society in the 1840s. Thomas Sharp's edition of two plays from the Coventry Guilds' cycle, published in 1818 and in 1825 expanded to include a "Dissertation on the Pageants, or Dramatic Mysteries, Anciently Performed at Coventry," is particularly important since the manuscript copy of one of the plays was later destroyed in a fire. Even though Sharp pointed out that his researches made it unlikely that the cycle then known as the *Ludus Coventriae* (now generally known as the N-Town Plays) was associated with Coventry, William Hone and others called it the Coventry Mysteries since a note on the manuscript identified them as such.[15] James Orchard Halliwell published it for the Shakespeare Society under the title *Ludus Coventriae: A Collection of Mysteries Formerly Represented at Coventry on the Feast of Corpus Christi* in 1841. The Surtees Society published what is now known as the Towneley cycle in the 1830s. My concern here, though, is less with the plays themselves than with the discussion of what their significance was for the idea of medieval communities.

The earliest antiquaries to draw attention to the medieval scripture plays noted that they were performed in summer, either at Whitsun, the seventh Sunday after Easter, or Pentecost, when the disciples received the Holy Spirit; or Corpus Christi,

---

[13]   Lucy Toulmin Smith, ed., *York Plays: The Plays performed by the Crafts or Mysteries of York on the Day of Corpus Christi in the 14th, 15th, and 16th Centuries* (Oxford: Clarendon Press, 1885), xxxiv.

[14]   E.K. Chambers provides a bibliographical overview of the editing of the plays in *The Medieval Stage*, 2:106–07.

[15]   Thomas Sharp, *A Dissertation on the Pageants or Dramatic Mysteries anciently performed at Coventry* (Coventry: Merridew, 1825), 5–6. As Sharp remarks, the identification of the collection of plays that Hone discusses with Coventry is due to an early librarian's manuscript note and a description of the plays by Dugdale; see also *Ludus Coventriae*, ed. J.O. Halliwell (London: Shakespeare Society, 1841), vi–x.

the Thursday after Trinity Sunday, the eighth Sunday after Easter. While post-Reformation Anglicans continued to recognize Whitsun as a Christian festival, Corpus Christi was more specifically a celebration in Roman Catholic countries, having been instituted by the pope in the thirteenth century to commemorate the "real presence" of Christ in the elements of the Mass. Theologically, then, both Whitsun and Corpus Christi acknowledge the continued presence of Christ and thus would seem suitable occasions to recall Christ's role in the history of the world, even though many of the episodes relate to Christ's birth and death, or Christmas and Easter. Practically, summer is a better time for outdoor plays for both actors and audience; it may still rain in an English summer, but it is unlikely to be unbearably cold. One of the first antiquarians to discuss the plays, Joseph Strutt in his *Þorða Anzel-cynnan, or, A compleat view of the manners, customs, arms, habits, &c. of the inhabitants of England* (1775–76), does not seem to have picked up on the possibility that the plays were acted in the open air, but quotes at length the proclamation to the Chester plays, demonstrating both that the plays were performed at Whitsun and that the different sections were the responsibility of the guilds.[16]

Thomas Warton was another early contributor to knowledge of medieval scripture plays: his *History of English Poetry*, first published in the 1770s but frequently reprinted, provides one of the earliest critical discussions of their contents. Warton's account of what he calls "the first of our dramatic exhibitions"[17] is important because he considers the role of community. Warton contradicts himself several times in responding to the works. He distinguishes between "moralities," which indicated "dawnings of the dramatic art," and (using both of the standard nomenclatures of the time) "miracle-plays, or MYSTERIES." These, he asserts, "were totally destitute of invention or plan; they tamely represented stories according to the letter of scripture, or the respective legend." Yet immediately after claiming the plays as literal envisionings of scripture, he mentions *The Massacre of the Holy Innocents* in the Digby manuscript in the Bodleian Library, which imagines how the mothers of the children, and the soldiers sent to kill them, might feel. Warton elaborates:

> It is in an enlightened age only that subjects of scripture history would be supported with proper dignity. But then an enlightened age would not have chosen such subjects for theatrical exhibition. It is certain that our ancestors intended no sort of impiety by these monstrous and unnatural mixtures. Neither the writers nor the spectators saw the impropriety, nor paid separate attention to the comic and serious part of these motley scenes; at last they were persuaded that the solemnity of the subject covered or excused all incongruities.

On the continuing theme of dramatic invention, he adds, "In these Mysteries I have sometimes seen gross and open obscenities." He cites the Chester Plays in which "Adam and Eve are both exhibited on the stage naked, and conversing about their nakedness," then tries to imagine how the community would have received such a scene:

---

[16]   Joseph Strutt, *Þorða Anzel-cynnan, or, A compleat view of the manners, customs, arms, habits, &c. of the inhabitants of England* (London, 1775–76), 3:130–42.
[17]   Thomas Warton, *The History of English Poetry*, 2:73. Subsequent references in text.

This extraordinary spectacle was beheld by a numerous assembly of both sexes with great composure: they had the authority of scripture for such a representation, and they gave matters just as they found them in the third chapter of Genesis. It would have been absolute heresy to have departed from the sacred text in personating the primitive appearance of our first parents, whom the spectators so nearly resembled in simplicity; and if this had not been the case, the dramatists were ignorant what to reject and what to retain. (Warton 2:75–78)

If the medieval audience for the play "so nearly resembled" the unfallen Adam and Eve in their "simplicity," Warton, perhaps subconsciously, is envisioning the medieval community as Edenic. Without the knowledge of good and evil, they can accept the spiritual truths in the dramas and look at nakedness without lust.

Warton's literal reading of the Chester stage direction presents a number of problems. Even beyond the possible chilliness of an English summer, if all the actors were male, as is generally believed, a naked Adam and Eve would not add to the verisimilitude of the performance. E.K. Chambers suggests, on the basis of directions for other plays, that the actors would have worn "fleshings."[18] The common belief, though, that Warton was right probably contributed to the belief that in an age of more "propriety," the plays were unperformable.

Even though he does not dwell on Adam and Eve, James Heywood Markland expressed similar sentiments in the two Chester plays that he edited for the Roxburghe Club in 1818. Markland selected to print *Noah's Flood* and *The Massacre of the Innocents*, probably because based on his reading of other plays he detected in them what he believed to be a uniquely English tradition of characterizing Noah's wife and the mothers of the slaughtered children. The Roxburghe Club restricted its publications to its few dozen gentleman members, and knowing that his edition was to be read only by the (supposedly) worldly-wise Markland printed such words as "shyte" and "arse" in full. He nevertheless felt some historical context was necessary, and reminded his readers that the Banes (Proclamation) "proves that the gratification of the populace was one of the chief motives for acting these plays, and that this end would not have been obtained had not the somber character of the plots been relieved by a species of buffoonery adapted to their taste."[19] Twice further he justifies the content by appealing to a sense of the Middle Ages: "We must be cautious not to judge of the simplicity of those times by the sensitive delicacy of our own. They at least conveyed *some* scriptural knowledge, and diverted the mind from an exclusive devotion to war and warlike sports." Conceding that "they may appear offensive to the taste of the present age," the plays remain "relics of the literature and

[18] E.K. Chambers, *The Medieval Stage*, 2:142–43: Adam and Eve's nakedness "is chiefly based on a too literal interpretation of the stage directions of the Chester plays. There is a fine *a priori* improbability about it, and as a matter of fact there can be very little doubt that the parts were played, as they would have been on any other stage in any other period of the world's history, except possibly at the Roman *Floralia* [fn. Cf. vol. i, p. 5] in fleshings. Jordan is quite explicit. Adam and Eve are to be 'aparelet in whytt lether,' and although Jordan's play is a late one, I think it may be taken for granted that white leather was sufficient to meet the exigencies even of medieval realism."

[19] [James Heywood Markland], *Chester Mysteries: De Deluvio Noe, De Occisione Innocentium* (London: Roxburghe Club, printed Bensley, 1818), ix.

amusements of our ancestors; and when we regard the spirit in which they were written, and the reverence with which they were viewed, suspicion of *intentional* profaneness or indelicacy cannot attach to the pen from which they proceeded" (*Chester Mysteries*, xv–xvi).

John Payne Collier provided another overview in his *History of English Dramatic Poetry* (1831). He prefers the term "Miracle Plays," and asserts that they "are the source and foundation of our national drama."[20] Collier notes that earlier references suggest that "Miracle-plays" were often performed in churches, but is aware that in "populous districts" the guilds were responsible for performances. To understand these plays, Collier urges his readers, "we must of course carry our minds back to the period when they were written or represented: we shall then find, that much that now seems absurd, ludicrous, or profane, was then pious, awful, and impressive" (2:136). Again, the editor's view is conflicted. Having suggested that the medieval mind was different, he finds in the Shepherds' plays in both the Chester and the Towneley cycles "the total abandonment of all dramatic propriety" (2:188). Yet he quotes what is now known as the *Second Shepherds' Play* at length, calling it "the most singular piece in the collection" (2:180).

William Marriott also addresses the question of propriety in his 1838 overview of what was known about medieval Bible plays that prefixes his edition of ten selected plays. Noting that "according to our ideas," his readers might find the onstage representation of God "highly improper and even irreverent," he maintains that as "one of the designs of the Miracle-pays was to instruct the people in the Scriptures, this character was partly necessary; at least our forefathers could have seen no great impropriety in it, or they would not have admitted it in these performances to the extent they did."[21] He nevertheless concedes that the "feeling of propriety that our ancestors entertained was certainly rather of a lax kind," and repeats (in untranslated Latin, presumably to avoid shock to those who did not understand it) Warton's contention that the actors playing Adam and Eve were literally naked onstage.

James Orchard Halliwell (later Halliwell-Phillips) and Thomas Wright edited the *Ludus Coventriae* and Chester cycles for the Shakespeare Society, the plays being valued, Halliwell notes, as "some of the most curious and valuable relics of bygone times; not merely as important records of our early stage, but also as illustrating, in a very interesting manner, the customs, language, and manners of the period to which they belong" (Halliwell, v). He makes little comment on the question of propriety, although he does remark that quite possibly actors were naked in the "Coventry" Adam and Eve pageant as in the Chester cycle. Thomas Wright's edition of the Chester Plays addresses decency in more detail, but uses it to stress difference: "The gross language frequently put into the mouths of the women give us but a mean opinion

---

[20] John Payne Collier, *History of Dramatic Poetry*, 2 vols (London: John Murray, 1831), 2:123. Subsequent references given as volume and page number.
[21] William Marriott, *A Collection of English Miracle-plays or Mysteries* (Basel: Schweigerhauser and Co., 1838), lvii.

of the delicacy of manners among the middle and lower classes in the fourteenth and fifteenth centuries."[22]

Medieval scripture plays are thus subject to multiple criticisms: they impiously represent Biblical figures, including God; they add apocryphal stories that are not in the Bible as British people know it; and they lack "propriety" in their public profanity and nudity. What they do have, however, is a sense of community, a point mentioned at least in passing by all the antiquarians but especially emphasized by William Hone, one of the earliest writers to attempt to present the plays to the kind of people who might have formed their original audience.

Hone and Community

When he unsuccessfully prosecuted William Hone for blasphemy in December 1817, Lord Chief Justice Ellenborough happened to comment that before Martin Luther, that is, in the Roman Catholic Middle Ages, "the habits of those times were totally different; the first scenic performances were mysteries or representations of incidents in Sacred Writ."[23] A few years later, Hone claimed this remark as the inspiration for his research into medieval mystery plays and other popular practices of the Middle Ages, which he published in 1823 as *Ancient Mysteries Described*. The subtitle adds:

> especially the English Miracle Plays Founded on Apocryphal New Testament Story, Extant among the Unpublished Manuscripts in the British Museum; including Notices of Ecclesiastical Shows, the Festivals of Fools and Asses – The English Boy Bishop, the Descent into Hell – The Lord Mayor's Show – The Guildhall Giants – Christmas Carols, &c.

Although the topics covered in *Ancient Mysteries Described* do not quite present a total vision of the Middle Ages, they do suggest that Hone's conception of England's medieval past took a form that one would hardly expect to find in the thinking of a man who started and ended his life as an evangelical Protestant and who spent most of the time in between in an antagonistic relationship with governmental structures. As in his discussion of Christmas, for Hone, the English Middle Ages represent a time of freedom of expression, especially in the form of parodic speeches and action initiated by the populace. Far from an age filled with decorous respect for hierarchy, as in the vision of many nineteenth-century British medievalists, the Middle Ages become a means of challenging the structures of oppression and suggesting that the story of the nation – and even of divine revelation – is not monolithic but multi-voiced.

William Hone is best remembered for printing Regency-era satires with illustrations, such as *The Political House that Jack Built*. These works passed through dozens

---

[22] Thomas Wright, ed., *The Chester Plays: A Collection of Mysteries founded upon Scriptural Subjects and formerly represented by the Trades of Chester at Whitsuntide* (London: Shakespeare Society, 1843, 1847), 1:xiii.

[23] *The Three Trials of William Hone*, ed. William Tegg (London: William Tegg, 1876), 133–34. See also *The Times* (December 20, 1817), 3.

of editions and were deliberately marketed at a price that working readers such as journalists, tradespeople, and educators were able to afford. While these pamphlets refer to directly contemporary events, such as the public quarrels between George IV and his wife Caroline of Brunswick and the government's attempts to suppress popular opposition to its policies, they hint that Hone has an idealized sense of the Middle Ages. For example, they characterize Magna Carta, for Hone the statement of English political rights, as "the WEALTH that lay in the house that Jack built."[24] In 1817, Hone published *The Late John Wilkes's Catechism of a Ministerial Member, The Political Litany Diligently Revised*, and *The Sinecurist's Creed*, each, as the titles suggest, patterned after parts of the Anglican Book of Common Prayer (*Three Trials*, 8). As a result, the government prosecuted Hone for blasphemy against the Anglican faith. Hone was tried for each publication on three successive days in December 1817; in each case he acted as his own counsel. Citing numerous historical precedents, Hone argued that he was writing parody for political purposes, and that far from attacking religion, he was deeply interested in religious history. Central to his argument was that religious language had always been used in parody, and that he was only being prosecuted because the government recognized itself as the target of the critique. For three days in a row, Hone spoke for hours, and each time at the end of the day, the jury found him not guilty.

Hone's trials are a landmark moment for political parody as a form of free speech, but they also seem to have been a turning point in Hone's self-conception. Although he continued to publish his cartoon collaborations with Cruikshank, Hone clearly enjoyed the kind of antiquarian research that he had used to support his case, and his last publications are a systematic attempt to recover the everyday world, and especially the self-organized celebratory pursuits of ordinary English people that parodied hierarchy. At the same time, Hone was planning a history of parody to secure its place as an ancient form for freedom of expression. Hone deserves credit not only as an important parodist, but also as a significant medievalist, one with an acute sense of seasonal celebration. In *The Rise and Fall of Merry England*, Ronald Hutton states that "Nobody has hitherto attempted to provide a systematic portrait of English seasonal rituals and pastimes in the half-century before the Reformation." With due respect to Hutton, I would suggest that Hone was attempting such a study, albeit with limited resources, and that he saw the re-creation of English recreation in *Ancient Mysteries Described* as a profoundly political act.[25]

Hone was able to do this in a way that his contemporaries could not for a number of reasons. The first was that he frankly acknowledged that medieval England drew its inspiration from religion. The post-Reformation myth of the late Middle Ages was that they were a time of religious superstition and corruption, and that ordinary English people were therefore eager to put Roman Catholicism behind them and become good Anglicans. Hone's research, in contrast, suggested that as late as

---

[24] William Hone, *The Political House that Jack Built* (London: William Hone, 1819), no page numbers.

[25] Ronald Hutton, *The Rise and Fall of Merry England*, 5. Hone's research has gone largely unrecognized by scholars of medieval theatre despite the fact that Hone was apparently the first to notice that the N-Town Plays are derived from the Apocryphal New Testament. E.K. Chambers was at least aware of Hone's work.

Tudor times, English townspeople used the religious year as the inspiration for their public celebrations, including the Corpus Christi play cycles, Christmas carols and rituals, the Feast of the Ass and Boy Bishop, and the Lord Mayor's Show in the City of London, which was originally associated with the Feast of St Simon and St Jude.

The second advantage Hone had over most other antiquarians of his time was that he was willing and able to reach a wider readership. Hone knew the work of Thomas Hearne, Thomas Warton, and particularly Joseph Strutt, whose histories of English sports and pastimes Hone was later to reprint in cheaper editions. By the standards of modern scholarship, it may appear that Hone quotes too extensively from the works of others. Very little of the work of other researchers from whom he prints excerpts, however, would have been affordable to Hone's readers. For example, at this time, the period of the so-called "Bibliomania," works by the early eighteenth-century antiquarian Thomas Hearne were in huge demand and commanded enormous prices, so Hone's use of Hearne's work made it available to a part of the reading public that could never have afforded access to it otherwise. Similarly, Hone mentions a "Coventry gentleman" – he means Thomas Sharp – who transcribed The Pageant of the Shearmen and Taylors from a manuscript owned by the city, and had a dozen copies printed for his friends around 1817. Hone obtained access to a copy, and was able to reprint a specimen for a far wider audience. Although Sharp later published his transcriptions of this and various related documents in a folio version, even this edition would have been beyond the reach of most of Hone's readers, so his publication of an excerpt broadened its circulation considerably.

Despite his extensive use of earlier printed works, Hone also made an original contribution to the recovery of scripture plays. First, he produced a low-cost edition of multiple plays from the so-called *Ludus Coventriae* and demonstrated their indebtedness to the apocryphal gospels. As far as I can determine, he was the first to make this point, even though in his 1841 edition of the complete play cycle J.O. Halliwell gives him no credit for it.[26] This alone was daring from a Protestant since the stories expand on the Biblical role of Mary. Hone read the plays as a prominent form of cultural expression at a time when few people knew anything about them. He may not have known the theory that the word "Mystery" derived from *misterium*, or craft, but he would probably have liked that idea, since his emphasis is on the community involvement of working people. In the 1820s Hone was among the few who took the plays seriously, as much as anything was serious to Hone.

The very fact that Hone assumed that his readers might care about the Middle Ages is also significant. It is likely that Lord Ellenborough's remark about the Mystery Plays was inspired by an offshoot of the Bibliomania, the Roxburghe Club, and Markland's edition of two Chester Plays. (Ellenborough, who died in 1818, was not a member of the Roxburghe Club, but he was in the Society of Antiquaries.) The Roxburghe Club's wealthy bibliophiles were a very different group from Hone's readers, who were literate but in general far from rich. Tradespeople and those working in modestly remunerated positions such as teachers and clerks had until this time tended to buy into the government stance that loyalty to the state church

---

[26]   Halliwell does mention Hone, but not in relation to the parallels with apocryphal writings.

was a civic duty, but by the 1820s Roman Catholicism no longer seemed a threat to the English nation, and Hone's work uncovering both religious traditions outside of orthodoxy and medieval civic practices centering on religion apparently did not prompt the "Church and King" indignation in his readers that, for example, Joseph Priestley's work had stirred up a generation earlier. Many readers were ready for a more tolerant view of the Middle Ages, and Hone supplied it.

Hone depicts the "Mystery Plays" as well-organized public performances, perhaps commissioned by clerics but, at least in the major cities, produced and acted by the trade guilds. Although it may appear that he anticipates Mikhail Bakhtin's theories of carnival, Hone does not draw as a clear a distinction between officially sanctioned forms of expression and festival expression. Bakhtin argues that "laughter in the Middle Ages remained outside all official spheres of ideology and outside all official strict forms of social relations. Laughter was eliminated from religious cult, from feudal and state ceremonials, etiquette, and from all the genres of high speculation."[27] Hone, in contrast, recognizes that the Church and local structures of power sanctioned, or at least, permitted, festival celebration, including parodic versions of scriptures, liturgies, and ceremonial practices. For Hone, then, parody is not simply a freedom that is taken; it is a freedom sanctioned by historic practice. For example, he explains of York:

> Every trade in the city, from the highest to the lowest, was obliged to furnish out a pageant at its own expense on this occasion. The subjects were from the history of the Old and New Testament, and each trade represented some particular part, and spoke suitable verses. Many orders and ordinances, existing in the city's registers, regulate the performance of this religious ceremony. (*Ancient Mysteries*, 210)

Yet the same time that Hone regrets the passing of such civic practices, he also suggests that modern society has progressed past such times. Transposing Warton's idea about Adam and Eve from the Chester cycle to the "Coventry" plays, he observes that "there can be no doubt that Adam and Eve appeared on the stage naked" (220). This is not for Hone, however, a condemnation of the people who produced and enjoyed such plays. He quotes a passage from *Cromek's Remains* observing that:

> The present age rejects as gross and indelicate those free compositions which our ancestors not only countenanced but admired. Yes, in fact, the morals of our forefathers were as strict and perhaps purer and sounder than out own; and we have been taught to look up to them as genuine models of the honest, incorruptible character of Englishmen.[28]

Hence rather than following most of his sources in relief that these crudely simple and superstitious times are past, Hone adopts the medievalist mode of mourning.

[27] Mikhail Bakhtin, *Rabelais and His World*, 73. Bakhtin nevertheless concedes that festivals such as "the feast of fools" had a semiofficial status (74).
[28] Quoted in *Ancient Mysteries Described*, 220. Cromek is actually discussing Scottish vernacular poetry, but he quotes the Biblical phrase "naked and unashamed," used as stage-prompt in the Chester plays. See R.H. Cromek, *Remains of Nithsdale and Galloway Song* (London: Cadell and Davies, 1810), 69–70.

He regrets that so many written records of the past were lost in the zeal of the Ref-ormation, and even waxes lyrical about Clerkenwell, which he and other antiquaries of his time believed to be a site for sacred drama. According to Hone, "a humble tenement occupied by a bird-seller" is now on the site, where:

> the present simplicity of the scene powerfully contrasts with the recollection of its former splendour. The choral chant of the Benedictine nuns accompanying the peal of the deep-toned organ through their cloisters, and the frankincense curling its perfume from priestly censors at the altar, are succeeded by the stunning sounds of numerous quickly plied hammers, and the smith's bellows flashing the fires of Mr. Bound's iron foundry, erected on the unrecognized site of the convent. (*Ancient Mysteries*, 207)

Hone made another important discovery about medieval drama through his work on an earlier publication, which he called the Apocryphal New Testament.[29] In 1820, Hone published a substantial selection of English translations of apocry-phal texts based on information he had learned from the works of Jeremiah Jones, Hone explaining a few years later that his own humble origins had not permitted him to learn Latin.[30] Hone adopted the provocative form of two columns to a page and chapter and verse divisions, so that the style resembled a King James Bible.[31] He justified the presentation of these texts to a wider audience by arguing that it provided insight into ecclesiastical history and especially into the Middle Ages:

> The lover of old literature will find here the obscure but unquestionable origin of several remarkable relations in the Golden Legend, the Lives of the Saints, and simi-lar publications concerning [the life of the Virgin]. Several of the papal pageants for the populace, and the monkish mysteries performed as dramas at Chester, Coventry, Newcastle, and in other parts of England, are almost verbatim representations of the stories. (*Apocryphal New Testament*, ix–x)

In *Ancient Mysteries Described* Hone prints a parallel text to demonstrate that the Coventry Mystery plays are directly derived from the apocryphal Life of the Virgin. Hone states in his Introduction that he himself made the transcription directly from Cotton Vesp. D.VIII, and that he is printing "quite enough to show largely the monkish playwright adopted the curious incidents, and the very language of the spurious Gospels" (*Ancient Mysteries*, 4). Yet at the same time that Hone imagines a single author creating a work, he suggests that the writer in question draws on

---

[29]   William Hone, ed., *The Apocryphal New Testament; Being all the Gospels, Epistles, and other pieces now extant...* (London: William Hone, 1820). Jeremiah Jones had published a translation in the 1720s, but in *Aspersions Answered* Hone cites the 1798 edition, *A New and Full method of Settling the Canonical Authority of the New Testament; To which is subjoined a Vindication of the former Part of St Matthew's Gospel from Mr. Whiston's Charge of Dislocation*, 3 vols (Oxford: Clarendon, 1798). The translations appear in volume 2. Jones's edition also uses columns, but for the purpose of presenting the Latin and English texts in parallel form. Hone's collection includes translations by William Wake.

[30]   William Hone, *Aspersions Answered* (London: William Hone, 1820), 19.

[31]   Disingenuously, Hone claimed in his pamphlet *Aspersions Answered* that he had not originated the division of verses for Apocryphal texts since chapters and verses were used in the Old Testament Apocrypha.

the plural voices of the Middle Ages through finding his source in the Apocrypha. Hence even though Hone states that the "multiform portion" of his work that follows his demonstration of how the "Coventry plays" were drawn from the Gospel of Mary is "skimble-skamble stuff" with "little appearance of cohesion in its parts," in fact, all parts of the work confirm the Middle Ages not as John Ruskin was to imagine it a few years later, as a time of united, collective vision, but as a time where self-organized groups found a variety of forms of celebratory expression, sometimes even drawing their inspiration not from Christian orthodoxy but from alternative scriptures.

Finally, that Hone examines the plays in the context of hierarchical-disrupting festivals such as the Feast of Fools and the Boy Bishop continues his lifelong campaign for free expression and critique of the structures of oppression. It might be argued, of course, that officially endorsed periods of disorder, particularly when that disorder takes the form of a simple reversal of normal hierarchies for a controlled period of time, are not really times of free expression. But as a Londoner, Hone had a model for how he imagined medieval festivals to work. The Lord Mayor's Show was at least contemporary with the Mystery Plays, and has tended to claim even earlier medieval origins in the Mayor of the City of London's obligation set out in the 1215 Magna Carta to pledge allegiance to the Crown in the Royal Courts of Justice. Like the Mystery Plays, the Lord Mayor's Show included organized craft participation; as late as the 1600s pageants were sponsored and performed by craft guilds. And although the Lord Mayor's Show was an officially sanctioned event, it was also a time for carnivalesque public celebration. Although carnival is not a word in Hone's vocabulary, his celebration of community festival resembles Mikhail Bakhtin's reading of medieval carnival as a time, to quote Bakhtin, when "life is subject only to its laws, that is, the laws of its own freedoms" (Bakhtin, 7). Hone's other connection with Bakhtin, of course, is that both are seeing in the Middle Ages the form of multi-vocal expression that their own societies suppress, especially through the literary form most dear to Hone's heart, parody. Hence although Hone never explicitly calls the Middle Ages a time of more freedom than his own, Hone's medieval vision represents both community and self-expression, a time when the texts and forms of established religion were prescriptive, but also provided the inspiration for free thought and collective fun.

7

Fragmented Autumn:
Harvest-Home to Lord Mayor's Show

AUTUMN AND ITS related connotations and activities provided subject-matter for multiple Romantic-era poems: examples would be Keats's celebration of the season in "To Autumn," Percy Shelley's inspiration from wind and dry leaves in "Ode to the West Wind," and Wordsworth's depiction of an observed harvester in "The Solitary Reaper."[1] The last is intriguing because the poem's speaker is unsure how to interpret either what he hears (the reaper's Gaelic song) or what he sees (a lone woman performing what might be expected to be a collective activity of cutting and binding "grain"). A single reaper is an anomaly, since bringing in the harvest required significant labor and was a time when everyone was expected to help: in *The Rural Life of England*, for example, William Howitt describes how everyone, male and female, old and young, was expected to help at harvest time.[2] In the early 1800s the successful completion of the harvest was still in some places followed by a community festival called Harvest-home.[3] During the first half of the nineteenth century, however, the simple and largely secular moral of harvest – that if everyone works together the result will be general prosperity and happiness that will defy the hardships of winter – became complicated by more metaphorical, more religious, and even apocalyptic, connotations. An ancient celebration of continuity served to remind nineteenth-century Britons both of the ending of ancient traditions and of the end of time.

The term "Harvest-home" was known to Shakespeare and Dryden, both of whom employ it in "medieval" contexts. Hotspur references Harvest-home in Shakespeare's *Henry IV Part 1*, set in the late fourteenth century.[4] In the final Act of Dryden's *King Arthur, Or the British Worthy* (1691), in which the Christian British King Arthur

---

[1]   Susan Wolfson and Peter Manning note that Wordsworth saw in manuscript Thomas Wilkinson's recollection of seeing such a scene, later published in *Tours to the British Mountains* (London: Taylor and Hessey, 1824), 12. See the *Longman Anthology of British Literature 2A*, 5th edition (New York: Longman, 2012). 558. Wilkinson later mentions summer hay harvests, but Wordsworth's reaper is cutting and binding grain, which would be an autumn activity.

[2]   Howitt, *The Rural Life of England*, 1:159.

[3]   "Harvest-home" is usually, but not always, hyphenated, and capitalization is inconsistent.

[4]   William Shakespeare, *Henry IV Part 1*, Act 1 Scene 3, line 34.

has just defeated the pagan Saxon Oswald, three "Peasants" sing a Harvest-home song with the chorus, "We'll merrily roar our Harvest-Home."[5] Although it comes directly before Venus – apparently, like Merlin, a friend to Britain – sings the patriotic song "Fairest Isle," the peasants' "Harvest-home" song reveals that they resent paying tithes of their harvest to the "Blockhead" of a parson. Even if purists might argue that these references apply more directly to Shakespeare and Dryden's own times than the Middle Ages, they suggest that audiences of the time would have understood what Harvest-home was. Robert Herrick's "The Hock-Cart, or Harvest-Home" (from *Hesperides*, 1648) invites his readers to see "the cart/Drest up with all the country art." The fun-filled reverence for the harvested grain – "Some bless the cart, some kiss the sheaves" – suggest that this is a traditional practice whose ancient origins the participants have no reason to investigate, especially since the ceremony will be followed by a feast provided by the "lord" with plenty of food and beer.[6] In some regions the term "Hock-Cart" seems to have become "Horkey," the name by which according to Robert Bloomfield the celebration of the last load of the harvest was known in Suffolk. His 1806 ballad "The Horkey" is related by an elderly woman who recalls how:

> Home came the jovial *Horkey load*,
> Last of the whole year's crop,
> And Grace among the green boughs rode
> Right plump upon the top.[7]

The "Advertisement" to the ballad explains that:

> I have endeavored to preserve the style of a gossip, and to transmit the memorial of a custom, the extent or antiquity of which I am not acquainted with, and pretend not to enquire.

> In Suffolk husbandry the man who, (whether by merit or sufferance I know not) goes foremost through the harvest with the scythe or sickle, is honoured with the title of "*Lord*", and at the Horkey, or harvest-home feast, collects what he can, for himself and brethren, from the farmers and visitors, to make a "frolick" afterwards, called "the largess spending."

"R.B.," as Bloomfield calls himself here, denies knowing the origins of a tradition that in *The Farmer's Boy* he had called "the long accustomed feast of HARVEST-HOME."[8] The theory that Harvest-home dated back to Saxon times, though, is found at least as early as Bourne's description of the harvest supper, where everyone involved in the gathering the harvest celebrates "without any Difference or Distinction" (Bourne, 229). Bourne believes that the custom derives from ancient Jewish practice but adds "it is certain this Custom was practiced by the *Saxons*, and is at least as ancient among us, as their Days. For among their Holy-days, we find

---

5   John Dryden, *King Arthur, Or The British Worthy* (1691), Act V.
6   Robert Herrick, "The Hock-Cart, Or Harvest-Home," *Complete Poems*, 1:175–78.
7   Robert Bloomfield, *Wild Flowers* (London: J. Wright, c. 1806), 37.
8   Robert Bloomfield, *The Farmer's Boy*, 5th edition, 45.

a week set apart at Harvest; of which our *Harvest-Home,* and *Mell-Supper,* in the *North,* are the only Remains." His source for this is Elizabeth Elstob's edition of the "Homily on the Birth-day of St Gregory," which lists the harvest holiday as "one whole week" at the beginning of September (Bourne, 232).[9] The discussion of harvest concludes Bourne's study of popular tradition, suggesting that this communal celebration bringing together both the "vulgar" and their employers is a fitting and thoroughly approved end to his study of which traditions "may be retained, and which set aside."

The second volume of Hone's *Every-Day Book* devotes twelve columns to Harvest-home, positioning the discussion between August and September. Predictably, most of the material is derived from John Brand's reworking of Bourne's notes in *Observations on Popular Antiquities,* once again providing a single source of transmission for most of the historic observations. A section borrowed from Brand proclaims of Harvest-home, "This festivity is undoubtedly of the most remote antiquity … Festivity is but the reflex of inward joy, and it could hardly fail of being produced on this occasion, which is a temporary suspension of all care" (*Every-Day Book* 2:1156). Multiple poems on the subject of harvest-home are reproduced, including Herrick's; of especial relevance here is "Harvest-Home," by "Mrs. Robinson" (2:1174–75).

Mary Robinson's description assumes that "harvest-home" will be familiar to her readers:

> Who has not seen the cheerful harvest-home,
> Enliv'ning the scorched field, and greeting gay
> The slow decline of Autumn.

Probably written during the year of the French Revolution, the passage depicts the "merry and artless throng" who bring in the harvest as one with the natural surroundings; the narrator calls them "Happy! More happy than the lords ye serve!" (*Every-Day Book* 2:1174–75). Yet although "Harvest-Home" as printed in the *Every-Day Book* celebrates rural virtue, the political content is slightly toned down from the description's context in Robinson's *Progress of Liberty.* The *Every-Day Book* drops a sentence critical of tithing: "On the plain/ The freckled gleaner gathers the scant sheaf,/ And looks, with many a sigh, on the tythe heap/ Of the proud, pampered pastor!"[10] The description of harvest-home is moreover followed by a reminder of Magna Carta: "Albion" is the place where "since the days/When her bold Barons ratified their deed,/ Freedom has smil'd triumphant and secure" (Robinson, 4:90). Given Hone's admiration for Magna Carta, it is curious that he cut these lines.

The *Every-Day Book* nevertheless features some new information, notably an account of the celebration at Hawkesbury in the Cotswolds, apparently submitted by a female eyewitness in September 1824. She reports that the parade included

---

[9]   The reference is Elizabeth Elstob's edition and translation of *An English-Saxon Homily on the Birth-day of St Gregory; Anciently used in the English Church* (London: W. Bowyer, 1709), 30. Elstob indicates her indebtedness to George Hickes for what she calls the "Dano-Saxon calendar."

[10]   Mary Robinson, *Memoirs of the Late Mrs Robinson, Written by herself,* 4 vols (London: R. Phillips, 1801), 4:88.

"a Maypole – that unsophisticated trophy of innocence, gaiety, and plenty"; a hay-wagon, and some kind of harvest queen on horseback that the observer, in this case interpreting the scene as Roman rather than Saxon-derived, takes as "no doubt representing Ceres." The editor invites other readers in the Cotswolds to "oblige him with particulars of what is passing under their eyes at this season every day" (*Every-Day Book* 2:1155–56).

The *Every-Day Book* editor's special request to receive more information on surviving harvest-homes supports the idea that the practice was becoming more uncommon. Following the general strain that we have seen over the course of this study, lovers of the seasons depicted harvest-home as a retreating rural custom. In *The Farmer's Boy* Bloomfield had described the harvest-home feast as a time when "once a year Distinction low'rs its crest,/ The master, servant, and the merry guest/ Are equal all," but concludes "Such were the days, ... of days long past I sing" (*Farmer's Boy*, 45). "R.B" explains of "The Horkey," "These customs, I believe, are going fast out of use; which is one great reason for my trying to tell the rising race of mankind that such were the customs when I was a boy" (*Wild Flowers*, 13). Leigh Hunt, writing in 1821, describes August as the start of harvest. He explains: "Harvest-home is still the greatest rural holiday in England," but:

> Our holiday-making is not what it was. Our ancestors used to burst into an enthusiasm of joy at the end of harvest, and even mingled their previous labour with considerable merry-making, in which they imitated the equality of the earlier ages. They crowned the wheat-sheaves with flowers, they sung, they shouted, they danced, they invited each other, or met to feast as at Christmas, in the halls of rich houses; and, what was a very amiable custom and wise beyond the commoner wisdom that may seem to lie on top of it, every one that had been concerned, man, woman, and child, received a little present, ribbons, laces, or sweetmeats.[11]

Hunt then quotes Herrick at length, but provides no other sources for his account;[12] the phrases "our ancestors" who were imitating the "equality of the earlier ages," though, suggest a medieval source, presumably based on the ascription of harvest-home to the Saxons. The reference to Christmas and present-giving elevates the importance of "harvest-home" to the rural community, almost as significant an event as Christmas, yet in Hunt's description the occasion is purely secular. Patmore's *Mirror of the Months* observes that "even the Harvest-home itself is fast sinking into disuse, as a scene of mirth and revelry, from the want of being duly encouraged and partaken in by the great ones of the Earth ..."[13] Patmore here ascribes the decline to the lack of support from the landowners expected to supply the feast. The Corn Laws, in effect from 1815 to 1846, which supported the price of grain to the extent that at times made bread unaffordable for working people, may also have diminished the enthusiasm for harvest-home. In 1838 William Howitt

---

[11]   Leigh Hunt, *The Months* (1821), 95–96.
[12]   Many poets embraced the subject of Harvest-home – for example, George Darley in the 1841 *Finden's Tableaux*, but few mention present-giving; in Robert Bloomfield's "The Horkey," shillings that the "Lord of Harvest" hoped to keep are shared among the group (40).
[13]   P.G. Patmore, *Mirror of the Months* (1823), 128.

Fig. 16. "Harvest-Home." R. Chambers, *Book of Days* (1863).

described the harvest-home celebration and supper as "the remaining links of the old chain of society."[14]

During the Victorian period, a secular holiday – even if, as few remembered, supposedly derived from the Saxon church calendar – merged into the English church "Harvest Festival."[15] Chambers's *Book of Days* contains a depiction of hock-cart (Fig. 16), but by the 1860s this would almost certainly have been inscribed not from life, but from memory or imagination. The invention of the "harvest festival" is attributed to Robert Stephen Hawker, who invited his Cornish parishioners to a

[14]   Howitt, *Rural Life of England*, 2:206.
[15]   Google ngram marks the precipitous decline of "harvest-home" by the second half of the nineteenth century, and the emergence of "harvest festival" in the 1840s.

harvest celebration of the Eucharist in 1843.[16] Hawker was an enthusiastic medievalist who was fascinated by the Saxon Saint Morwenna after whom his parish was named and who was later to publish his own "Holy Grail" poem, "The Quest of the Sangraal," in 1864. At a time when manual workers could barely afford food and farmers had apparently become reluctant to sponsor harvest-home dinners, local clergy assumed leadership, and the "harvest festival" became an Anglican tradition within a few years.

Harvest-home had, of course, always been associated with gratitude, but now that thankfulness was specifically Christian. Martin Farquhar Tupper, for example, wrote a "Thanksgiving Hymn and Chant for the Harvest Home of 1847." The hymn encourages the "Christian nation" to give thanks for a bounteous harvest, yet acknowledges that conditions have been dire for poor people, especially those affected by the Irish famine:

> O, ye famine-stricken glens, whose children shrieked for bread,
> And noisome alleys of the town where fever fed on hunger –
> O ye children of despair, bitterly wailing Erin,
> Come and join my cheerful praise, for God hath answered prayer ...[17]

Best-remembered is the clergyman Henry Alford's "After Harvest" in his *Poetical Works* (1845). The opening lines, "Come, ye thankful people, come,/ Raise the song of Harvest-home!" have helped preserve the term "Harvest-home" in English-speaking countries.[18] The "Lord of harvest" is not, as in Bloomfield's memory, an elected leader, but the Creator. Like Tupper's poem, "After Harvest" reminds the "thankful people" that "God our Maker doth provide/ For our wants to be supplied." All this seems benign, if overoptimistic at the time of the Irish famine, but the hymn then reworks one of Christ's stories from the Gospels, the parable of the Wheat and Tares, to remind those paying attention to the words that the Last Judgement will come:

> For the Lord our God shall come,
> And shall take His Harvest home:
> From His field shall in that day
> All offences purge away:
> Give his angels charge at last
> In the fire the tares to cast;
> But the fruitful ears to store
> In His garner evermore.[19]

---

[16]   Sabine Baring-Gould, *The Vicar of Morwenstow: A Life of Robert Stephen Hawker* (New York: T. Whittaker, 1879), 236–37.

[17]   [Martin Farquhar Tupper], *Hactenus* (Boston, MA: Pierce, 1848), 88.

[18]   In the United States, this has become a Thanksgiving hymn, but since Thanksgiving is celebrated in late November, "all" has been "safely gathered in" for some week in most regions. The text sung is usually not the 1845 version from *Poetical Works* but the 1867 version in *The Year of Praise* (London: A. Strahan, 1867), 273. Alford was an enthusiast for the Christian year and compiled both prayers and hymns for the entire year.

[19]   Quoted from the more familiar words in *The Year of Praise* (1867), 273; the most significant change is that the third and fourth line of the earlier version read "From His fields shall purge away/ All that doth offend that day."

Despite its association with collective hope, harvest should, this hymn suggests, remind the singers of the end times when the righteous "fruitful ears" will receive their heavenly reward, and the disruptive "tares" will be cast into the flames.

Hallowe'en

In the earlier nineteenth century, many years before Frazer's *Golden Bough*, if it occurred to those participating or witnessing harvest-home that it might be a relic of pre-Christian ritual the standard explanation would be that ultimately all religious practice was derived from the descendants of Noah. Harvest celebrations seemed self-explanatory since the community activity of harvest led naturally to a shared celebration at its successful conclusion, and if any justification was needed, such thanksgiving was sanctioned by the Bible. Harvest-home was celebrated in both England and Scotland, where it was sometimes called the Kirn (*Every-Day Book* 2:1177–78). In the Scottish weaver John Strachan's "Harvest Home," the poet differentiates Harvest home from other celebrations:

> The Scottish Muse has woke to sing
> O' Yule and Halloween,
> And Beltane games that May do bring
> To clad the earth in green,
> But ah! They bear the stamp o' Beast
> O'er seven hill'd Rome that reigns,
> Or days when Druids wont to feast
> On human blood and brains,
> On ony night.
>
> But gie's the merry Harvest Home –
> No pagan dress it wears;
> Nor has it aught to do wi' Rome,
> Nor stamp o' Beast it bears;
> But just God's creatures social come
> For gifts his goodness sent,
> Their gladsome thanks to offer him,
> On's altar ca'd content,
> Sae free this night.[20]

To Strachan, harvest-home is distinct from some of the Scottish traditions celebrated by Burns, Scott and others[21] since it is not derived from Catholicism (in this context, the Middle Ages) or paganism – apparently, he assumes the Druids were

---

[20]   John Strachan, *Walter and Emma; or, A Tale of Bothwell Bridge; with other poems* (Forres: printed for author, 1829), 69–70. John Strachan, a weaver resident at Forres in the Scottish Highlands is identified as the poet in an approving notice in the *Edinburgh Literary Journal* 43 (September 5, 1829), 194–95.

[21]   Burns does not specifically mention Beltane, but Scott explains it in the notes to "Glenfinlas, or Lord Ronald's Coronach." Walter Scott, *Ballads and Lyrical Pieces* (Edinburgh: Ballantyne, 1806), 4, 18.

cannibals and fed on "human blood and brains." Instead it is a natural and almost spontaneous celebration of God's goodness, hosted by the farmer but shared by all.

Strachan's reference to Hallowe'en and Beltane is significant because although used in parts of Scotland, these terms were largely unfamiliar to the English until the nineteenth century. In John Galt's 1823 historical novel *Ringan Gilhaize, Or The Covenanters* government troops are billeted on the Scottish Covenanters to quell their resistance to Stuart rule. After the arrest of the Covenanter preacher and leader Mr Swinton in 1666, an English-born soldier, Lieutenant Swaby, seeks to "lure" Swinton's sixteen-year-old daughter Martha to "his wicked will." When Martha resists, he tries to enlist an old woman, Mysie Gilmour, to "lend a cast of her skill to bring about a secret meeting between him the bonny defenceless Martha Swinton."[22] Mysie, however, lets others know of Swaby's plan to rape the girl, and they inform the soldier that not only is Mysie a witch, but that her power is greatest on Hallowe'en, the night agreed for Mysie to give Martha over to him.

Although he is superstitious, Swaby has never heard of Hallowe'en. Mysie's brother-in-law warns him that "mony a ane has met with things on Hallowe'en that they never after forgot." He elaborates that "Hallowe'en among us is a dreadful night! Witches and warlocks, and a' lang-nebbit things, hae a power and dominion unspeakable on Hallowe'en." It is the night where "Cluty [the devil] plays on the pipes!" (179). Swaby nevertheless persists, until he finds that the creature waiting for him in Mysie's bed is not a girl but a bad-tempered black ram.

The Covenanters know about Hallowe'en, but do not believe in it. Swaby the Eng-lishman, in contrast, has not heard of Hallowe'en, which is not in the English church calendar. A stranger in Scotland, Swaby believes in the continued power of ancient forces, and is easily persuaded that the ram is "the real Evil One" (181). Galt also mentions Hallowe'en in *Annals of the Parish*, where the annalist Micah Balwhid-der, Presbyterian minister in a rural parish, notes that the local fortune-teller Mizy Spaewell's death on Hallowe'en "made everybody wonder" – implicitly, whether she had made a pact with the devil.[23]

Hallowe'en is "All-Hallows Eve," the night before November 1, or All Saints' Day, which in the English church tradition was a celebration of the righteous dead and close to the end of the liturgical year, before Advent. The Collect was a prayer that the faithful might "come to those unspeakable joys, which thou hast prepared for them that unfeignedly love thee" (Book of Common Prayer). All Saints' Day was a carry-over from the Roman Catholic calendar, a papal institution having its origins in the rededication of the Pantheon in Rome as a Christian church in the early seventh century; the date of November 1 was fixed as early as the ninth century. *The Oxford Book of the Year* notes that November 1 "is the Irish *Samhain*

---

[22] John Galt, *Ringan Gilhaize, Or, The Covenanters* (1823), ed. Patricia J. Wilson (Edinburgh: Scottish Academic Press, 1984), 176. Subsequent page references given in text. Although the threat of rape is humorously averted in this case, Jacobite Highlanders later rape Ringan's niece, who never recovers from the trauma, while the fates of his own wife and daughters are too terrible for him to contemplate, let alone narrate.

[23] John Galt, *Annals of the Parish* (Edinburgh: Cadell, 1822), 17. "Spae" is a Scots word for "tell fortunes."

and the Scottish *Samhuin*, celebrated with bonfires, a festival of the dead..."[24] Yet as Ronald Hutton has observed, our knowledge of paganism in the British Isles is so scant that we cannot be sure how much Christianity impacted earlier forms of religion. Hutton himself feels that the preponderance of evidence suggests that "the opening of November was the time of a major pagan festival," although there is "no evidence that it was connected with the dead, and no proof that it opened the year, but it was certainly a time when supernatural forces were to be guarded against or propitiated; activities which took different forms in different regions" (Hutton, *Stations*, 369–70).

Popes Gregory III and IV are unlikely to have cared much about festivals in regions that were never really part of the Roman Empire when they declared November 1 All Saints' Day, and thus it is reasonable to suspect either that the date of Hallowe'en has an early medieval origin; or that the coming of Christianity may have changed the nature of a pre-Christian festival. The beliefs and practices of Hallowe'en as represented in literature, though, suggest that this is a night first, when the power of the Church is weakened; and second, when otherwise good Christians can invoke non-Christian powers. Witches and fairies emerge from their hiding places, and mortals can work charms. I cannot claim that none of these beliefs carried over from pagan times; even before James Frazer made some very specific claims about Hallowe'en in *The Golden Bough* some antiquarians believed that they did.[25] I would suggest, though, that the practices of Hallowe'en were not simply passed down through generations from ancient tradition, but sustained and expanded by literature.

By the time of publication of *Ringan Gilhaize*, English readers probably would have heard of Hallowe'en, after Robert Burns's 1784 poem of that title: Strachan's "Harvest Home" poem is likely modeled on "Halloween," using a similar verse-form. Before Burns's poems reached a wide readership, English knowledge of Hallowe'en may have been limited to isolated rural communities, or none at all. In the 1770s, Thomas Pennant, one of the earliest sources on Beltane, made a brief mention of Hallowe'en in a list of Scottish superstitions: "The young people determine the figure and size of their husbands by drawing cabbages blindfold on All-Hallows even; and like the *English* fling nuts into the fire..."[26] The reference to the English is interesting; possibly Pennant was aware of some regional practices in the north of England. Yet Burns himself, writing a decade later, considered that his readers needed the explanation in standard English that "Halloween" is "thought to be a night when Witches, Devils, and other mischief-making beings are all abroad on their baneful, midnight errands; particularly those aerial people, the Fairies, are said on that night to hold a grand Anniversary."[27] The references might seem to refer to pre-Christian times, but after an initial description of the Fairies' moon-light dance, Burns takes the reader to the banks of the River Doon in western

---

[24] *Oxford Book of the Year*, 440–41.

[25] See Frazer, 3rd edition, 3:222–45, where Hallowe'en is connected with pre-Christian fire rituals.

[26] Thomas Pennant, *A Tour in Scotland and Voyage to the Hebrides* (London, 1776), 156.

[27] Robert Burns, *Poems, Chiefly in the Scottish Dialect*. New edition (Edinburgh: Cadell, 1798), 1:171.

Scotland, the area in medieval times "Where BRUCE ance rul'd the martial ranks,/ An' shook his *Carrick* spear." Continuing the traditions of the past, "Some merry, friendly, countra folks" come together to "haud their *Halloween*." The youth of the party are all well dressed, but the goal is not merely to impress potential lovers but to find out their identity by the kinds of ritual attributed in England to midsummer and St Agnes' Eve. According to Burns's notes, the state of pulled cabbage stalks, ears of oats, and burned nuts are treated as predictors of future partners. Other spells actually charm apparitions – as in the St Agnes charm, visions of one's true love, or otherwise of one's future role in life.

In Burns's poem some of the rituals simply disappoint those who participate in them, such as elderly "uncle John," to whom the ritual of the three dishes (a kind of matrimonial shell game) leaves no hope of marriage: clean water in the dish means marrying a virgin, foul a widow; and no water no marriage at all. The outcome is not unreasonable, since "uncle John" was already a hopeful bachelor in the early years of the century, and has desired matrimony since "Mar's year" (the Jacobite rising of 1715). Other stanzas make it clear, however, that some of the practitioners of charms might seriously frighten themselves. Jamie Fleck, for example, is convinced that he will be unafraid of the throwing out hemp seed, but ends up "sae fley'd and eerie" that he thinks he has seen an unattractive future life-partner when it was really "but Grumphie" (that is, the family's pig). Widow Leezie tries dipping her sleeve in water "where three lairds' lands meet at a burn," and when she hears "the Deil, or else an outler Quey," she ends up in the water. The narration leaves the reader a choice as to whether the "croon" that startles Leezie is from the devil or from a wandering heifer, but given the playful tone of the narration the latter seems most likely.

Robert Chamber's edition of *The Life and Works of Robert Burns* (1853) makes some significant observations on "Halloween." First, a note explains that:

> The most of the ceremonies appropriate to Halloween, including all those of an adventurous character, are now disused. Meetings of young people still take place on that evening, both in country and town, but their frolics are usually limited to ducking for apples in tubs of water (a ceremony overlooked by Burns), the lottery of the dishes, and pulling cabbage stalks. The other ceremonies are discountenanced as more superstitious than is desirable, and as somewhat dangerous.[28]

Second, the notes undermine the sense that Burns was familiar with all these rituals through oral tradition by pointing out the similarity to a poem by John Mayne published in *Ruddiman's Weekly Magazine* in November 1780. The poem notes that among festive occasions:

> There's few in Scotland held mair dear
>   For mirth, I ween,
> Or yet can boast o' better cheer,
>   Than Hallowe'en.

---

[28] See *The Life and Works of Robert Burns*, ed. Robert Chambers. 4 vols (Edinburgh: W. and R. Chambers, 1853), 1:153.

The second stanza makes an interesting claim:

> Langsyne indeed, as now in climes
> Where priests for siller pardon crimes,
> The kintry 'round in Popish rhymes
>   Did pray and graen;
> But customs vary wi' the times
>   At Hallowe'en.[29]

John Mayne, or Jockie Mein, as he calls himself, suggests that the Hallowe'en practices of (supposedly Presbyterian) Scotland are an adaptation of the vigils of Roman Catholic countries, where people would pray for the souls of the dead. This does not quite explain the references to other supernatural beings invoked in storytelling. Mayne's poem describes how after work – hence evening – all gather at a farmer's house, where the farmer's wife reminds them that

> Bogle's ha'e gart folks tyne their wits
>   At Hallowe'en.

> Grieved, she recounts how, by mischance,
> Puir pussy's forced a' night to prance
> Wi' Fairies, wha in thousands dance
>   Upon the green,
> Or sail wi' witches ower to France
>   At Hallowe'en.

The potential dangers related in stories told on Hallowe'en – being enchanted and losing one's wits – are undermined by the fact that it is the household cat who is forced to be the companion of fairies and witches, and even then, only according to the story. After dinner, the main task of the young is to "Search a' the dark decrees o' fate" and thus "ken their matrimonial mate," and a number of examples are similar to those that Burns describes. Both poems mention throwing a "clew" or "clue" of ribbon into the "kiln," which according to Burns's note will upon command reveal the name of one's partner.

Burns's poem thus provides a "how-to" guide for Hallowe'en that was replicated in later publications such as Hone's *Every-Day Book*. The first volume provides a list of Hallowe'en customs derived largely from Burns and Pennant, supplemented by some antiquarian observations about bonfires. The second volume's entry for "Hallow Eve" merely observes that:

> The superstitious observances of this night, in the former volume, are fast disappearing. In some places where young people were acustomed [*sic*] to meet for purposes of divination, and frequently frighten each other to fits, as of ancient custom, they have little regard to the old usages. The meetings on Hallow-eve are becoming pleasant merrymakings; the dance prevails till supper-time, when they take a cheerful glass and drink to their next happy meeting. (2:1360)

[29]   Mayne's poem is reproduced in full in the *Abbotsford Series of the Scottish Poets*, ed. George Eyre-Todd, 7 vols (Glasgow: W. Hodge, 1891–96), 7:162–64.

The charm has become the most benevolent form of foresight: "Until we meet again."

Autumn Festival: The Lord Mayor's Show

Hallowe'en involved a simple gathering of friends, but autumn was also the occasion for a surviving civically organized festival, the London Lord Mayor's Show. The official website for the Lord Mayor's Show explains its origins as in the time of King John:[30]

> For years London had been trying to organise itself into a "commune": a sort of early city state that would be able to declare its borders, make treaties and defend itself. The King may have thought it a clever move to go along with this, and in 1215 he issued a Royal Charter creating the commune and allowing the City to elect its own Mayor every year.
>
> The King added a careful condition: every year the newly elected Mayor must leave the safety of the City, travel upriver to Westminster and swear loyalty to him. The Mayor has now made that journey nearly 700 times, despite plagues and fires and countless wars, and pledged his or her loyalty to 34 kings and queens of England… The Mayor became the "Lord Mayor" about a century later but it remained an elected office and for the next few hundred years, Lord Mayor of London was by far the grandest position to which a commoner could aspire.
>
> The Mayor's journey was the celebrity spectacle of its day and over the centuries it grew so splendid and so popular that by the 16th century it was known everywhere as the Lord Mayor's Show.[31]

This is a rethinking of the narrative that appeared on the website in 2012:

> The Lord Mayor's Show is the longest, oldest and most popular civic procession in the world. It winds through nearly 800 years of London history to arrive in the 21st century more splendid than ever. In 1213 a grateful King John awarded the City of London the right to choose its own Mayor, but he had a condition: every year, when a new Mayor took office, he had to make his way upriver to Westminster and pledge loyalty to the Crown. The Lord Mayor of London is one of the world's oldest elected officials, and the Lord Mayor's Show is the public festival that has grown up around his journey.[32]

In both versions, the reference to King John places the practices that led to the show firmly in the medieval period. Yet the narrative as given in 2012 suggests that John willingly granted London rights, implicitly in contrast with the forced concessions of Magna Carta. The official voice of the Lord Mayor's Show at that time continued

---

[30] This section is a revision of an article that appeared in *Studies in Medievalism* XXII (2013).

[31] https://lordmayorsshow.london/history/origins (accessed January 7, 2020).

[32] www.lordmayorsshow.org (accessed April 5, 2012). Elsewhere on the website the charter date is given as 1215. On King John's Charters, see, for example, Lindsey German and John Rees, *A People's History of London* (London: Verso, 2012), 22–23.

to identify its origins in loyalty to political structures, rather than as a form of resistance to them. By pairing the phrase "one of the world's oldest elected officials" with the idea of "public festival" the introduction also supports the suggestion that the Lord Mayor's Show, claimed as the "longest, oldest, and most popular civic procession in the world," originated in the medieval period.

The change by 2019 downplays the angle of civic loyalty just a little, but the emphasis on the show as "the celebrity spectacle of its day" continues. The Lord Mayor's procession certainly dates from the Middle Ages, but the Lord Mayor's Show came to prominence after the English Reformation, providing a partial substitute for earlier forms of public performance suppressed during the sixteenth century. The show is thus an intriguing example of how a public event that took form after the Middle Ages has traditionally claimed legitimacy and official sanction through the strategy of historical claims to medieval practice.

Not only has the Lord Mayor's Show utilized medieval motifs drawn from history and myth since the later sixteenth century, but, as the current financial support of the London Stock Exchange Group suggests, from its development by the London Livery Companies to the present, it has also historically united public spectacle with corporate funding and image creation. The emergence of the show as a major public event in the early modern period has been well studied, but my focus here is on historicizing and myth-making since the beginning of the nineteenth century, especially the Victorian period; and how it creates a medieval story for the post-medieval format of Lord Mayor's Show that justifies its continued existence as both as an antiquarian curiosity and a popular festival.

From early times, the Lord Mayor of the City of London was not considered just a politician but also a representative of trade, being elected from one of the major trade companies; according to tradition the first mayor of London was Henry Fitz-Alwin, a mercer, who was mayor until 1211. Occasionally, claims were made for even earlier origins. For example, the introduction to the 1761 *Guide to the Lord Mayor's Show* maintains that the position of Lord Mayor was "so constituted from and before the time of William the Conqueror; yet going under various Denominations."[33] There can be no doubt that during the medieval period, the king chartered trade and craft companies for, as W. Carew Hazlitt was later to describe it, "valuable consideration."[34] The reign of Henry V was a particularly active period in the granting of charters, and it was also the era of the future London folk-hero Richard Whittington, who left his mark on London in the form of a college, prison improvements, and other charitable endowments. Ballads and narratives about "Dick Whittington" dating from the seventeenth and eighteenth centuries sometimes include a woodcut of Whittington on horseback in a parade, with what Tracey Hill has suggested are fireworks.[35] This is less evidence that Whittington himself was part of a grand Lord

[33] The "Dissenting Report" in the Royal Commission of the 1880s points to references that guilds existed in Anglo-Saxon times. *The Report of the Royal Commission on the City of London Livery Companies*, 5 vols (London: Eyre and Spottiswoode, 1883–85), 1:58.

[34] William Carew Hazlitt, *The Livery Companies of the City of London* (London: Swan Sonnenschein and Co., 1892), 63.

[35] Tracey Hill, *Pageantry and Power: A Cultural History of the Early Modern Lord Mayor's Show, 1585–1639* (Manchester: Manchester University Press, 2010), 130–32.

Mayor's Show than an indication that later audiences liked to think that he was. As we have seen, in the nineteenth century, this hero of the Mercers' Guild was to become the pantomime character Dick Whittington.

From the monarch's point of view, the charters, renewed at least until the early 1700s, were a useful source of revenue; presumably, the London Guilds of Henry V's time were helping finance the Hundred Years' War. From the Livery Companies' point of view, charters granted to their trades were a historic validation. It is beyond the scope of this book to determine whether companies really had a continued existence and membership, or whether later charters were in effect creations of new companies. In terms of mythmaking, however, post-Reformation companies made much of their medieval origins. The first Royal Charter for the Mercers, whose first charitable establishment was built in the 1200s on a location once owned by Thomas Becket's family, was in 1394.[36] While the Mercers had a continuous tradition of sorts at least since the time of Richard Whittington, the Butchers' Company had no written evidence of their existence before 1592; they nevertheless pointed to references to a Butchers' Guild late in the reign of Edward III and in 1573.[37]

As Hill and others have demonstrated, while the Lord Mayor had traveled to Westminster to show his allegiance to the monarchy since the time of King John, the Lord Mayor's Show did not take the form of a major public event until the late 1500s. Claims for antiquity were common, though, even in the early 1600s.[38] By this time, most religious pageants organized by craft guilds had succumbed to Protestant suspicions of saints' days; fears that the representation of Biblical figures onstage was idolatrous; and concerns about the social dangers of large-scale gatherings. The London tradition of the Midsummer Watch, celebrated with bonfires and religious pageants, was also suppressed after the Reformation, and some of its practices transferred to the Lord Mayor's Show, celebrated on October 29, the Feast of St Simon and St Jude.[39] After Britain's move to the Gregorian Calendar in 1751, the show moved to November 9 and that date effectively became a public holiday in the City of London.[40] Depending on the era, the Lord Mayor traveled by barge, horse,

---

[36] Timeline of the Mercers' company, www.mercers.co.uk/our-history/700-year-timeline (accessed June 19, 2020).

[37] *Report of the Royal Commission on the City of London Livery Companies*, 3:212.

[38] Hill remarks that the "mayoral Shows' roots" can be traced back to late medieval pageants but that any "exploration of the early days of civic pageantry is inhibited by a lack of certainty as to when pageantry on Lord Mayor's Day began to be established practice, although the Shows' continuities with existing traditions were, on the whole, numerous" (Hill, 27). Given the amount of documentation that the Livery Companies were able to produce for the Royal Commissions in the nineteenth century, it is significant that none of it points to major celebrations of Lord Mayor's Day before the 1580s. For the borrowing of earlier public traditions connected with other calendar dates, see also Ronald Hutton, *The Rise and Fall of Merry England*, 76.

[39] For a brief period, some religious pageants may have been transferred to the Lord Mayor's Show but its performances were usually symbolic rather than drawn from Bible stories. See David Cressy, *Bonfires and Bells: National Memory and the Protestant Calendar in Elizabethan and Stuart England*.

[40] Tradespeople grumbled throughout the nineteenth century at the loss of a day's income; only in 1959, however, was the show moved to the second Saturday in November. See, for example, a letter signed "An Old City Subscriber" who objected to paying a day's

foot, and coach to Westminster, returning back to the Guildhall for a banquet; by the nineteenth century the travel was primarily by the mayor's state coach, which, as the 2019 website points out, is still in use.

The advantage of the Lord Mayor's Parade was that it was primarily secular; although originally on the Feast Day of St Simon and St Jude it required no direct celebration of saints and thus retained its status as England's identity changed from Roman Catholic to Anglican Protestant. It was moreover centered on a public act of loyalty to the crown and thus could be safely sanctioned both by rulers and by conscientious citizens. In an age when the period now known as the Middle Ages was still often characterized as filled with ignorance and superstition, the show chose to celebrate what was good about the past as seen through the eyes of the London Livery Companies. These companies claimed their origins in medieval guilds, the groups of craftsmen in a specific trade who banded together for mutual benefit ratified by royal charter; such a group would have apprentices learning the needed skills and trained craftsmen (journeymen). In his extensive 1892 study of the Livery Companies, W. Carew Hazlitt notes the "obscurity of origin" of the companies but identifies the continuity by calling them "Livery Gilds" and explaining, "The LIVERY is so called from the ancient practice of periodical delivery of clothing" to the group. Even then Hazlitt concedes "an inherent tendency on their part to diverge from their original gospel and *role*, and, whereas the incidence of apprenticeship was the very essence and foundation for their being, to develop a cliental and charitable principle into a sub-municipal autocracy..."[41]

For as the focus on apprenticeship waned, in London many of the most powerful groups were not practicing a craft but a trade, and protecting the interests of that trade. In using the show to create myths of origin for themselves, the Livery Companies and the productions that they commissioned did not only draw from the medieval period. For example, in the early modern period, rather than using the term "pageant," which was connected with the medieval religious-themed dramas performed on specific dates in the Christian calendar, companies tended to prefer the word "triumph," which has classical associations. Moreover, some of the entertainments devised to celebrate the show in the early modern period hinted at myths of origins of the early British people, such as the story that the Ancient Britons were escapees from the Fall of Troy. Even a production titled *Troia-Noua Triumphans*, which was written by Thomas Dekker, pays almost as much attention to the medieval origins of the Livery Companies as to the Ancient Britons; after a prologue emphasizing how much expense has gone into the production and scenes on land and water, "Fame" provides a list of medieval royalty and other leaders who have worn the Merchant Taylors' livery.[42]

Despite these assorted influences, because the Livery Companies tended to choose show themes that solidified the historical importance of their trade, the medieval period was a fruitful source of inspiration. One example of the combination of specifically medieval history and myth in the early modern period is Anthony

---

wages to his employees for no work (*Times*, November 12, 1849). As an added complication, November 9 was also the birthday of the Prince of Wales, later Edward VII.

[41]   Hazlitt, *Livery Companies*, 19–21.

[42]   Thomas Dekker, *Troia-Noua Triumphans; or, London Triumphing* (London, 1612).

Munday's *Chrysanaleia: the Golden Fishing* (1616). In 1616 the new Lord Mayor was John Leman, from the "auncient and worthie Companie of Fishmongers." Munday's pageant therefore features the fourteenth-century Lord Mayor Sir William Walworth, who may have been a dealer in kippers. In some accounts, Walworth is portrayed as an opportunist who treacherously struck down Wat Tyler while he was parleying with King Richard II and thus helped end the democratic promise of the Peasants' Revolt. For example, in Robert Southey's *Wat Tyler* (which appeared in an unauthorized edition in 1817), Walworth remarks that if the "rabble" lose their leaders, they will be easily dispersed, and strikes down Tyler from behind.[43] For the Fishmongers, in contrast, Walworth is a hero who proved the loyalty of their trade to the Crown. *Chrysanaleia* opens with a medievalist justification of the association between the Fishmongers and the Goldsmiths, asserting that during the Crusades, the two trades began working together.[44] The procession includes some symbols without historical specificity such as a fishing boat and a lemon tree to honor the name of the new mayor John Leeman (Lemon);[45] but it also features figures representing the time of the Crusades and of the Peasants' Revolt: among these are "the King of Moores, gallantly mounted on a golden Leopard, he hurling gold and siluer euery way about him"; King Richard II and the Virtues; and finally a "goodly Bower" containing the tomb of Sir William Walworth.[46] Walworth rises from his tomb and explains the pageant elements, and notes that "as my Dagger slew the Rebell then," it is represented in the London coat of arms:

> To honor *London* more (if more it may)
> The *Red-Crosse* , in a *Siluer-field* before,
> Had *Walworths* Dagger added to it more.
> And now my Lord, this goodly Monument
> Or Chariot of *Triumphall Victory*
> Some shape of that daies honour doth present,
> By *Heauens protection* of *True Maiestie*,
> And beating downe *Treason* and *Mutinie*.[47]

[43]   Robert Southey, *Wat Tyler, A Dramatic* Poem (London: Sherwood, Neely, and Jones, 1817), 35. This was an unauthorized edition of a play written during the 1790s and published to embarrass Southey at a time when he would probably have been more sympathetic to Walworth. For nineteenth-century ideas of Wat Tyler, including his adoption as a folk-hero by groups such as the Chartists, see Stephen Basdeo, *The Life and Legend of a Rebel Leader: Wat Tyler* (Barnsley: Pen and Sword Books, 2018).

[44]   Anthony Munday, *Chrysanaleia, Or the Golden Fishing* (London, 1616), introduction. Very possibly this medievalist preamble describing the association between the Fishmongers and the Goldsmiths was added for the printed edition.

[45]   The Lemon Tree was not simply a pun on the Lord Mayor's name. It was "richly laden with the fruite and flowers it beareth" and under it was a Pelican, emblematic of self-sacrifice and hence an "excellent type of gouernment in a Magistrate, who, at his mere entrance into his yeares Office, becommeth a nursing father of the Family."

[46]   Tracey Hill reproduces some of these in her study of the Lord Mayor's Show (140–41; 235); they are mentioned in William Herbert's 1836–37 history.

[47]   The spirit of Walworth is referring to coat of arms of the City of London, which is the cross of St George with a sword or dagger in one quarter; folklore claimed that this represents Walworth's weapon. According to most accounts, Walworth struck down Tyler with a sword or mace, and then later had the wounded man dragged from his bed and beheaded.

Walworth's return from the shades like a corporate King Arthur recalls the "honor" of the events of medieval times, the triumph of loyalty over rebellion, and the importance of fishmongers to the destiny of London.

The lavish productions of the late sixteenth and early seventeenth century had waned by the eighteenth century. In the early 1800s, the Lord Mayor's Show did not aspire to their scale, yet the Livery Companies continued their emphasis on medieval origins. The Lord Mayor of London[48] was still elected from one of the twelve "great" Livery Companies and they appointed "bachelors in foins and budge" to form part of the procession at their personal expense. The Elizabethan terms "foins and budge" refer to grades of fur, one being fur from martens or similar animals and one from lambs; by the 1880s these terms seem to have been used exclusively by Livery Companies in reference to their members' obligations in the Lord Mayor's procession. Usually, bachelors in foins (also spelled foynes) were expected to pay more than bachelors in budge; for example, in the 1880s the Haberdashers expected the bachelors in foynes to pay £10 and the bachelors in budge to pay £6.13.6d.[49] Over the course of the nineteenth century two strands of medievalism develop: an antiquarian justification for continuing the power of the Livery Companies as manifested in the show; and the popular appreciation for medieval elements.

The main antiquarian justification for the show was not, as might reasonably be expected, that it was a celebration of corporations, but that it was a surviving emanation of lost traditions of the medieval period. William Hone included an account of the Lord Mayor's Show in *Ancient Mysteries Described* in support of his goal of reclaiming medieval scripture plays as a form of popular drama. Hone identifies the Lord Mayor's Show as "the only stated exhibition in the metropolis that remains as a memorial of the great doings in the time of the pageants" and for this reason he provides "some account of its ancient appearance" (*Ancient Mysteries*, 246). Immediately, Hone performs the historical elision that recurs in accounts of the show. Having identified it as a "memorial" of medieval religious drama, he then provides an account of its "ancient" practices that dates from the Elizabethan period, specifically 1575. Hone is well aware that the secular "London Pageants" emerged about this time since he cites printed sources that make this point. He is especially interested, though, in finding continuities with medieval scripture plays, suggesting that the Livery Companies are the true successors of the craft guilds that sponsored them.

Scholars of the later nineteenth century found another way to claim continuity by asserting that the term "mystery play" itself derived not from religious revelation but from the trade companies that sponsored and performed them. According to Hazlitt's study of the Livery Companies,

---

[48] The Lord Mayor is the honorary title of the head of the aldermen of the City of London at the heart of London's commerce. The areas that the aldermen represent are often in combination called the Corporation. The Lord Mayor is chosen from one of the twelve Livery Companies. The Lord Mayor's Procession pointedly makes a distinction between London and Westminster. The office is distinct from the very recent position of Mayor of London, an elected American-style local administrator and head of the City Council.

[49] *Report of the Royal Commission*, 2: xx.

The ordinary orthography of the term *mystery* is calculated to favour an erroneous impression on the part of those who do not remember that the true word is mistery, the old French *maistre* and *maistrie* having been translated indifferently into English *master* and *mister, mastery* or *mistery*. Mistery, mester, maistrie, are all closely allied to *mestier* or *métier*, a trade.[50]

Even if this is correct, it has little to do with the Lord Mayor's Show, which is Hazlitt's purpose for including this questionable derivation.

The continued importance of the Lord Mayor's Show to London celebration is indicated by its inclusion in many almanacks as soon as the genre emerged in the 1830s, where almanacks produced in London mark "Lord Mayor's Day" on November 9. Yet because they owned extensive property, ran many charitable institutions, and controlled so much of the commercial market, at least twice during the nineteenth century, the London Livery Companies found that they needed to defend their structures and practices to government commissions. As early as the government "Commission for Inquiring into Municipal Corporations" in the reign of William IV, the Companies claimed their origins in ancient guilds and that they were the original corporations that led to the growth of commerce. William Herbert, Librarian of the Corporation of London, published two large volumes in 1836–37 tracing the London Guilds back to Anglo-Saxon times, and especially focusing on the origins of "the ancient trading Corporations," the twelve great Livery Companies.[51] In describing their ancient halls and banquets, Herbert explains that the "city Guildhall, on the lord mayor's day, now affords the best idea of the company's ancient halls and feasts, though certainly on a scale of greater magnitude and splendour" (1:87). Herbert mentions multiple medieval instances of the mayor of London and the Livery Companies riding in their regalia to meet the monarch or to celebrate other significant occasions. He hints that the Lord Mayor's Show of the late 1500s and 1600s was the successor to such "ridings" and the Midsummer Watch:

> *The Lord Mayor's Show*, as exhibited with all the increased splendour we have alluded to, was the king of City sights. – To the simple procession of minstrels, whom we have seen with the Companies' beadle on horseback, first succeeded spectacles on the water, chiefly in the nature of sham fights, with a few allegorical characters on land, who sang or recited complimentary verses. (1:199)

Herbert's account of the evolution of the Show follows Hone's in assuming a continuity with, although a development from, medieval practices. F.W. Fairholt published *Lord Mayors' Pageants: Being Collections towards a History of these Annual Celebrations* for the Percy Society in 1844. Assuming, like Hone, that the celebrations were connected with craft guilds' plays, he provided many early possible parallels, but

---

50   Hazlitt, *Livery Companies*, 24.
51   William Herbert, *The History of the Twelve Great Livery Companies of London*, 2 vols (London: printed for author, 1836–37), 1:iii. Herbert notes that that Anglo-Saxon guilds "were, at first, political" (1:3); the early pages of study intermingle trade guilds with other kinds of companies.

conceded that little was known about the actual pageantry before 1523.[52] A generation later, in 1864, Joshua and Lucy Toulmin Smith similarly claimed that corporations had their origins in the medieval guilds. They also insisted that: "Charters of
Incorporation do not and cannot *create* Corporations. They have always depended,
and still depend, for even their validity upon the pre-existence of the 'Commu-
nitas.'"[53] Corporations, then, were founded for the welfare of their members and
interests that they supported.

By the Victorian period some of the Livery Companies had major power in
London, having assumed the role of quality control officers for their trades.[54] All at
least in theory offered aid to the sick and elderly among their numbers; and many
sponsored charitable institutions such as schools and housing; certainly, today, the
Livery Companies, whose members are frequently not associated with the trade that
gave the company its name, claim that their main function to is support and admin-
ister their charitable foundations.[55] The companies were thus seeking to maintain
status in the community. While it could certainly be argued that the ultimate intent
of achieving such status was to increase profits, community standing was a more
immediate goal, and the public spectacle of the Lord Mayor's Show was a means of
celebrating a collective history.

Historians who stressed the medieval "pageant" origins of the show may, though,
have influenced some new Lord Mayors to try to recreate the glories of the past.
The Times usually reported both on the parade and the lavish dinner in the Guildhall hosted by the new Lord Mayor that followed soon after. These descriptions
reveal that most years, the parade had a visible connection with the medieval past.
During the nineteenth century it was not often, however, the figures of Gog and
Magog, whom current websites claim to have been part of the parade since the time
of Henry V. The official Lord Mayor's Show website explains that the two giants are
"the traditional guardians of the City of London" and that they have been "carried in
the Lord Mayor's Show since the reign of Henry V."[56] Acknowledging the vagueness
of the history surrounding the Guildhall Giants, the site adds, "we do know that by
the reign of Henry V there were carved giants guarding the gates of Guildhall. In
1554 they appeared in the Lord Mayor's Show, and in 1605 the Pageantmaster of the
day alluded to the giants who appeared in the Procession on Lord Mayor's Day as
Corineus and Gogmagog." The appearance of Gog and Magog in the Lord Mayor's

[52]   Frederick W. Fairholt, *Lord Mayors' Pageants: Being Collections towards a History of
these Annual Celebrations…* Part 1 (London: Percy Society, 1843), 9.

[53]   Joshua and Lucy Toulmin Smith, *English Gilds: The Original Ordinances* (London:
Early English Text Society, 1870), xii. Joshua, Lucy's father, died a number of years before
publication.

[54]   For example, the Royal Commission reported that "The Fishmongers' Company,
relying on its charters but without authority by any Fish-statute, appoints and pays 'fish meters'
who attend at Billingsgate Market, examine the fish offered for sale there, and condemn any
which may be proved to be unsound. The company defrays the expense of deodorizing and
removing the fish thus condemned" (1:19).

[55]   See, for example, the history of the Merchant Taylors company, www.merchant-taylors.
co.uk/about/company-history (accessed June 20, 2020).

[56]   https://lordmayorsshow.london/history/gog-and-magog (accessed February 1, 2020).

Show, however, is not quite that consistent; they are not in the parades described by *The Times* in the early Victorian period.

The Guildhall Giants are large carved wooden figures kept in the building at least since the earlier 1600s. Often described as the "traditional guardians of London" (www.lordmayorsshow.org) they are not representations of medieval characters but rather mythological figures; their usual names, Gog and Magog, are from the Bible. In some sources they were Trojans who migrated with Brutus the great-grandson of Aeneas to Ancient Britain, and in others they were already resident and defeated by the Trojans. Further myth also suggests that after being defeated (by the Trojans or by the Cornish giant Corinaeus) the giants were chained to a palace on the site of the Guildhall. In 1819 John Galt published a playful children's book explaining not only their origin, but the foundation of many other London landmarks, comically dating them long before the medieval period. The antiquarian-minded narrator tells how in a November 9 in "a rude age, long before the Roman legions," the brave young warrior twins Gog and Magog agreed to give themselves up to release the Princess Londona, from the Giant Humbug, which explains the name of the London Exchange and led to the institution of the Lord Mayor.[57] In imagining this happening on Lord Mayor's day before the concept of November existed, Galt is making fun of antiquarian quests for origins, but in a format that may have confused some young readers about the history of London.

The very confusion over who the Giants are and what they represent suggests that their story has largely been handed down by oral tradition. Although they are associated with the Ancient Britons, for William Hone they are a remnant of the medieval pageants ended at the Reformation, marking the continuity between the Middle Ages and the present. Hone includes in his 1823 *Ancient Mysteries Described* an engraving of the Giants of his time, themselves replacements of earlier figures. The Giants are a significant aspect of the Guild tradition that has survived to the present day, although the figures have changed over the years. Early wooden statues were destroyed in the Great Fire of London in 1666; the replacement pair known to Galt, Hone and others was destroyed in the Second World War; and a new pair was sponsored by a former Lord Mayor in 1953.[58] Guildhall Giants were certainly part of London folk-culture, but seemingly only rarely a part of the parade for the Lord Mayor's Show until their recent recreation as giant basketwork parade figures.[59] Eighteenth- and nineteenth-century antiquarians, possibly drawing on European

---

[57] Robin Goodfellow [John Galt], *The History of Gog and Magog, The Champions of London* (London: printed for J. Souter [also John Galt], 1819), 2. Princess Londona proves to be well capable of looking after herself.

[58] In the nineteenth century the giants flanked a doorway and were brightly painted wood, spruced up with a new coat of paint from time to time. The current pair might be described as "mid-century modern," and are distinct from the basketwork parade figures that have been used recently.

[59] On the role of giants in festival culture, see Dorothy Noyes, *Fire in the Plaça: Catalan Festival Politics After Franco* (Philadelphia, PA: University of Pennsylvania Press, 2003), particularly pp. 42–46. The Catalonian Corpus Christi celebrations coincide with the traditional time of English mystery plays on the Christian calendar. Noyes identifies the 1890s as the point when the festival moved to become a more directly orchestrated tourist event (45).

analogues, made the assumption that the pasteboard and wood figures of before the Great Fire were paraded in the "triumphs." Hone goes so far as to assert: "That wicker was used in constructing figures for the London pageants is certain" (*Ancient Mysteries*, 273), implying that the early Guildhall Giants were such parade figures even though the evidence is scanty. Hone's *Table-Book* mentions the inclusion of "extremely well contrived" wicker-work figures of Gog and Magog in the 1827 Lord Mayor's Show, but they are said to be a "novelty," which suggests that they had not appeared in previous years.[60] F.W. Fairholt's 1859 account of the giants theorized that they were paraded in the distant past, but provides no other nineteenth-century instance of their inclusion.[61]

But even without giants, the procession had a medieval element. For much of the nineteenth century, the "men in armour" represented for the crowds the imagined medieval past of Lord Mayor's Day. A 1761 guide to the show mentions a man in armor with attendants as representative of the "Armourers and Brasiers" company.[62] Spectators, though, seem to have interpreted the men in armor as a tradition in its own right. The "men in armour" were clearly annual favorites with ordinary Londoners, who, unless they had a life story like Dick Whittington's, would never have the opportunity to share in the lavish banquets that followed the day's events.

In 1790, *The Times* stated that the "man in armour, the last of the city pageants, who, with his attendants, formed a spectacle that gratified the curiosity of many, has ceased to grace the show" (November 10, 1790). In 1808, however, the "man in armour was restored to this ancient ceremony, after a lapse of some years, to the great satisfaction of the spectators" (*The Times*, November 10, 1808). "Ancient Knights" on horseback were particular crowd favorites. Fairholt, who describes them as the "great feature of modern shows,"[63] notes that three knights and their attendants appeared in the 1822 show, and adds that the steel armor was "Henry the Fifth's from the Tower" (of London), although a footnote dutifully points out the uncertainty of the attribution to Henry V. Mr Marriott, a Fleet Street ironmonger, had manufactured one suit of brass armor, and "Mr Elliston" (probably Robert William Elliston) loaned another from his theatre. Other pieces of armor used by attendants were apparently trophies from the Battle of Waterloo.

Despite the mixed origins of the armor, "Ancient Knights" were apparently revived as a crowd expectation. An account of the parade in 1826 mentions a "Man in brass chain armour, mounted on a black charger"; the parade also included two men in copper armor and another in "brass scale" armor (*The Times*, November

---

[60]   William Hone, *The Table-Book* (London: William Hone, 1827), 609.

[61]   F.W. Fairholt claims that giants were included in the 1837 parade (*Lord Mayors' Pageants* 138); this appears to be a typographic error for 1827 since he names the Lord Mayor as "Alderman Lucas," Mayor in 1827. In his later study of the Guildhall Giants, *Gog and Magog, The Giants in the Guildhall* (London: J.C. Hotten, 1859), the mistake is repeated even though it disrupts the chronology (69).

[62]   *A Guide to the Lord Mayor's Show, or the gentleman and lady's companion to that magnificent procession* (London, 1761), 8. In 1761 the newly crowned George III and family attended, and the banquet cost £4,889.4.0, roughly equivalent to $750,000 today.

[63]   Fairholt, *Lord Mayors' Pageants*, 137.

ILLUSTRATIONS OF THE MAYORALTY.
The 8th and 9th of November, falling on the days of our publication, we are prevented from giving any representations of the events | of the great civic ceremonies of those days; but, as we are familiar with the observances of past years, and by the favour of the public officers, fully acquainted with the details of those which are at this | moment passing before the public eye, we may safely introduce a few sketches of the more remarkable points of the successive pageants, without identifying them with the persons through whom

Fig. 17. "Ancient Knights" in the Lord Mayor's Show. *Illustrated London News*, November 1844.

10).[64] Most Lord Mayors of the 1820s and 1830s included knights in armor in their shows, although Barber Cox would probably have had to borrow armor for his son to wear in the Tournament at Tuggeridge from the owners, not the Lord Mayor himself.[65] Even the fairly modest 1848 procession included an "Ancient Knight, mounted on a charger, armed *cap-à-pié*, in a suit of polished Steel Armour, and plumed." Another "Ancient Knight" was costumed in a "suit of burnished Brass Scale Armour, and plumed" (*The Times*, November 10, 1848, 5) (Fig. 17).

In 1850, the new Lord Mayor Sir John Musgrove, probably inspired by the Great Exhibition planned for his mayoral year, decided to abandon the knights and to present an allegorical display of British triumph. *The Times* reported that "the olden

[64] The different colored suits of armor, some apparently chain mail rather than plate armor, may possibly be a response to the immense popularity of Walter Scott's *Ivanhoe* (1819), which was to become a leading inspiration for arms, armor, and tournaments.

[65] See Chapter 2.

procession" had "undergone a change" and that the "old knights in armour" had been "replaced by the more pleasing figures of England's glory – Peace, Industry, Arts, and Manufactures." Peace, represented by a winged young woman on a "white palfrey" and bearing an olive branch, was accompanied by mounted figures representative of the continents of Europe, Asia, Africa, and America. Following were live animals: a horse for Europe, a camel for Asia, an elephant for Africa, and two deer for America (*The Times*, November 11, 1850, 6).[66] Furthermore, the parade featured a "Splendid Allegorical Car," drawn by six horses and representing a "State Barge, Rowed by British Tars, Tritons and Dolphins at the stem, supporting the Civic Shield, Sword of Justice and Mace, together with a Royal Standard and Union Jack, in the centre bearing a Gigantic Car, with Britannia and Happiness, personated by young ladies, allegorically robed…" This would seem to be an attempt not to modernize the parade but to return it to the masque tradition of allegory seen in seventeenth-century accounts; the *Illustrated London News* noted that "Mr. George Godwin, F.R.S." had read Fairholt's book and suggested a revival of pageants to the new Mayor.[67] Despite *The Times*'s approval, however, there may have been resistance to this attempt a creating a new – or perhaps reviving an old – tradition. The following year the knights were back in force, the parade including some individual knights as champions of dignitaries in the attendance and a "Troop of Twenty Knights"; all were wearing armor of the reigns of Henry VIII and Francis I (*The Times*, November 11, 1851, 3). The fact that the new Lord Mayor and his supporters had come to the conclusion that the more knights, the better suggests that the "Allegorical Car" was no substitute for what had become a tradition.

The 1870s and 1880s were a crucial point in the history of the Lord Mayor's Show since opinions were so strongly divided as to what it meant. In 1870 Lucy Toulmin Smith claimed the Show as a true medieval survival. In her Preface to the records of medieval Guild activity that she edited with her late father, she remarks that "In the present day, when the race of life is to the swift, and there is scarcely any time left for anything else, these popular pageants are despised, and a barren imagination can see in the last relic of them, the Lord Mayor's Show, nothing but 'a bore.'" She goes on to quote Canon Rock's *Church of our Fathers*:

> such an age will not understand the good which, in a moral and social point of view, was bestowed upon this country by the religious pageants, and pious plays and interludes of a by-gone epoch. Through such means, however, not only were the working-classes furnished with a needful relaxation, but their very merry-making instructed while they diverted them.[68]

For Toulmin Smith, the Lord Mayor's Show is indicative of the popular nature of civic pageants. *English Gilds* also contains a lengthy treatise by Lujo Brentano arguing that medieval guilds were the forerunners of present-day trade unions.

---

[66]   When the plan was announced, a prankster claiming to represent the hippopotamus that had arrived in London earlier that year wrote to *The Times* protesting his client's lack of inclusion (*Times*, November 7, 1850, 5 [signed O. Possum]).

[67]   *Illustrated London News*, November 9, 1850, 366.

[68]   J. and L. Toulmin Smith, *English Gilds*, xxxiv–v.

In 1880 a new Royal Commission was appointed to inquire into the state of the London Livery Companies. The government was interested in how charitable trusts were administered; whether the companies were functionally monopolies; whether their administrative structures should be revised; and whether they were paying appropriate taxes. Hazlitt explains that:

> the hostile critics of the Corporation and the Companies made a good deal of the serious loss to the Imperial revenue from the enormous amount of property held in mortmain and exempt from succession-duty in perpetuity ... There was also a contention that the Companies were independent of the Corporation, and were, at least no longer, what they nominally or ostensibly professed to be—representatives, guardians, and promoters of various trades and callings. (*Livery Companies*, 2)

It also seems possible that in an era of growing fears about the spread of anarchy and communism, the government may have believed the Toulmin Smiths' observation that the Livery Companies were a form of working-class organization, even though by this time most companies were run by prosperous businessmen who claimed them as the founders of "commerce."[69] In 1884 the Commission produced a five-volume report which began with a historical overview of the medieval origins of the Livery Companies. Drawing on some of the Toulmin Smiths' archival work, the Commission repeated the evidence for medieval survivals claimed by the Companies. Quoting other authorities, the introduction to the Commission conceded that "it is doubtful whether any primitive merchant guild ever existed in London, and the process by which a popular form of the livery local government became established at the period just mentioned is obscure." Yet it emphasizes the importance of the companies to London's development: "There is no doubt, however, that some of the corporations which are the subject of this inquiry (some had existed before the Norman conquest), were, to a great extent, the instruments through which the municipal independence of London was achieved."[70]

While the Royal Commission's final report did not present a threat to the continued existence of the Livery Companies, William Carew Hazlitt's *Livery Companies of the City of London* seems to have been composed in anticipation of a need to defend them. Hazlitt stresses the respectable nature of the Companies in a quiet refutation of the idea that they were a crucible for socialist rebellion, and even justifies their expenditure on banquets as "almost the only survivals of ancient English hospitality" (*Livery Companies*, 5). In fact, they hardly needed it; they became liable to the Corporation Tax of 1884, but the government did not interfere with their administrative structures. In keeping with his emphasis on the respectability of the Livery Companies, Hazlitt treads lightly over the issue of the Lord Mayor's Show, but in his summary of the history of each company he provides an extensive list of the pageants of early modern times.

---

[69] The original guilds appear not to have been gender exclusive but by the Victorian period, members were all male. Women Livery Company members made a resurgence in the twentieth century, but the current picture of the Merchant Taylor leadership shows them as mainly male.

[70] *The Report of the Royal Commission*, 1:9.

Hazlitt's reluctance to address the Lord Mayor's Show directly, even though it would seem the most obvious emanation of the continued relevance of the Livery Companies, is probably because the "popular" elements of the show lack antiquarian dignity. Yet the element that contemporary commentary reveals still to have been particularly welcome to the large crowds who attended the parade was the continued inclusion of "men in armour." In 1865, the parade was once again scaled down and the "men in armour" abandoned: in 1868 *The Times* noted with satisfaction: "The men in armour will be 'conspicuous in their absence.' Two or three years ago that grotesque part of the spectacle was abolished, and will probably henceforward exist only in the popular recollection as a subject of ridicule" (*The Times*, November 9, 1868).

This prognostication proved, however, to be incorrect. In the 1870s the parade took on an imperial flavor and the 1876 parade included "Indian elephants, in Oriental trappings with howdahs, guided by Mahouts; attendant equestrians in State costumes; [and] six Knights in armour, with each a lance and pennon" (*The Times*, November 10, 1876). The word "pageant" began to be used more frequently, as, returning to the early modern practices and the one-year attempt in 1850, parades once again started to include carts drawing displays. In 1877, *The Times* noted that "in spite of the wishes of some who look with no friendly eyes upon the Corporation and its surroundings, the Lord Mayor's Show is still as it has been from the earliest recollection of all." Even in rain, the procession was more ambitious and more topical than ever, and included:

> Two immense dromedaries from Sangers Circus, ridden by "Egyptians," and after them came an ornamental car, drawn by six horses, carrying an insignificant model of Cleopatra's Needle, surrounded by a group of persons representing Egypt. It had been originally intended to carry the model perpendicularly, but Temple-bar again proved a thorn in the side of the Civic authorities, and so this "Egyptian loan," as it was called, had to recline on its car, amid representations of the Sphinx and the Pyramids. A pair of elephants followed the Needle, and then came what was described as an elaborate ornamental tableau car, drawn by ten horses, and representing "Peace and Plenty," – questionably appropriate at this juncture; – the Muses, the Four Seasons, and other trophies and emblems, more or less absurd. (*The Times*, November 10, 1877)

The parade therefore seems to have resembled that of 1850 in looking back to the early modern period, where representations of camels (possibly at that time horses in pasteboard trappings) were sometimes included as part of the emblem of the Mercer's Company. Thematically, the camels connected with an awkward representation of the obelisk known as Cleopatra's Needle then on its way from Egypt to London. Yet the subject matter was not merely topical; to keep everyone happy, it also included six men in armor.

The 1884 Show included "floats" with episodes in London history:

> There was, for instance, a car drawn by 12 ponies, with the immortal Dick Whittington beside the Highgate mile-post in the act of listening to Bow Bells, and in close proximity to a representative of his famous cat…William the Conqueror was represented, and so was Richard Coeur de Lion, Henricus Fitz-Alwyne, the first Mayor of London,

Richard II, and Queen Elizabeth, all beautifully mounted and carefully costumed after the manner of the habits in which they lived. Lord Mayor Walworth standing over the slain Wat Tyler was not a popular figure. It evoked groans and hisses. (*The Times*, November 11, 1884)

The reaction to William Walworth indicates the class divisions in the reception of the Lord Mayor's Show. For the Guilds, especially the Fishmongers who claimed him as one of their own, Walworth was a hero who maintained order in London by defeating the rebel Wat Tyler. Many in the crowd may have felt more kinship with Wat, who in popular tradition attempted to stand up for the rights of working people against oppression.

The Show was thus to some degree a means for the disenfranchised to voice their opinions. While the Livery Companies took the opportunity to assert their status in the city, the show itself gave the people of London an opportunity to show approval or disapproval of the new and retiring mayors. As early as 1787, *The Times* remarked that the new mayor's parade through the City "gives the vast multitude of citizens and inhabitants an opportunity of knowing his person, and paying him every proper degree of reverence and respect. Here too, the former Lord Mayor goes through the popular ordeal; and his conduct is generally marked with approbation, or reproach" (*The Times*, November 8, 1787)

As the parade expanded to become more like a carnival, the editors of *The Times* felt entitled to point out the absurdity of the some of the representations, even though these scenes endorsed the crown, the Empire, and trade. Still, while *The Times* conceded that "some iconoclasts maintain that Lord Mayor's Show is only meant for bumpkins and children," it also defended it as "by no means an empty fiction. It symbolizes in a manner the power and repute of the Corporation of London, which are no shadows, but substantial realities" (*The Times* editorial, November 9, 1882).

Yet the public celebration of the ancient Corporations' continued existence, the Lord Mayor's Show, was moving more in the direction of folk tradition and carnival. Far from an occasion of civic pomp, then, the Lord Mayor's Show is a chance to escape the everyday world of London commerce. The Square Mile of the City has few residential properties, and on a typical Saturday, the area is very quiet. On the day of the Lord Mayor's Show, however, an estimated quarter of a million people come out to watch the parade, which now claims to have participants in the "thousands."[71] In the later twentieth and early twenty-first century, as the Lord Mayor's show of allegiance to the Crown has become irrelevant and London's economy has grown increasingly dependent on heritage culture, traditions themselves become the justification.

Despite the antiquarians' detection of the remains of medieval pomp, some nineteenth-century observers were apparently aware of the dubious medieval origins of the Lord Mayor's Show, again raising the question comically presented by Galt in 1819 of whether traditions might be fantasy, or even lies. In an expanded version of the Baron Munchausen stories published around 1860 by an anonymous but

---

[71]   See the website https://lordmayorsshow.london/ (accessed May 27, 2020).

presumably American author,[72] during the Baron's fantastic adventures he is protected from Don Quixote's attack by Gog and Magog, who ride on a Sphinx. Don Quixote quotes Burke: "But the age of chivalry is gone, and the glory of Europe is extinguished forever!" Yet the knight has his medieval defenders: "Lord Whittington, at head of all his raree-show, came forth, armor antique of chivalry, and helmets old, and troops, all streamers, flags, and banners glittering gay, red, gold, and purple, and in every hand a square of gingerbread all gilded nice, was brandished awful."[73] The chapter summary beginning the book simply describes this as "Lord Whittington with the Lord Mayor's Show." In the Preface, Gulliver, Sinbad and Aladdin solemnly swear to the truth of the Baron's stories, and sign their attestation, "Sworn at the Mansion House, 9th Nov. last" – that is, Lord Mayor's Day.

[72] Sarah Tindal Kareem traces the development of the Munchausen stories from Rudolph Raspe's originals by largely anonymous hands in *Eighteenth-Century Fiction and the Reinvention of Wonder* (New York: Oxford University Press, 2014), especially 154–85.
[73] *The Travels and Surprising Adventures of Baron Munchausen* (New York: James Miller, 1860), 206. Although this edition was illustrated by the Englishman Alfred Crowquill, I accept the *Christian Examiner*'s contention that the authorship was American (*Christian Examiner* 71, 151). George Cruikshank later illustrated the same text with English spellings.

Epilogue: Christmas Ghosts

MEDIEVALISM HAS A ghostly aspect, as the past continues to haunt the present.[1] In the traditions noted in this study, the past tends to function as a friendly, helpful shadow, if all too ready to slip away. Accounts of British folk beliefs suggest that ghosts do *not* appear at Christmas: for example, W. Howells, in *Cambrian Superstitions* (1831), states of ghosts, "the usual time of their appearance is midnight, seldom before it is dark, and no ghosts can appear on Christmas eve."[2] This suggests that ghostly behavior had changed since medieval times, when spirits of the dead sometimes become visible in the hours before Matins or even in broad daylight;[3] they almost invariably have a message that they convey to a living person.[4] Peter the Venerable's *De Miraculis* moreover notes a number of miraculous events around Christmas, and makes specific mention of a ghost that appeared on Christmas Eve (Joynes, 44); Peter himself, who was Abbot of Cluny, was to die on Christmas Day, 1156.

Despite the absence of ghosts, British popular tradition clung to the idea of Christmas as a time of wonders. The constant present of Christmas so central to the Christmas carol takes a somewhat different form in other cultural practices associated with the disruption of nature and natural order. Antiquarians pointed to Christmas social activities that broke down hierarchies, and to folk beliefs that at Christmas Eve, the night that God took the form of humanity, nature itself might assume some supernatural aspects. The ghost story, however, is not a medieval genre but, as Joynes remarks, "a relatively recent literary development" (Joynes, xi), and the Christmas ghost story is still more recent. Even the most famous and the most presentist Christmas ghost story, Dickens's *A Christmas Carol*, makes use of, then expands, a newly invented tradition.

---

[1] David Matthews, for example, starts *Medievalism, A Critical History* with the statement, "The ghosts of the Middle Ages are unquiet" (1).

[2] W. Howells, *Cambrian Superstitions* (Tipton: Longman, 1831), 13.

[3] M.R. James remarks on a "daylight ghost" in "Twelve Medieval Ghost-Stories," *English Historical Review* (1922), 419.

[4] Andrew Joynes provides a fascinating selection of medieval narratives featuring ghosts in *Medieval Ghost Stories* (Woodbridge: Boydell Press, 2001, rpt 2006). Most of the accounts of spirits that survive were recorded by ecclesiastics, who usually state or imply a moral lesson. See also Peter the Venerable's *De Miraculis libri duo,* especially Part 2, chapters 22, 23, and 27, in *Patriologiae Cursus Completus,* ed. J.-P. Migne (Paris, 1844–65).

Gift-Books and Ghosts

In *The Sketch Book*, following the Christmas dinner, Geoffrey Crayon provides some hint of ghost stories. Sitting in a "venerable" oak chair, the parson shares "strange accounts of the popular superstitions and legends of the surrounding country," including "several anecdotes of the fancies of the neighbouring peasantry, concerning the effigy of the crusader, which lay on the tomb beside the church altar." The figure "was said to get up from the tomb and walk the rounds of the churchyard in stormy nights, particularly when it thundered." The crusader's walks are particularly associated with "Midsummer eve, when it was well known all kinds of ghosts, goblins, and fairies, become visible and walk abroad" (*Sketch Book* 2:86–87).

Significantly, the parson ascribes such beliefs not to the Bracebridge family but to the "neighbouring peasantry." In relating ghost stories, educated men almost invariably ascribe their transmittal to women and the uneducated, particularly servants, who have passed them down orally – and then proceed to tell them themselves. Even then, these stories are often depicted as in decline. For example, the *Ladies' Monthly Museum* for 1819 warns readers "Of the DANGERS of entrusting CHILDREN to the CARE of Unprincipled DOMESTICS." Parents should not employ servants of "unenlightened minds" who will give children "erroneous opinions." Yet the writer adds that "fortunately for the rising generation, those tales of ghosts and goblins, which, during the period of my childhood, obtained such universal credit amongst servants, are now no longer believed in them."[5] *Professional Anecdotes, Or Ana of Medical Literature* (1825) notes, "In the good old times of our ancestors, it was the usual custom, on winter evenings, when the family was assembled around the blazing fire, for some maiden aunt, some gossiping nurse, or tattling dairy-maid, to relate a number of wonderful stories about ghosts and goblins, until their auditors became afraid of their own shadows…" Yet now "the skepticism of the metropolis has spread over the country; and in consequence, these fearful pleasures are at an end."[6] The phrase "fearful pleasures" is significant, since unlike most medieval accounts of apparitions, the early nineteenth-century ghost story does not seem to need a moral purpose. In an age privileging heightened emotion, stories that elicit fear in their audience can themselves be a source of satisfaction.[7]

Also in the 1820s, the publisher Henry Colburn began a new series of *The Monthly Magazine*, which provides useful insights on developing attitudes towards Christmas as less of a time for reverence than a season for pleasure. The magazine's title had been used earlier for a conservative-leaning journal focusing on politics, but this new series is aimed more at the general reader. The journal's official editor was Thomas Campbell, best known for his 1799 poem *The Pleasures of Hope*, and

---

[5]   *Ladies Monthly Museum*, May 1819, 272.

[6]   *Professional Anecdotes; or Ana of Medical Literature* (London: John Knight and Henry Lacey, 1825), 1:286–87.

[7]   Edmund Burke's *Philosophical Inquiry into our Ideas of the Sublime and Beautiful* (London: Dodsley, 1759) connected "terror," including that produced by darkness, obscurity, and "ghosts and goblins," with the extreme emotional state of the "sublime" (97–100), a concept very influential on Romantic-era Gothic.

Christmas is largely represented as a season of both pleasure and hope. In the first decade of publication, multiple essays discuss Christmas traditions and practices.

In 1829, although the *New Monthly Magazine* had not previously associated Christmas with ghosts, Campbell published "A Few Ghosts for Christmas-Time" under his usual pseudonym MEM. MEM, having encountered what proves to be not a ghost-horse but a simply lost horse, reflects to himself that had he been able to relate a real ghost story "what a treasure I should have been to the fire-sides of the cottages which I passed." He then relates two local stories of ghosts, a woman in white and Highgate's ghostly coach and horses, to which the local "plebeians" – belief in ghosts is related to social standing – add a sheep: "The coach-and-six is always turning round before you; and if you turn about yourself to avoid it, you encounter the dreadful sheep."[8] Of particular interest in the development of the Christmas ghost story is the reference to one of Sir Walter Scott's contributions to *The Keepsake* of the 1828–29 Christmas season, "The Tapestried Chamber."

MEM professes not to have read the story himself, but claims that "a lady was good enough to repeat to me the principal circumstances; and in the vivacity of her recital, the story, I conceive, lost nothing" ("A Few Ghosts," 79). The narrative move is important here, since even if MEM had not read the story, the details included suggest that Thomas Campbell most likely had. Although Sir Walter Scott was the most famous novelist of the time, having recently acknowledged his authorship of the Waverley series, *The Keepsake* was marketed to ladies, and the masculine persona of the *New Monthly Magazine* contributor denies having read the story himself. Instead, the story is conveyed to him through a woman's oral retelling – and thus becomes like the traditional ghost story, a tale to be shared by the fireside.

Scott's effectively frightening tale also uses the motif of a woman's oral tradition: the narrator of "The Tapestried Chamber, Or, The Lady in the Sacque," implicitly Scott himself, claims to have heard the story from the writer Anna Seward, who had died in 1809. The story recounts how an army general, a veteran of the American War of Independence who seems to others to have "retained possession of his cool judgment under the most imminent dangers," spends a night in an ancient room in a medieval castle, partly "as old as the wars of York and Lancaster," but with Elizabethan and Jacobean additions.[9] The unemotional General, however, finds himself the victim of an experiment in terror. He later explains that he was visited in the night by a "horrible spectre" wearing "an old-fashioned gown, which, I think, ladies call a sacque" ("Tapestried Chamber," 136). The General's masculinity has been challenged by the necessity of telling a ghost story and admitting his terror, and he here cautiously enters female territory by not only being able to describe a woman's garment but to name it.[10]

---

[8]   [Thomas Campbell], "A Few Ghosts for Christmas-Time." *New Monthly Magazine* 25 (January 1829), 78.

[9]   The Author of Waverley [Sir Walter Scott], "The Tapestried Chamber, or, The Lady in a Sacque." *The Keepsake for 1829*: 143–45.

[10]   The General – and Scott's – masculinity is preserved by the wrong nomenclature for the dress. The term "sacque" seems to be an eighteenth-century word, but the ghostly ancestor presumably predates the 1700s, the event itself taking place in the 1780s.

Yet it is surely telling that the General gains admittance to the castle through "a modern Gothic lodge, built in that style to correspond to the castle itself" ("Tapestried Chamber," 127). Scott's tale is not merely an example of the modern Gothic, but the start of a new sub-genre, the ghost story in a Christmas book. Admittedly, the story does not take place at Christmas but during hunting season, and ends not on a note of reconciliation but rather a loss of friendship. The General realizes that he has been the subject of a terrifying experiment by his host to find out whether a brave unimaginative man will see the family ghost, and his host realizes that the dark secrets of his family's past are still within his castle walls. Nevertheless, its presence in a Christmas annual, and Campbell's article "A Few Ghosts for Christmas," contribute to a new sub-genre that perversely does not claim novelty but that revels in its tenuous connection with the past.

Tara Moore, one of the few authors to explore the phenomenon of the Christmas ghost story, sees them as an offshoot of the Christmas publishing industry. As she notes, a fireside ghost story collection, *Round About our Coal Fire*, existed as early as the 1730s. This much-reprinted book claims that part of "Christmas Entertainment" is stories of goblins, witches, ghosts, and fairies, yet those that follow, told both humorously and skeptically, make no specific connection with Christmas.[11] Moore mentions Washington Irving's account of fireside stories, but is inclined to see the Christmas ghost story as a development of Victorian print culture. She points out that in Hervey's *Book of Christmas* ghost stories are associated with the ancient ballad tradition: "The song and the story, the recitation and the book read aloud are, in town and in village, mansion and farmhouse, amongst the universal resources of the winter nights now, as they or their equivalents have at all times been."[12] Moore adds, "While other elements of the seventeenth- and eighteenth-century Christmas were cast aside in favor of the dominant London midwinter narrative, ghost stories survived and, in print at least, multiplied. References to ghost stories at Christmas became much more numerous after 1800, and the ritual was both accepted and well practiced by the end of the 1830s" (Moore, 82). As other supposed medieval traditions faded away, the Christmas ghost story provided a popular bridge between the medieval world and the present.

Finden's Tableaux, edited by Mary Russell Mitford, provides some intriguing examples. Published from 1835 to 1844, this was the engravers William and Edward Finden's entry into the Christmas annual craze; the format was larger than most of the other annuals, giving particular prominence to the illustrations.[13] It was Mary Russell Mitford's task as editor to find authors who would draw inspiration from the images; she produced many pieces of fiction herself, but commissioned other stories and poetry, mainly from personal acquaintances, to accompany the rest of the pictures. Elizabeth Barrett (later Browning) was willing to help out her friend by supplying poems, but since she was away from London at the time, she could not

---

[11]   Tara Moore, *Victorian Christmas in Print*, 81–82; see also *Round About Our Coal Fire, Or, Christmas Entertainments* (London, 1734).

[12]   Hervey, *The Book of Christmas*, 228.

[13]   Frederick Winthrop Faxon's *Literary Annuals and Gift Books: A bibliography with a descriptive introduction* (Boston, MA: Boston Book Company, 1912) contains a list of known annuals; in Britain they peaked in the 1830s and had faded away by the mid-1850s.

actually see the pictures that her poetry was supposed to illustrate. For her contribution for the 1839 annual, Mitford sent her a copy of the engraving in April 1838 (*Brownings' Correspondence* 4:27); and Barrett used it as inspiration for the medieval "Romaunt of the Page." The engraving (Fig. 18), which shows a womanly figure dressed as a page looking at a knight from behind a tree, is very likely inspired by Sir Walter Scott's 1808 poem *Marmion*, in which Constance follows Marmion in such a guise, becomes his lover, and ends her life bricked up in a convent wall. Barrett presumably picked up on this, since she named the knight Sir Walter;[14] *Marmion* was also in her mind when she wrote her "ghost-story" contribution the following year.[15]

While over "The Romaunt of the Page" lies the spectral figure of Scott's Constance, there is a further allusion to Marmion in the form of an actual ghost in one of Barrett's contributions for the following year, "The Legend of the Brown Rosarie." In June 1839 she told a friend, "I have begun already a wild & wicked ballad" with "so many monks & nuns" in the engraving that she exclaims, "think of the very annuals turning papistical!" (*Brownings' Correspondence* 4:169). The image shows a young woman, a rosary in her right hand, slumped in front as an altar or tomb covered by a cloth with a cross, on which is a wreath (Fig. 19). The young woman is supported by an older woman, and they are watched by a young boy. There are monkish figures in the background, but only two. I suspect that in order to include the line drawing frame that illustrates scenes from the poem the picture has been trimmed down and that originally the figures might have been looking at the statue of a saint, since the end of the poem mentions the Shrine of St Agnes.

The image may also have suggested to the poet the ballad of Lenore, since in the *Findens'* version of the poem the woman is called Lenora: Barrett suggested to Mitford that her poem might be titled "The Ballad of Lenora." In Auguste Gottfried Bürger's ballad, well known in Britain through translations by Scott and others, a young woman is in despair because her lover has not returned from battle. One of the earliest translations, that of William Taylor, medievalized Bürger's poem so that the lover, William, is not a modern soldier but away at the Crusades; Taylor's translation uses the identical form of the name to Barrett's poem.[16] At midnight, "William" arrives on a black horse to take her to her wedding; as the ride continues, however, she realizes that she being carried away by Death: the spirits around her remind her somewhat belatedly,

> "Be patient; though thyne herte should breke,
> Arrayne not Heaven's decree;
> Thou nowe art of thy bodie reft,
> Thie soule forgiven bee!" (Emerson, 85)

[14] Very likely Barrett also knew "Child Waters" in the version printed in Thomas Percy's *Reliques of Ancient English Poetry*, where the pregnant Ellen follows her lover on foot; "Walter" and "Waters" are obviously close.

[15] It is not the only Scott-inspired story about a woman dressing as a boy in *Finden's Tableaux*; the same issue contains John Hughes's "The Minstrel of Provence," set in the eleventh century, where the minstrel proves to be a girl called Constance.

[16] See Oliver Farrar Emerson, *The Earliest English Translations of Bürger's Lenore: A Study in English and German Romanticism* (Cleveland, OH: Western Reserve University Bulletins, 1915), 81.

Fig. 18. "Romaunt of the Page." By W. Perring. *Finden's Tableaux* for 1839.

Fig. 19.   "Legend of the Brown Rosarie." By J. Browne. *Finden's Tableaux* for 1840.

Barrett's Lenora commits a similar, if not worse, offense, but she herself proves to be the demon lover who sends her partner to his grave. When Lenora's mother asks her little brother "where is Lenora," he first tells her that she is "At the tryst with her lover." To this the mother replies, that Lenora's "lover to battle is gone,/And the saints know above that she loveth but one."[17] At this, he confesses that she is meeting with "The ghost of a nun with a brown rosarie/ And a face turned from heaven"; this nun, like Scott's Constance, was "buried alive" in the convent walls (16).

The same volume contains another ghost story in ballad form: J.R. Chorley's "The Maid's Trial: A Sea Tale" tells how a sea-captain slain by pirates returns to as a ghost to defend his daughter from dishonor and to steer the ship to safety. Richard Hengist Horne contributed "The Fetches," a miniature tragedy set in a medieval castle in which a man sees the apparitions of himself and his betrothed, and takes this as an omen that their death is near (Fig. 20).[18] This proves correct: when he stays away from his fiancée so that she need not share his fate, she takes poison, and he jumps off a cliff. The volume was generally well reviewed, so that Barrett told John Kenyon, who had also contributed to the volume, that it "prospered this year, above any annual." She mentioned the quality of the engravings and some of the contributions, and then added, "As for me I only sate in the corner & told a ghost story" (*Brownings' Correspondence* 4:252).[19] Barrett and her friends, then, were well aware that Christmas gift books could include ghosts, and were prepared to contribute to the development of the genre; what is more, here she portrays her written story as an oral tale, a "ghost story" told by the fireside.

In December 1841 Barrett and Mary Russell Mitford had a discussion of ghosts, that seems to have started with reflections as to whether Joan of Arc really did commune with supernatural beings. In late November Barrett had sent Mitford two books, *The Keepsake* for 1842 and Jung-Stilling's *Theory of Pneumatology*. They had already discussed one of the most striking contributions to *The Keepsake*, a ballad by Theodosia Garrow (later Trollope) titled "The Doom of Cheyneholme." Like many contributions to annuals of this period, the poem has both a ghostly and a medieval aspect: one of the last surviving members of a family driven to their deaths by the local landowners lays a curse on the family, dooming the men to dishonorable deaths and the women to unhappiness in love. As the last member of the Cheyneholme family perishes, mute "simple Agnes" dying infatuated with a man who does not know of her existence, witnesses think they catch a glimpse of the "ghastly phantom" of the mother who years earlier had uttered the curse.[20]

---

[17] "The Legend of the Brown Rosarie," *Finden's Tableaux: The Iris of Prose, Poetry, and Art for MDCCCXL*, ed. Mary Russell Mitford (London: Charles Tilt, 1839), 15. My quotations follow this edition by page number. "EBB" later revised the poem as "The Lay of the Brown Rosary," renaming the central character Onora. See *The Works of Elizabeth Barrett Browning*, 1:309–31.

[18] John Aubrey provides multiple examples of seeing one's own apparition as a presage of one's death (*Miscellanies*, 76–78).

[19] The letter is dated March 7, 1840, the day of *Sordello*'s publication.

[20] Theodosia Garrow, "The Doom of Cheyneholme." *The Keepsake* (1842), 88–117. The illustration shows characters in seventeenth-century costume yet the text refers to barons, knights, and a monk.

Fig. 20. "The Fetches." By J. Browne. *Finden's Tableaux* for 1840.

Barrett may have had the "ghostly" aspects of *The Keepsake* and similar Christmas annuals in mind when she asked Mitford for her opinion of the second book, an 1834 translation of Johann Heinrich Jung-Stilling's work, *Theory of Pneumatology, in reply to the question, what ought to be believed or disbelieved concerning presentiments, visions, and apparitions, according to nature, reason, and scripture.* Jung-Stilling argued that:

> Presentiments, visions, and apparitions of spirits, testify of an invisible world of spirits, which is the abode of departed souls, and of good and evil angels and spirits. They prove the existence of the soul after death, with the full consciousness of its present existence, and the recollection of the whole of its earthly past life.[21]

On December 3, 1841, Mitford wrote back to Barrett with a sample of each: the "presentiment" of a man who dreamed of a murder and was able to prevent it happening; a "vision" of a sailor seen by her maid K. (which was short for Kerenhappuch), foretelling of losses in her own family; and the "apparition" of a churchyard ghost. Mitford concludes, "I do not disbelieve in the possibility of such appearances, though I heartily agree with Stilling in the sinfulness and danger of seeking them" (*Brownings' Correspondence* 5:80). Barrett, who had lately lost her beloved brother, was less convinced. She responded,

> Our dead are our absent ones! – and if as Stilling thinks their spiritual abode be in the midst of us, it is not less a state of separation, – & our cry (happily for that new blessed peace they have won) cannot more reach & wound them. How can they hear any cry of ours? – Does Death invest them with ubiquity – with omniscience – with God's own attributes? – or are they forced to walk step by step with us – they in their divine sympathy, and we in our earthly sorrowfulness – the one rent by the other? – No – it is not reasonable, I think, that we shd. wish it – nor is it scriptural that we shd. believe it. (5:182)

Barrett continued the discussion of ghosts on December 8, where she criticized the Gothic novelist Ann Radcliffe for creating a sense of the supernatural, then deflating it: "She made the instinct toward the supernatural too prominent, to deny & belie the thing. It was want of courage & power in her imaginative faculty... Can anything be much more irritating than the Key to her mysteries, – & the undressing rooms of her ghosts?" (5:184). For Barrett, then, the idea that the souls of the dead might actually be around the living is contrary to religious truth – but a mainstay of the literary imagination. And she certainly understood that, ghosts sell books, especially at Christmas.

Dickens's Christmas Ghosts

Barrett was lukewarm in her response to the most famous Christmas ghost story of all, noting on December 27, 1843 that while she liked the Cratchits she did not like "the machinery – which is entangled with allegory and ghostery" (*Brownings'*

---

[21] Johann Heinrich Jung-Stilling, *Theories of Pneumatology*, trans. Samuel Jackson (London: Longman, 1834), 8.

Correspondence 4:113). As we have seen, Charles Dickens did not invent the concept of the ghost story at Christmas, which had successfully been grafted into the British imagination as an ancient tradition by the 1840s. Just as, however, *A Christmas Carol* helped establish the idea of a snowy Christmas, it also helped cement the thematic connection between the ghost story and Christmas. Dickens had first written a ghost story about Christmas in the December 1836 episode of the calendar novel *The Pickwick Papers*. In the December 1836 installment Mr Pickwick and friends return to the home of the hospitable Mr Wardle at the Manor Farm in Dingley Dell for a traditional Christmas. They arrive on December 22, attend a wedding on December 23, which would have been a Sunday in the real-life 1827; and partake of Christmas festivities on Christmas Eve. In Chapter XXVIII the narrator sets the scene: "Christmas was close at hand, in all his bluff and hearty honesty; it was the season of hospitality, merriment, and open-heartedness…"[22] Traditions are apparent in the marriage on December 23, which is followed by food, toasts, and a wedding cake ritual that recalls the St Agnes traditions: "the cake was cut, and passed through the ring; the young ladies saved pieces to put under their pillows to dream of their future husbands on; and a great deal of blushing and merriment was thereby occasioned" (345). In the evening a ball follows, where the narrator self-consciously medievalizes the scene:

> seated in a shady bower of holly and evergreens were the two best fiddlers, and the only harp, in all Muggleton. In all sorts of recesses, and on all kinds of brackets, stood massive old silver candlesticks with four branches each. The carpet was up, the candles burned bright, the fire blazed and crackled on the hearth, and merry voices and lighthearted laughter rang through the room. If any one of the old English yeomen had turned into fairies when they died, it was just the sort of place in which they would have held their revels. (347)

The reference to the non-Christian beliefs associated with the Christmas season is fitting since the only visit to church over the Christmas period is for a wedding.

The next day is Christmas Eve, where in the kitchen all observe the "annual custom… observed by old Wardle's forefathers from time immemorial" of kissing under the "mystic branch" of the mistletoe that Wardle himself hangs from the kitchen ceiling (350);[23] at Christmas in the Wardle household, the proprietors come together with their employees in the servants' space. After games and drinks, Wardle tells Pickwick of the family's "invariable custom" of having the whole household sit down by the fire: "and here we wait, until the clock strikes twelve, to usher Christmas in, and while away the time with forfeits and old stories." By this time, it is snowing, although Wardle's mother implies this is a rare event at Christmas. It reminds her of one Christmas Eve five years before Wardle's father died, the "very night he told us the story about the goblins that carried away old Gabriel Grub" (352–53).

---

[22]   Charles Dickens, *Pickwick Papers*, ed. James Kinsley, 334. Subsequent references in text, by page number from this edition.

[23]   "Time immemorial" implies the medieval period – in legal parlance the reign of Richard I – but as noted in Chapter 3, no writers mention kissing under the mistletoe until the eighteenth century.

A ghost story on Christmas Eve is not out of keeping with custom; a ghost story *about* Christmas actually violates British oral tradition. A century before Howells's *Cambrian Superstitions* Henry Bourne had noted that in popular belief Christmas actually limits the powers of ghosts: the "Midnight Spirits who wander about the World... always fly away at Cock-crow" because this time is associated with the Saviour's birth and when "the Angels sung the first Christmas-Carol to the poor Shepherds, in the Fields of Bethlehem" (Bourne, 49). Most likely without knowing it, then, Dickens recaptures some of the characteristics of medieval stories of apparitions, including the idea that spirits might roam at Christmas; and that unlike Scott's story that focuses on terror, spirits have a message to give to the living.

Wardle's mother points to the fact that at some time the story of Gabriel Grub and the goblins must have been new to the family, but in a few years telling it appears to have become a tradition. Mr Pickwick is eager to hear it, and there follows – in a new chapter[24] – "The Story of the Goblins who Stole a Sexton." If tales of "ghosts and goblins" go together, this is a true Christmas ghost story, since it takes place "one Christmas Eve," and although the inhabitants of Manor Farm have not been to church, they do imaginatively visit a churchyard. In this churchyard the sexton Gabriel Grub, who finds other people's Christmas happiness "gall and wormwood" and is not above describing a coffin as "a Christmas Box," encounters a goblin king in medieval dress (Fig. 21) who drags him down into a cave (355–56). Yet while the goblins are associated with the underworld, they seem to have a reformative purpose in showing Grub a more complex view of humanity than he has previously held. The Goblin King orders his under-goblins to reveal to "the man of misery and gloom" images of human happiness and loss. Grub comes to "the conclusion that it was a very decent and respectable sort of world after all," and learns to be cheerful. Although Grub wakes in the churchyard on Christmas Day still feeling what he ascribes to kicks of the Goblins, as in *A Christmas Carol*, there is space to think of this as a dream. After he has learned more about the world and about himself from the Goblin visions Grub leaves the community, who until his return years later believes he has been "carried away by the goblins" (362).

The Pickwick Papers came to an end before the following Christmas, probably partly because the publishers Chapman and Hall had Christmas in mind; the last double installment was published on November 1, 1837, ahead of the complete novel, announced as available on November 14, in perfect time to become a Christmas present; Dickens himself gave it to his friend the actor William Macready, famous for his Christmas dinners.[25] Yet the title page to the final double issue refers back to the previous Christmas, as goblins of the Gabriel Grub story draw back a curtain to show Mr Pickwick and Sam Weller reading stories in a Gothic room in their new – but apparently old – house in the London suburb of Dulwich, which according to Pickwick combines "comfort" with "elegance" (Fig. 22). The businessman Pickwick has become lord of his own manor. Sam has shown a sense of feudal

---

[24]   In early editions, this is a "ghost chapter," also numbered chapter 28.

[25]   Advertisement in issue 18, dated September 29, 1837; according to Macready's journal Dickens held a dinner to celebrate *Pickwick* on November 18, and sent Macready a copy on December 12. *The Diaries of William Charles Macready*, ed. William Toynbee. 2 vols (New York: Putnam's, 1912), 1:426; 431.

Fig. 21. "Gilbert Grub and the Goblin King." By Phiz. From *The Posthumous Papers of the Pickwick Club* (1836–37).

Fig. 22. "Mr. Pickwick and Sam." By Phiz. From *The Posthumous Papers of the Pickwick Club* (1836–37).

loyalty towards his master Samuel (never Sam) Pickwick, even arranging to join him in the Fleet prison, but as Sam sits in a Gothic wooden chair and Mr Pickwick in an armchair, they are still master and servant but at least elbow to elbow.

Dickens's fully planned venture into the territory of Christmas publishing came in the form of his Christmas books, of which the first, *A Christmas Carol*, has become a Christmas tradition of its own. Particularly in the United States, a "Dickens Christmas" has become synonymous with tradition – ironic since first, as we have seen, nineteenth-century Britons regarded Christmas as in decline and in need of artificial supports to maintain tradition; and second, Dickens seems on the surface to be concerned with the present. Still, as in the "Goblins" story, Dickens successfully melds his ghost story told at Christmas with Christmas themes, to make it, as in the subtitle, "a Ghost Story of Christmas" – not merely to be told at Christmas, but about Christmas.

Unlike most Christmas ghost stories, but somewhat like the Christmas carols that give the story its title, the narrative begins very directly; the narrator makes no claims to have heard the story at second hand or passed down orally through others, and apologizes only for his[26] use of the simile "as dead as a door-nail."[27] In keeping with the direct tone of the narration and its insistence on verisimilitude, I am initially approaching the narrative literally, and only then metaphorically. First, let us consider *A Christmas Carol* as a ghost story. The traditional ghost-lore is seen largely in Stave One, where Scrooge sees first Marley's face on the door knocker to his chambers; and then the death hearse going up the stairs. The narrator has been at pains to point out that Scrooge is unimaginative and that he has not been thinking about Marley when he sees his face "with a dismal light about it, like a bad lobster in a dark cellar"; but he will only say that Scrooge "thought he saw" the "locomotive hearse going on before him in the gloom" (42–43). The ghostly hearse is not a major problem for Anglican Christian theology since in legend it appears at the moment of death, or as a presage of death, after which the soul would presumably move on to heaven or hell; Dickens has, however, transposed the tales of phantom funerals from remote areas of Wales and Scotland to present-day London.[28] Yet when Marley appears dragging chains – something that in the late eighteenth century Francis Grose had noted as "not the fashion of English ghosts" – [29] his explanation of his

---

[26]   Although ghost stories are frequently described as told by, or preserved in form by, women, Dickens was a well-known personality by 1843 and readers would be inclined to identify him as or like the storyteller, hence my use of "he."

[27]   Charles Dickens, *A Christmas Carol In Prose, Being a Ghost Story of Christmas* (1843), 33. References are by page number from Michael Slater's edition. Unlike many of the annuals and other books marketed as gifts for Christmas and New Year, which bore the imprint of the year to come, this book was produced for December 1843.

[28]   Welsh phantom funerals presaging death are mentioned in William Howells's *Cambrian Superstitions*; in 1839 *Bentley's Miscellany* 6 (August 1839) featured a Scottish tale by G.R. Gleig titled "The Phantom Funeral" (195–205). I have not found stories earlier than *A Christmas Carol* specifically mentioning a phantom hearse, although many accounts of phantom hearses appear later, especially in the United States. Opinions are divided on whether by "locomotive hearse" Dickens refers to a horse-drawn vehicle in motion, or whether Scrooge sees a hearse moving without horses.

[29]   Francis Grose, *Provincial Glossary – Popular Superstitions* (1790), 8.

present state as one of perpetual unrest and remorse suggests a kind of Purgatory like that proposed by Jung-Stilling, and not out of keeping with medieval accounts of ghosts hoping for help from the living to purge their sins.[30] Anglican Britons, though, did not accept the concept of Purgatory, so when Scrooge asks Marley about "comfort," he replies, "I have none to give" (48), the only slight relief to his torment being his attempt to save his friend from a similar judgment. On this Christmas Eve, far from being the night when according to British tradition ghosts cannot walk, it seems that ghosts must walk: the air is "filled with phantoms, wandering hither and thither in restless haste, and moaning as they went" (52). The theological confusion is well represented by Scrooge's fireplace, where the Bible stories depicted on the tiles become overwhelmed with the image of Marley.

Marley is nevertheless a conventional ghost in being the specter of a deceased person come to warn the living. Two of the spirits that appear to Scrooge in the "staves" that follow identify themselves as "Ghosts" (the third does not speak), but seem more in the tradition of supernatural beings: angelic messengers, or perhaps the "goblins" of Gabriel Grub, who have a similar monitory function.[31] The narrator refers to the visitors as "Ghosts," but until he is forced to speak for the Ghost of Christmas Yet to Come, Scrooge addresses his guides not as ghosts, but by the name "Spirit," which is striking since with the exception of Marley, in Stave 1 neither he nor the narrator referred to anybody by name. When the Ghost of Christmas Past announces itself, Scrooge inquires "Long Past?" since he is "observant of its dwarfish stature" (55). Perhaps Scrooge thinks the Ghost has dwindled over the centuries, as suggested by the narrator, or perhaps he imagines that people in ancient times were smaller; yet the "traditional" Christmas revealed by the old but childlike Ghost proves not to be of "ancient times" but that of old Scrooge's own youth.

When they travel back through time, the Ghost's explanation that Scrooge is invisible to those he observes because they are "but shadows of the things that have been" (57) works for the past, but not quite so well for the present and future. Presumably, the Christmas mood that Scrooge observes throughout society in the present is consistent with what happens when he awakes the following morning, but the Cratchits' and Fred's Christmas Days do not unfold as Scrooge observes them since the Cratchits receive a prize turkey and Scrooge himself attends Fred's Christmas dinner. The Scrooge of the past is not able to see the Scrooge of the present observing him, but if he were, the older Scrooge would be a "fetch," which, as in Horne's story, usually predicts the observer's death. In combination with Marley's warning and the phantom hearse, the supernatural elements of the story predict Scrooge's own lonely demise. Yet in Staves 3 and 4, Scrooge is witnessing a version of the future in an apparently non-deterministic cosmos, where redemption remains a possibility and neither Tiny Tim nor Scrooge has to die.

Scrooge has already been reminded of the benevolent traditionalism of the Fezziwigs, whose seasonal generosity to the community extends not just to their own

---

[30] Joynes's *Medieval Ghost Stories* includes many such examples, including two selections from the Dialogues of Gregory the Great (Joynes, 9–11).

[31] Changes to the manuscript of *A Christmas Carol* suggest that Dickens had hesitations about calling the spirits Ghosts. See *A Christmas Carol, By Charles Dickens: A Facsimile of the Original Manuscript* (London: Chapman and Hall, 1903).

employees, but also to poor workers of the neighborhood whose employers are not so kind: for example, the underfed "boy from over the way" and the "girl from next door but one, who was proved to have had her ears pulled by her Mistress" (62). The Ghost of Christmas Present points out to the businessman Scrooge the effective return in happiness on an investment of perhaps "three or four" pounds, and Scrooge himself notes that as an employer Fezziwig "has the power to render us happy or unhappy" (64). Fezziwig, like Mr Pickwick and Scrooge, is a businessman and not an ancestral Lord of the Manor as is Squire Bracebridge; but he seems to manage better than the Squire in understanding his ability to affect his workers' happiness, and unlike Bracebridge, he leaves his doors open to all.

Fig. 23. "Scrooge and Bob Cratchit." By John Leech. From *A Christmas Carol* (1843).

Scrooge takes the lesson to heart. Learning that the future can be changed, Scrooge awakes on Christmas Day, sends the Cratchits a turkey to supplement the small goose (giving a generous Christmas Box in the process); makes amends with the charity gentlemen; and goes to church – a detail easily overlooked since the narrator simply states "He went to church" – before interacting with people in the streets (114–15). He then changes what the Ghost of Christmas Present showed him by going to dinner with his nephew, whom he now addresses as "Fred" (115). Back in his office on Boxing Day, the day of giving to workers and the poor but still at this time not a work holiday, Scrooge orders, "Make up the fires, and buy another coal-scuttle before you dot another i, Bob Cratchit." He becomes "as good a friend, as good a master, and as good a man, as the good old city knew, or any other good old city, town, or borough, in the good old world" (116).

The final picture, by John Leech, shows Scrooge not in his office but in his nightgown by the fireplace in his rooms sharing "a Christmas bowl of smoking bishop" with Bob Cratchit (Fig. 23); Christmas greenery is overhead and on the mantlepiece. For all its reminders of the presence of the poor, *A Christmas Carol* is not advocating major social and economic change but shares with the *Pickwick Papers* a benevolent sense of feudal obligation that will ultimately maintain the roles of master and servant not just among the landowning aristocracy but also among those who have earned wealth through business. Early in the story Ebenezer Scrooge famously refuses to give to charity, observing that the poor are for him statistics; now, he shares a celebratory drink with Bob. The illustration is generally assumed to be the same Boxing Day, but the greenery and the nightgown – Scrooge must have been dressed to go to the office earlier in the day – raise the possibility that this may not be the Christmas of the spirits' visit, but a future year, a new tradition having been created. Through the spirits' intervention, Scrooge has been in the homes of the poor, and now his employee is welcome in his home – at least at Christmas. The ghosts have done their work, and readers of *A Christmas Carol* have a present-day ghost story that truly unites traditions old and new: medieval community, feudal generosity, ghostly storytelling, and the Christmas gift book's healthy dose of consumerism.

Bibliography

A'Beckett, Gilbert A. *Babes in the Wood; Or, Harlequin Robin Hood and his Merry Men.* London: J. Miles, 1867.

Alford, Henry. *Poetical Works of Henry Alford.* 2 vols. London: James Burns, 1845.

—. *The Year of Praise.* London: A Strahan, 1867.

Anderson, Benedict. *Imagined Communities.* 1983, 2nd edition. London: Verso, 1991.

Armstrong, Isobel. *Language as Living Form in Nineteenth-Century Poetry.* Brighton: Harvester Press, 1982.

Aristotle's Last Legacy; Or, His Golden Cabinet of Secrets opened, for Youth's Delightful Pastime. London, 1710.

Aubrey, John. *Miscellanies.* London: Edward Castle, 1696.

The Babes in the Wood. London: Sampson and Low, 1861.

Bailey, Nathan, et al. *Dictionarium Britannicum.* London: T. Cox, 1730.

Bakhtin, Mikhail. *Rabelais and His World* (1965), trans. Helene Iswolsky. Cambridge, MA: MIT Press, 1968.

Barham, R.H. *The Ingoldsby Legends.* 1839–42; London: T. Nelson, n.d.

Baring-Gould, Sabine. *Curious Myths of the Middle Ages.* London: Rivingtons, 1866.

—. *Lives of the Saints.* 3rd edition. 16 vols. London: J. Hodges, 1872–82.

—. *The Vicar of Morwenstow: A Life of Robert Stephen Hawker.* New York: T. Whittaker, 1879.

Barczewski, Stephanie L. *Myth and National Identity in Nineteenth-Century Britain.* Oxford: Oxford University Press, 2000.

Basdeo, Stephen. *The Life and Legend of a Rebel Leader: Wat Tyler.* Barnsley: Pen and Sword Books, 2018.

Berdoe, Edward, ed. *The Browning Cyclopaedia.* London: George Allen, 1912.

Betts, Laura Wells. "Keats and the Charm of Words: Making Sense of the Eve of St. Agnes." *Studies in Romanticism* 47:3 (2008), 299–319.

Biddick, Kathleen. *The Shock of Medievalism.* Durham, NC: Duke University Press, 1998.

Blackburn, Henry. *Art in the Mountains: The Story of the Passion Play.* London: Sampson Low, Son, and Marston, 1870.

Blackburn, Bonnie, and Leofranc Holford-Strevens, eds. *The Oxford Companion to the Year.* Oxford: Oxford University Press, 1999.

Bloomfield, Robert. *The Farmer's Boy.* 5th edition. London: Vernor and Hood, 1801.

—. *May Day with the Muses,* 2nd edition. London: printed for author, 1822.

—. *Wild Flowers.* London: J. Wright, c. 1806.

Blunt, John Henry, ed. *The Annotated Book of Common Prayer.* London: Rivingtons, 1867.

Booty, John E., ed. *The Elizabethan Prayer Book.* Charlottesville, VA: Folger Shakespeare Library, 1976.

Bourdieu, Pierre. *Outline of a Theory of Practice,* trans. Richard Nice. Cambridge: Cambridge University Press, 1977, rpt 1988.

Bourne, Henry. *Antiquitates Vulgares, Or, The Antiquities of the Common People*. Newcastle: Printed for author, 1725.

Bowdler, Thomas. *The Family Shakespeare in Ten Volumes; In which nothing is added to the original text; but those words and expressions are omitted which cannot with propriety be read aloud in a family*. London: Longman, 1818.

Brady, Ciaran. *James Anthony Froude, An Intellectual Biography of a Victorian Prophet*. Oxford: Oxford University Press, 2013.

Brady, John. *Clavis Calendaria, Or, A compendious analysis of the calendar*. 2 vols. London: Longman, 1812–13.

Brand, John, ed. *Observations on Popular Antiquities, including the whole of Henry Bourne's Antiquitates Vulgares, With addenda to every chapter of that Work*. Newcastle: J. Johnson, 1777.

—, ed. Henry Ellis. *Observations on Popular Antiquities; Chiefly illustrating the Origin of our Vulgar Customs, Ceremonies, and Superstitions. Arranged and Revised with Additions*. 2 vols. London: Rivington, 1813.

Browning, Elizabeth Barrett. *The Works of Elizabeth Barrett Browning*, ed. Sandra Donaldson et al. 5 vols. London: Pickering and Chatto, 2010.

Browning, Elizabeth Barrett and Robert. *The Brownings' Correspondence*, ed. Philip Kelley and Ronald Hudson. 14 vols. Winfield, KS: Wedgestone Press, 1984–.

Browning, Robert. *Christmas-Eve and Easter-Day*. London: Chapman and Hall, 1850.

—. *The Poetical Works of Robert Browning*, ed. Ian Jack and Margaret Smith. 9 vols. Oxford: Clarendon Press, 1984.

Burke, Edmund. *A Philosophical Inquiry into our Ideas of the Sublime and Beautiful*. 2nd edition. London: Dodsley, 1759.

—. *Reflections on the Revolution in France*. 5th edition. London: Dodsley, 1790.

Burns, Robert. *Poems, Chiefly in the Scottish Dialect*. New edition. Edinburgh: Cadell, 1798.

Busk, Mary Margaret. *Plays and Poems*. 2 vols. London: T. Hookham, 1837.

Byron, H.J. *The Babes in the Wood, and the Good Little Fairy-Birds*; reprinted in *H.J. Byron's Select Plays*, ed. Jim Davis. Cambridge: Cambridge University Press, 1986.

Carlyle, Thomas. *Past and Present*. London: Chapman and Hall, 1843.

Cary, H.F., translated and ed. *The Vision; or Hell, Purgatory, and Paradise of Dante Alighieri*. 2nd edition. London: Taylor and Hessey, 1819.

Chambers, E.K. *The Medieval Stage*. 2 vols. Oxford: Clarendon, 1903.

Chambers, Robert, ed. *The Book of Days: A Miscellany of Popular Antiquities*. 2 vols. London: W. and R. Chambers, c. 1863.

—, ed. *The Life and Works of Robert Burns*. 4 vols. Edinburgh: W. and R. Chambers, 1853.

Chandler, Alice. *A Dream of Order: The Medieval Ideal in Nineteenth-Century British Literature*. Lincoln, NE: University of Nebraska Press, 1970.

Chaucer, Geoffrey. *Works: The Riverside Chaucer*. 3rd edition, ed. F.N. Robinson and Larry D. Benson. Boston, MA: Houghton Mifflin, 1987.

Christmas Carols; Or. Sacred Songs suited to the festival of our Lord's Nativity. London: J.W. Parker, 1833.

Clough, Arthur Hugh. *The Poems and Prose Remains of Arthur Hugh Clough*. 2 vols. London: Macmillan, 1869.

Cobbold, Richard. *Valentine Verses; Or Lines of Truth, Love, and Virtue*. Ipswich: Shalders, 1829.

Collier, John Payne. *History of English Dramatic Poetry to the Time of Shakespeare*. 2 vols. London: John Murray, 1831.

Cressy, David. *Bonfires and Bells: National Memory and the Protestant Calendar in Elizabethan and Stuart England*. London: Weidenfeld and Nicholson, 1989.

Cromek, R.H. *Remains of Nithsdale and Galloway Song.* London: Cadell and Davies, 1810.

Cruikshank, George, et al. *The Comic Almanack, An Ephemeris in Jest and Earnest, Containing Merry Tales, Humorous Poetry, Quips, and Oddities, by Thackeray, Albert Smith, Gilbert à Becket, The Brothers Mayhew, With many hundred Illustrations by George Cruikshank and Other Artists.* London: Tilt, 1835–53. Rpt First Series, 1835–43. London: Chatto and Windus, n.d.

D'Arcens, Louise, ed. *The Cambridge Companion to Medievalism.* Cambridge: Cambridge University Press, 2016.

Darley, George. *Sylvia, Or, The May Queen, A Lyrical Drama.* London: John Taylor, 1827.

Dekker, Thomas. *Troia-Noua Triumphans; or, London Triumphing.* London, 1612.

Dickens, Charles. *A Christmas Carol. In Prose. Being a Ghost Story of Christmas.* London: Chapman and Hall, 1843.

—. *A Christmas Carol and Other Christmas Writings,* ed. Michael Slater. London: Penguin, 2003.

—. *A Christmas Carol, By Charles Dickens: A Facsimile of the Original Manuscript.* London: Chapman and Hall, 1903.

—. *The Pickwick Papers,* ed. James Kinsley. Oxford: Oxford University Press, 1986, rpt 1992.

—. *The Posthumous Papers of the Pickwick Club.* London: Chapman and Hall, 1836–37.

Duncan, Thomas G., ed. *Medieval English Lyrics and Carols.* Cambridge: D.S. Brewer, 2013.

Dundes, Alan, ed. *International Folkloristics: Classic Contributions by the Founders of Folklore.* Lanham, MD: Rowan and Littlefield, 1999.

Elliott, Emily Elizabeth Steele. *Copsley Annals Preserved in Proverbs.* Boston, MA: Dutton, 1868.

Elstob, Elizabeth, edited and translated. *An English-Saxon Homily on the Birth-day of St. Gregory; Anciently used in the English Church.* London: W. Bowyer, 1709.

Emerson, Oliver Farrar. *The Earliest English Translations of Bürger's Lenore: A Study in English and German Romanticism.* Cleveland, OH: Western Reserve University Bulletins, 1915.

Emery, Elizabeth, and Richard Utz, eds. *Medievalism: Key Critical Terms.* Cambridge: D.S. Brewer, 2014.

English, Clara. *The Affecting History of the Children in the Wood.* c. 1801.

Eyre-Todd, George, ed. *Abbotsford Series of the Scottish Poets.* 7 vols. Glasgow: W. Hodge, 1891–96.

Faber, George Stanley. *The Origin of Pagan Idolatry Ascertained from Historical Testimony and Circumstantial Evidence.* 3 vols. London: Rivingtons, 1816.

Fairholt, Frederick W. *Lord Mayors' Pageants: Being Collections towards a History of these Annual Celebrations ...* Part 1. London: Percy Society, 1843.

—. *Gog and Magog, The Giants in the Guildhall.* London: J.C. Hotten, 1859.

The Famous and Remarkable History of Sir Richard Whittington. London, 1656.

Faxon, Frederick Winthrop. *Literary Annuals and Gift Books: A bibliography with a descriptive introduction.* Boston, MA: Boston Book Company, 1912.

Fisher, Devon. *Roman Catholic Saints and Early Victorian Literature.* London: Ashgate, 2013.

Forsyth, Mark. *A Christmas Cornucopia.* London: Viking, 2016.

Frazer, J.G. *The Golden Bough: A Study in Comparative Religion.* 1890. 2 vols. New York: Macmillan, 1894.

—. *The Golden Bough: A Study in Magic and Religion.* 3rd ed. 12 vols. London: Macmillan, 1911–15.

Garvin, Katharine. "The Christianity of St Agnes' Eve: Keats' Catholic Inspiration." *Dublin Review* 234 (Winter 1960–61), 356–64.

Galt, John. *Annals of the Parish.* Edinburgh: Cadell, 1822.

—. *The History of Gog and Magog, The Champions of London.* London: J. Souter, 1819.

—. *Ringan Gilhaize, Or, The Covenanters* (1823), ed. Patricia J. Wilson. Edinburgh: Scottish Academic Press, 1984.

Gay, John. *Dramatic Works*, ed. John Fuller. 2 vols. Oxford: Clarendon, 1983.

Genlis, Stéphanie Félicité, comtesse de. *Les veillées du château, ou Cours de morale à l'usage des enfans.* 1784; Paris: Maradan, 1803.

—. *Tales of the Castle; or, Stories of Instruction and Delight*, trans. Thomas Holcroft. London: G. Robinson, 1785.

Gilbert, Davies. *Some Ancient Christmas Carols, with the Tunes to which they were sung in the West of England.* 2nd edition. London: J. Nichols, 1823.

Gilbreath, Marcia. "The Etymology of Porphyro's name in Keats's 'Eve of St. Agnes.'" *Keats Shelley Journal* 37 (1988), 20–25.

Girouard, Mark. *The Return to Camelot: Chivalry and the English Gentleman.* New Haven, CT: Yale University Press, 1981.

Gissing, George. *The Odd Women.* New York: Macmillan, 1893.

Gittings, Robert. "Rich Antiquity." *Twentieth-Century Interpretations of "The Eve of St. Agnes.",* ed. Allan Danzig. Englewood Cliffs, NJ: Prentice-Hall, 1971, pp. 86–98.

Gleig, G.R. "Legends of the Lochs and Glens II: The Phantom Funeral." *Bentley's Miscellany* 6 (August 1839), 195–205.

Glover, Jimmy. *Jimmy Glover and His Friends.* London: Chatto and Windus, 1913.

Gregory, Troy. "Mr. Jorrocks's Lost Sporting Magazine." *Victorian Periodicals Review* 36:4 (2003), 331–50.

Grimes, Kyle, ed. *The Every-Day Book.* honearchive.org/etexts/edb/home.html (accessed September 21, 2018).

Grose, Francis. *A Provincial Glossary, With a Collection of Old Proverbs, and Local Superstitions.* 2nd ed. London: S. Hooper, 1790.

A Guide to the Lord Mayor's Show, or the gentleman and lady's companion to that magnificent procession. London, 1761.

Hair, Donald S. *Domestic and Heroic in Tennyson's Poetry.* Toronto: University of Toronto Press, 1981.

Halliwell, James Orchard, ed. *Ludus Coventriae.* London: Shakespeare Society, 1841.

Hampson, Robert Thomas. *Medii aevi kalendarium; or, Dates, Charters, and Customs of the middle ages; with calendars from the tenth to the fifteenth century; and an alphabetical digest of obsolete names of days: forming a glossary of the dates of the middle ages; with tables and other aids for ascertaining dates.* 2 vols. London: H.K. Causton, 1841.

Harris, Katherine D. *Forget Me Not: The Rise of the British Literary Annual, 1823–1835.* Athens, OH: Ohio University Press, 2015.

Harvey, Karen. "The Trouble About Merlin: The Theme of Enchantment in 'The Eve of St. Agnes.'" *Keats-Shelley Journal* 34 (1985), 83–94.

Hawlin, Stefan. "Merlin's Debt in Keats's 'The Eve of St. Agnes.'" *Notes and Queries* 66 (2019), 273–78.

Hazlitt, William Carew, ed. *Dictionary of Faiths and Folk-Lore.* 3 vols. London: Reeves and Turner, 1905.

—. *The Livery Companies of the City of London.* London: Swan Sonnenschein and Co., 1892.

Herbert, William. *The History of the Twelve Great Livery Companies of London.* 2 vols. London: printed for author, 1836–37.

Herrick, Robert. *Complete Poems.* 3 vols, ed. Alexander Ballach Grosart. London: Chatto and Windus, 1876.

Hervey, Thomas Kibble, and Robert Seymour. *The Book of Christmas.* London: William Spooner, 1836.

The History of Dick Whittington, Lord Mayor of London; With the Adventures of his Cat. Banbury: J.G. Rusher, n.d.

Hill, Tracey. *Pageantry and Power: A Cultural History of the Early Modern Lord Mayor's Show, 1585–1639.* Manchester: Manchester University Press, 2010.

Hobsbawm, Eric J., and Terence Ranger. *The Invention of Tradition.* Cambridge: Cambridge University Press, 1983; rpt 2019.

Holloway, Gerry. *Women and Work in Britain since 1840.* Abingdon: Routledge, 2005.

Hone, William, ed. *Ancient Mysteries Described.* London: William Hone, 1823.

—, ed. *Apocryphal New Testament.* London: William Hone, 1820.

—. *Aspersions Answered.* London: William Hone, 1824.

—. *The Every-Day Book.* London: William Hone, 1826–27.

—. *Political House that Jack Built.* London: William Hone, 1819.

—. *The Table-Book.* 2 vols. London: William Hone, 1827.

—. *The Three Trials of William Hone*, ed. William Tegg. London: William Tegg, 1876.

Horne, Richard Hengist, ed., *The Poems of Geoffrey Chaucer, Modernized.* London: Whittaker, 1841.

—. *The New Spirit of the Age.* 2 vols. London: Smith, Elder, 1844.

Hovelaque, Henri-Léon. *Browning's English in "Sordello."* Paris: Les Presses Modernes, 1933.

Howells, William. *Cambrian Superstitions.* Tipton: Longman, 1831.

Howitt, Anna Mary. *An Art-Student in Munich.* 2 vols. London: Longman, 1853.

Howitt, William. *The Rural Life of England.* 2 vols. London: Longman, 1838.

Howitt, William, [and Mary Howitt]. *The Book of the Seasons, Or, The Calendar of Nature.* London: Henry Colburn and Richard Bentley, 1831.

Huizinga, Johan. *Homo Ludens; a Study of the Play-Element in Culture.* 1949. London: Routledge and Kegan Paul, 1980.

Hughes, Maureen. *A History of Pantomime.* Barnsley: Pen and Sword History, 2013.

Hutton, Ronald. *Stations of the Sun: A History of the Ritual Year in Britain.* Oxford: Oxford University Press, 1996.

—. *The Rise and Fall of Merry England, 1400–1700.* Oxford: Oxford University Press, 1994.

Illustrated London Almanack. London: Illustrated London News, 1845–94.

Irving, Washington. *The Sketch Book of Geoffrey Crayon, Gent.* 2 vols. London: Thomas Davison, 1821.

Jarvis, Stephen. *Death and Mr. Pickwick.* New York: Farrar, Straus and Giroux, 2015.

Jones, Jeremiah. *A New and Full method of Settling the Canonical Authority of the New Testament; To which is subjoined a Vindication of the former Part of St. Matthew's Gospel from Mr. Whiston's Charge of Dislocation.* New edition. 3 vols. Oxford: Clarendon, 1798.

Jones, Richard. *The Growth of the Idylls of the King.* Philadelphia, PA: Lippincott, 1894.

Joynes, Andrew. *Medieval Ghost Stories.* Woodbridge: Boydell Press, 2001, rpt 2006.

Jung-Stilling, Johann Heinrich. *Theories of Pneumatology*, trans. Samuel Jackson. London: Longman, 1834.

Kareem, Sarah Tindal. *Eighteenth-Century Fiction and the Reinvention of Wonder.* New York: Oxford University Press, 2014.

Keats, John. *Lamia, Isabella, The Eve of St. Agnes, and Other Poems.* London: Taylor and Hessey, 1820.

—. *The Eve of St. Agnes.* Illustrated by Edward H. Wenhert. London: Joseph Cundall, 1856.

Keble, John. *The Christian Year.* 2 vols. Oxford: J. Parker, 1827.

Keightley, Thomas. *Fairy Mythology*, 2 vols. London: Whittaker, 1833.

—. *Tales and Popular Fictions.* London: Whittaker, 1834.

Kent, Charles. *The Land of the Babes in the Wood.* London: Jerrold, c. 1910.

King, Joshua. "John Keble's *The Christian Year*: Private Reading and Imagined National Religious Communities." *Victorian Literature and Culture* 40 (2012), 397–420.

—. *Imagined Spiritual Communities in Britain's Age of Print*. Columbus, OH: Ohio State University Press, 2015.

Knight, Richard Payne, and [Thomas Wright]. *A Discourse on the Worship of Priapus and On the Worship of the Generative Powers*. 1865; rpt New York: Julian Press, 1957.

Landon, Laetitia Elizabeth (L.E.L.), *The Easter Gift: A Religious Offering*. London: Fisher, 1832.

Landow, George P. *Victorian Types, Victorian Shadows: Biblical Typology in Victorian Literature, Art, and Thought*. Boston, MA: Routledge and Kegan Paul, 1980.

Latané, David E. *Browning's* Sordello *and the Aesthetics of Difficulty*. University of Victoria English Literary Studies Monograph Series, 1987.

Lawson, Jonathan. *Robert Bloomfield*. Boston, MA: Twayne, 1980.

Life of Sir Richard Whittington, compiled from authentic documents by the author of memoirs of George Barnwell. London: M. Jones, 1811.

The Life and Times of Dick Whittington, An Historical Romance. London: H. Cunningham, 1841.

Lysons, Samuel. *The model merchant of the Middle Ages, exemplified in the story of Whittington and his cat*. London: Hamilton, Adams, and co., 1860.

Macready, William Charles. *The Diaries of William Charles Macready*, ed. William Toynbee. 2 vols. New York: Putnam's, 1912.

Maidment, Brian. "Re-Arranging the Year: The Almanac, the Day Book and the Year Book as Popular Literary Forms, 1789–1860." *Rethinking Victorian Culture*, ed. Juliet John and Alice Jenkins. Basingstoke: Macmillan Press, 2000, pp. 91–113.

—. "Beyond Usefulness and Ephemerality: The Discursive Almanac, 1828–1860." *British Literature and Print Culture*, ed. Sandro Jung. Cambridge: D.S. Brewer, 2013, pp. 158–94.

Malory, Sir Thomas. *La [sic] Mort D'Arthur: The Most Ancient and Famous History of the Renowned Prince Arthur and the Knights of the Round Table*. London: R. Wilkes, 1816.

—. *The History of the Renowned Prince Arthur and His Knights of the Round Table*. London: J. Walker, 1816.

—. *The Byrth, Lyf, and Actes of Kyng Arthur*, ed. Robert Southey. 2 vols. London: Longman, 1817.

—. *Le Morte Darthur*, ed. P.J.C. Field. Woodbridge: D.S. Brewer, 2017.

[Markland, James Heywood]. *Chester Mysteries: De Deluvio Noe, De Occisione Innocentium*. London: Roxburghe Club, 1818.

Marriott, William. *A Collection of English Miracle-plays or Mysteries*. Basel: Schweigerhauser and Co., 1838.

Matthews, David. *Medievalism, A Critical History*. Cambridge: D.S. Brewer, 2015.

Mayhew, Henry, ed. *London Labour and the London Poor*. 4 vols. 1861–62. Rpt New York: Dover, 1968.

MacColl, Malcolm. *The Ober-Ammergau Passion Play*. New edition. London: Rivington, 1880.

Mill, John Stuart. *Collected Works of John Stuart Mill*. Toronto: University of Toronto Press, 1981.

Mitford, Mary Russell, ed. *Finden's Tableaux*. London: Charles Tilt, 1837–40.

—, ed. *Schloss's English Bijou Almanac*. London: A. Schloss, 1843.

Moore, Tara. *Victorian Christmas in Print*. New York: Palgrave Macmillan, 2009.

Morris, William. *The Earthly Paradise*. 1868–70. Hammersmith: Kelmscott Press, 1896–97.

—. *The Earthly Paradise*, ed. Florence S. Boos. 2 vols. New York: Routledge, 2002.

Morton, Thomas. *The Children in the Wood, An Opera*. 3rd edition. London, 1794.

Munday, Anthony. *Chrysanaleia, Or the Golden Fishing.* London, 1616.

Neale, John Mason, and Thomas Helmore. *Carols for Christmas-Tide, Set to Ancient Melodies.* London: Novello, 1854.

—. *Deeds of Faith.* 1849. 2nd edition. London: Mozley, 1860.

—. *The Letters of John Mason Neale, D.D., edited by his daughter* (Mary Sackville Lawton). London: Longman, 1910.

Newell, Venetia. *An Egg for Easter: A Folklore Study.* Bloomington, IN: Indiana University Press, 1971.

Newman, John Henry. *Apologia Pro Vita Sua.* 1864. Oxford: Clarendon Press, 1967.

—. *The Letters and Diaries of John Henry Newman,* ed. Francis J. McGrath et al. 32 volumes. Oxford: Oxford University Press, 2004–08.

—, ed, et al. *Lives of the English Saints.* London: James Toovey, 1844–45.

—, ed. *Newman's Lives of the English Saints,* ed. Arthur Wollaston Hutton. 6 vols. London: S.T. Fremantle, 1900–01.

Nicoll, Allardyce. *A History of English Drama 1660–1900.* 2nd edition. Volume 4. Cambridge: Cambridge University Press, 1963.

Noyes, Dorothy. *Fire in the Plaça: Catalan Festival Politics After Franco.* Philadelphia, PA: University of Pennsylvania Press, 2003.

Oates, John. *The Teaching of Tennyson.* London: Elliott Stock, 1903.

Old Moore's Almanack. London, 1697–.

"On the Holy Plays or Mysteries of the Middle Ages, with an account of a Sacred Drama which was performed in the year 1840 at Oberammergau in Upper Bavaria." *Christian Teacher* 3 (1841), 150–60.

Opie, Amelia. *Valentine's Eve.* 3 vols. London: Longman, 1816.

Paden, W.D. *Tennyson in Egypt: A Study of the Imagery in his Earlier Work.* Lawrence, KS: University of Kansas Humanistic Studies No. 27. Kansas, 1942.

Pennant, Thomas. *A Tour in Scotland and Voyage to the Hebrides.* London, 1776.

Percy, Thomas. *Reliques of Ancient English Poetry.* New edition. 3 vols. London: J. Dodsley, 1767.

Porter, George Richardson. *The Progress of the Nation in its Various Social and Economical Relations.* 2nd edition. London: John Murray, 1847.

Palgrave, Sir Francis. *History of the Anglo-Saxons.* London: John Murray, 1831.

Professional Anecdotes; or Ana of Medical Literature. London: John Knight and Henry Lacey, 1825.

Pugin, A.W.N. *Contrasts; A Parallel between the Noble Edifices of the XIVth and XVth Centuries and Similar Buildings of the Present Day, Shewing the Present Decay of Taste.* Alderbury: printed for author, 1836.

Punch, Or, The London Charivari, ed. Mark Lemon et al. London, 1841–1992.

Raby Jr., Richard. "The Mystery of the Passion at Ober-Ammergau." *The Rambler* 6 (1855), 119–33.

—. (?). "The Miracle-Plays of the Middle Ages." *The Rambler, A Catholic Journal and Review* n.s. 4 (1855), 323–36; 403–14.

Ranke, Leopold von. "On the Character of Historical Science." *The Theory and Practice of* History, trans. and ed. Georg G. Iggers, Wilma A. Iggers and Konrad von Moltke. Indianapolis, IN: Bobbs-Merrill, 1973, pp. 33–44.

Reed, Edward Bliss. *Christmas Carols Printed in the Sixteenth Century.* Cambridge, MA: Harvard University Press, 1932.

The Report of the Royal Commission on the City of London Livery Companies. 5 vols. London: Eyre and Spottiswoode, 1883–85.

Rejzl, Jan. *Good King Wenceslas, The Real Story.* Norwich: 1st Choice Publishing, 1995.

Richards, E.G. *Mapping Time: The Calendar and its History.* Oxford: Oxford University Press, 1999.

Rickert, Edith. *Ancient English Christmas Carols MCCCC to MDCC.* London: Chatto and Windus, 1914.

Ricks, Christopher. *Tennyson.* New York: Macmillan, 1972.

Ritson, Joseph, ed. *Ancient Engleish Metrical Romanceës.* 3 vols. London: Bulmer, 1832.

—. *Ancient Songs, from the Time of King Henry the Third, to the Revolution.* London: J. Johnson, 1790.

Robinson, Mary. *Memoirs of the Late Mrs. Robinson, Written by herself.* 4 vols. London: R. Phillips, 1801.

Rossetti, Christina Georgina. *New Poems,* ed. William Michael Rossetti. London: Macmillan, 1896.

—. *The Poetical Works of Christina Georgina Rossetti,* ed. William Michael Rossetti. London: Macmillan, 1904.

—. *Time Flies, A Reading Diary.* London: SPCK, 1885.

Round About Our Coal Fire, Or, Christmas Entertainments. London, 1734.

Ruskin, John. *The Seven Lamps of Architecture.* London: J. Wiley, 1849.

Sandys, William. *Christmas Carols, Ancient and Modern.* London: R. Beckley, 1833.

Schichtman, Martin B. "Percival's Sister: Genealogy, Virginity, and Blood." *Arthuriana* 9:2 (1999), 11–20.

Scott, Sir Walter. *Ballads and Lyrical Pieces.* Edinburgh: Ballantyne, 1806.

—. *Marmion, A Tale of Flodden Field.* Edinburgh: Ballantyne, 1808.

—. *The Antiquary.* 1816, ed. David Hewitt and David Punter. London: Penguin, 1998.

—. *Ivanhoe.* 1819, ed. Ian Duncan. Oxford: Oxford University Press, 1996.

Sedding, Edward. "Christmas Carols." *Once A Week,* December 26, 1863, pp. 10–13.

Seymour, Robert. *Seymour's Humorous Sketches, comprising Eighty-Six Caricature Etchings,* ed. Alfred Crowquill. London: Bohn, 1866.

Sharp, Thomas. *A Dissertation on the Pageants or Dramatic Mysteries anciently performed at Coventry.* Coventry: Merridew, 1825.

Smith, Lucy Toulmin, ed. *York Plays: The Plays performed by the Crafts or Mysteries of York on the Day of Corpus Christi in the 14th, 15th, and 16th Centuries.* Oxford: Clarendon Press, 1885.

Smith, Joshua Toulmin, and Lucy Toulmin Smith. *English Gilds: The Original Ordinances.* London: Early English Text Society, 1870.

Southey, Robert. *Wat Tyler, A Dramatic Poem.* London: Sherwood, Neely and Jones, 1817.

Spenser, Edmund. *The Shephearde's Calender.* London, 1579.

Stillinger, Jack. *Reading the Eve of St. Agnes: The Multiples of Complex Literary Transaction.* New York: Oxford University Press, 1999.

Strachan, John. *Walter and Emma; or, A Tale of Bothwell Bridge; with other poems.* Forres: printed for author, 1829.

Stubbes, Philip. *Anatomie of Abuses.* 3rd edition, ed. William B.D.D. Turnbull. London: Pickering, 1836.

Strutt, Joseph. *Þorða Anzel-cynnan, or, A compleat view of the manners, customs, arms, habits, &c. of the inhabitants of England.* London, 1775–76.

—. *Glig-gamena angel-deod, Or, The Sports and Pastimes of the People of England.* 2nd edition. London: Bentley, 1810.

Tennyson, Alfred, Lord. *Poems in Two Volumes.* London: Moxon, 1842.

—. *The Holy Grail and Other Poems.* London: Strahan, 1870.

—. *Idylls of the King.* London: Moxon, 1859.

—. *Locksley Hall Sixty Years After Etc.* London: Macmillan, 1886.

—. *The Poems of Tennyson*, ed. Christopher Ricks. London. Longmans, 1969.

Tennyson, Hallam. *Alfred, Lord Tennyson, A Memoir*. 2 vols. London: Macmillan, 1898.

—, ed. *The Works of Tennyson*. 9 vols. London: Eversley, 1907–09.

Thackeray, William Makepeace. *Barber Cox, The Cutting of his Comb*. Serialized in the *Comic Almanack*, 1840.

—. *Stubbs's Calendar; Or, The Fatal Boots*. Serialized in the *Comic Almanack*, 1839.

—. *The Fatal Boots and Cox's Diary*. London: Smith, Elder and Co., c. 1880.

Thomson, James. *The Seasons*. 1730. London: Stockdale, 1794.

Thorpe, Benjamin. *Yule-Tide Stories: A Collection of Scandinavian and North German Popular Tales and Traditions*.

Tiddy, R.J.E. *The Mummer's Play, With a Memoir*. Oxford: Clarendon, 1923.

Towle, Eleanor A. *John Mason Neale D.D., A Memoir*. 2nd impression. London: Longmans, 1907.

The Travels and Surprising Adventures of Baron Munchausen. New York: James Miller, 1860.

Tucker, Herbert F. *Epic: Britain's Heroic Muse 1790–1910*. Oxford: Oxford University Press, 2008.

Tupper, Martin Farquhar. *Hactenus*. Boston, MA: Pierce, 1848.

Twitchell, James. *The Living Dead: A Study of the Vampire in Romantic Literature*. Durham, NC: Duke University Press, 1981.

Wagner, Leopold. *The Pantomimes and All About Them*. London: John Haywood, 1881.

Warton, Thomas. *The History of English Poetry*. Revised edition. 4 vols. London: Thomas Tegg, 1821.

Westwood, Thomas. *The Sword of Kingship: A Legend of the "Mort d'Arthure."* London: privately printed, 1866.

—. *The Quest for the Sancgreall, The Sword of Kingship, and Other Poems*. London: John Russell Smith, 1868.

The Whimsical Valentine-Writer. London: T. Hughes, n.d.

Wilkinson, Thomas. *Tours to the British Mountains*. London: Taylor and Hessey, 1824.

Wolfson, Susan, and Peter Manning, eds. *The Longman Anthology of British Literature 2A*. 5th edition. New York: Longman, 2012.

Wood, Sarah. *Robert Browning, A Literary Life*. Basingstoke: Palgrave, 2001.

Wordsworth, William (and S.T. Coleridge). *Lyrical Ballads*. London: J and A. Arch, 1798.

—. *Lyrical Ballads*, ed. R. L. Brett and A.R. Jones. London: Methuen, 1963.

—. *The Excursion, Being a Portion of the Recluse*. London: Longman, 1814.

Wortley, Lady Emmeline Stuart, ed. *The Keepsake for MDCCCXXXVII*. London: Longman, 1837.

Wright, Thomas, ed., *The Chester Plays: A Collection of Mysteries founded upon Scriptural Subjects and formerly represented by the Trades of Chester at Whitsuntide*. London: Shakespeare Society, 1843, 1847.

—., ed, *Songs and Carols; Now First Printed from a Manuscript of the Fifteenth Century*. London: Percy Society, 1847.

—, ed. *Songs and Carols Printed from a Manuscript in the Sloane Collection*. London: W. Pickering, 1836.

—, ed. *Songs and Carols from a Manuscript in the British Museum of the Fifteenth Century*. London: T. Richards, 1856.

Yonge, Charlotte Mary. *The Heir of Redclyffe*. 1853, ed. Barbara Dennis. Oxford: World's Classics, 1997.

Index

Medievalism

I
Anglo-Saxon Culture and the Modern Imagination
edited by David Clark and Nicholas Perkins

II
Medievalist Enlightenment: From Charles Perrault to Jean-Jacques Rousseau
Alicia C. Montoya

III
Memory and Myths of the Norman Conquest
Siobhan Brownlie

IV
Comic Medievalism: Laughing at the Middle Ages
Louise D'Arcens

V
Medievalism: Key Critical Terms
edited by Elizabeth Emery and Richard Utz

VI
Medievalism: A Critical History
David Matthews

VII
Chivalry and the Medieval Past
edited by Katie Stevenson and Barbara Gribling

VIII
Georgian Gothic: Medievalist Architecture, Furniture and Interiors, 1730–1840
Peter N. Lindfield

IX
*Petrarch and the Literary Culture of Nineteenth-Century France:
Translation, Appropriation, Transformation*
Jennifer Rushworth

X
*Medievalism, Politics and Mass Media:
Appropriating the Middle Ages in the Twenty-First Century*
Andrew B.R. Elliott

XI
Translating Early Medieval Poetry: Transformation, Reception, Interpretation
edited by Tom Birkett and Kirsty March-Lyons

XII
Medievalism in A Song of Ice and Fire *and* Game of Thrones
Shiloh Carroll

CPSIA information can be obtained
at www.ICGtesting.com
Printed in the USA
JSHW051315120723
44634JS00003B/129